SMALL GAME AND
VARMINT HUNTING

Dedication
For Janet, Brendan, Brad, and Blair.

SMALL GAME AND VARMINT HUNTING

Wilf E. Pyle

Stoeger Publishing Company

Other books by the author:

The Hunter's Book of the Pronghorn Antelope (with Bert Popowski)

Hunting Predators for Hides and Profit

PHOTO CREDITS

Chuck Cadieux: 19, 29, 64, 84, 236; Canadian Bureau of Sport Fisheries and Wildlife: 16 (2), 66; Jerome J. Knap: 32, 34, 35, 49, 50, 51, 52, 54, 56, 57, 58, 59, 229, 266, 267, 268 (2), 269 (2), 270 (2), 271, 272, 287.

Published by Stoeger Publishing Company
55 Ruta Court
South Hackensack, New Jersey 07606

ISBN: 0-88317-150-3
Library of Congress
Catalog Card Number: 89-61258
Manufactured in the United States of America

Distributed to the book trade and to the sporting goods trade by Stoeger Industries, 55 Ruta Court, South Hackensack, New Jersey 07606.

In Canada, distributed to the book trade and to the sporting goods trade by Stoeger Canada, Ltd., Unit 16, 1801 Wentworth Street, Whitby, Ontario L1N 5S4.

Acknowledgments

Authoring a book requires resources, research, recall, and rewriting. It also requires help. I want to express my gratitude to those who provided valuable assistance with this project.

Thanks to my good friend Jerome Knap, himself a well established writer and active outdoorsman, for allowing me to use many of the photos that accompany this text. Also a tip of the hat to Chuck Cadieux for his photo input.

A very special thanks to my wife Janet for her continued help in editing my manuscripts. I also thank Jim Haley for computer advice during the early part of the work.

Finally, to all my hunting partners, and you know who you are, who have helped make my outdoor trips more fun, I offer a special thanks.

Preface

This book is about putting skills together for the purpose of successfully hunting small game. It's about having fun while doing this. It's also about doing these things well.

The world seems full of hunters and shooters, but every year these groups drift further apart. I attribute this trend to increased specialization in outdoor sports and the resulting lack of interest in activities other than one's own. It seems that hunters don't know a lot about shooting, and shooters don't care to know much about hunting.

If this book has a goal, it's to put some hunting back into shooting and a little shooting back into hunting. Each group must learn more and adopt the skills of the other. Trigger control has to be joined with woodsmanship, and special equipment added to the basics of marksmanship. Small game hunting provides the opportunity to do this well.

Hunters going after small game participate in one of the oldest of all sports. Squirrel and rabbit hunting are traditional—as traditional as apple pie and the stars and stripes. Deep in our heritage is the lone hunter outfitted with squirrel gun and hunting knife.

Good shooting puts good meat on the table. Shooters usually discover that it's smart to keep game meat and learn the skills of preparing it for the table. Small game hunting offers the biggest variety of table fare. Small game meat, especially squirrel and rabbit, have been tested by generations of hunters. Man's road to success is paved with the bones of countless squirrels and heaps of rabbits.

Small game hunting is for everyone. Any age group can derive enjoyment from this kind of hunting. There is no need for expensive trips— plenty of game is available close to home. This contrasts with other types of hunting, where long distance travel is necessary. This is the working man's kind of hunting. No fancy guides are required and the hunting travel agency crowd is totally absent. It's also a great outing for the whole family.

In this book we'll tell the outdoorsman everything he needs to know to hunt small game: the animals, the rifles, the optics, the cartridges, the clothing, and the techniques. It's all here, and I hope you'll find it makes for absorbing reading for the beginner and the old hand alike.

Widely distributed small game is covered in detail. The mistake many books make (at least the ones I've seen) is to take a broad-brush, superficial approach to small game hunting. What I've tried to do here is to approach the

sport from a fun and learning point of view.

We'll explore the important facets of riflery, marksmanship, woodcraft, and special tools. This kind of hunting knowledge can lead to improved outdoor skills, with applicability to other hunting. Want some really specialized information? We'll also cover blackpowder arms.

In this book, varmints get detailed treatment, because this area has frankly *never* been adequately covered. Mastery of long range varmint shooting is the culmination of years of practice. Varmint shooting really is the last great playground for the active shooter and experimenter. Varmints give rise to the need for specialized rifles, well developed reloading skills, and a good understanding of tools and techniques.

Above all, I hope readers will enjoy the book. Let the details sink in, and weigh and consider the historical information. Read the woodcraft setions critically; take what you need to make small game hunting work in your area. Come away from this book a better hunter and shooter, a skilled outdoorsman.

If you have as much fun reading the book as I did living and writing it, I will have done my job.

Wilf E Pyle

Wilf E. Pyle
Regina, Canada

Contents

Chapter 1

For the Fun of It

I'm not sure when I started hunting small game. It might have been the big jackrabbit I took back in grade five—around 1958. The trees are gone now, but I could take you to the very spot where it happened. I used a .22 short rimfire in a single-shot rifle. For years I kept the case, and only recently lost track of its whereabouts. Anyway, by early grade school, hunting and shooting were important parts of my life.

It seemed like everybody shot rifles and hunted game. Hunting on your own, without guidance from parents or uncles, was a source of great personal pride to us kids. Bringing home game, usually rabbits, was a major accomplishment that elicited praise from the entire family. Although rural life was changing, a good hunter still held special status in the community. While others drifted off to the passive land of watching television, I stayed interested in hunting.

I am sure most shooters back then hunted for fun rather than for any contribution to the family food supply. Whether together or alone, doing something outdoors was the real attraction. We didn't associate hunting with wilderness skills, marksmanship, or survival ability. All of those things were second nature, part of our daily lives.

Long range varmint shooting, close-in hunting for jackrabbits, and long distance crow shooting, all highly specialized skills, were things I learned long after I had put hundreds of rabbits through our stew pot and taken countless ground squirrels as agricultural pests.

Varmint hunting in its modern forms didn't exist when I was a kid on the farm. You stalked close for any game, whether rabbit or ground squirrel, and the mark of a true woodsman was economy in shooting. If somebody had ever admitted taking ten gophers with 50 shots he would have been hooted out of the school yard. Many young hunters, especially in the upper grades, were taking 52 or 53 rabbits with a box of 50 cartridges. By passing up many simpler shots, the hunter could choose opportunities where two or more rabbits were lined up so that the bullet passing through one would lodge in the other. This was always at close range, probably never more than 30 yards. Status accrued to those few fellows who could achieve the same feat with crows. All in all, varmint hunting in rural North America was different back then.

The origins of small game hunting lie in man's desire to be outdoors. Some claim that varmint

Unlike the big game variety, most small game hunting is close to home. It is easy to set aside time for this kind of hunting.

hunting grew out of gun-tinkering, but I disagree. Gun building was only an excuse to be outdoors, to sample the smell of newly-plowed fields in the spring, to feel the sun on your back in the summer, and to listen to the sounds of harvest in the fall.

Shooting rabbits and tree squirrels for the pot helped legitimize being outdoors. Shooting ground squirrels and woodchucks provided an excuse for helping rural friends or kin folk. These activities gave us a strong tie to the land, and they all happened to be fun. I had fun filling my grandmother's larder with fresh-skinned jacks or bragging to my classmates about recent gopher takes.

Small game hunting differs from all other types of hunting. Unlike big game, most small game animals are taken close to home. Less travel is involved, and hunting can be planned around small bits of time like after school or a Sunday afternoon. This means more hunting opportunities throughout the season.

It's nice, too, when hunts can be impromptu affairs involving a few friends or relatives, with little preplanning and prehunt arranging. I like the more spontaneous atmosphere that comes with this kind of hunting. Compared to that, big game hunting often requires lots of planning and complicated trips across several states.

There is often a close relationship between landowners and small game hunters. Most hunters are state residents. Usually, somebody in the hunting party knows the landowner, and this leads to an uncomplicated, more laid-back hunter/landowner relationship. In big game hunting, guides, trespass fees, and inflated expenses are part of the mix. Many small game hunting outings include the landowner as a member of the party. This is almost unheard of in big game hunting.

There's also a tendency for the same groups of hunters to work the same areas. This builds trust between landowner and hunter. When the same hunters return year after year, they feel a loyalty to the land. The hunter benefits, because

he becomes intimate with a specific area.

Mastery of an area, knowing where animals travel, familiarity with the best habitat locations, and an overall understanding of the landscape all put the hunter ahead. In the typical big game situation, hunters don't gain this intimate knowledge of specific areas. They probably don't want it, because it's unlikely they'll ever return to the exact locality.

There are other more obvious differences that impact on the small game picture. The size of small game compared to any of the deer family—whitetails, mule deer, moose and elk—widens our choice in equipment, especially in rifles and cartridge selection. A host of different firearms can be chosen, and all produce excellent results.

On the other hand, there are numerous similarities between the two kinds of hunting. Certain principles are the same. For example, it's necessary for all hunters to have at least a minimal knowledge of their territory. Scouting, reading, and interpreting sign are critical skills necessary in all types of hunting.

In practice, many small game hunters become year-round hunters. Even after deer and bear season are over, there are often opportunities to go after woodchucks, squirrels, and rabbits. Hunters new to small game will find themselves becoming more attentive to their hunting environment. They will no longer pass over rabbit sign when they are after deer. They'll remember and file away the observations as possible rabbit territory when the deer season closes. A deer hunter may well stumble upon a pasture replete with woodchuck sign. This, too, is filed away.

Certainly one of the nicest benefits of small game hunting is the contact hunters gain with other outdoor people. Active hunters get to know landowners, trap shooters, four-wheel-drive buffs, pistol shooters, natural history types, military personnel, deer hunters, varmint shooters, bench rest experts, and big game devotees. Most of these folks, you'll find, hunt small game to some extent.

You learn, too, where to hunt, the conservation attitude in the area, the political positions of wildlife groups, and the concerns of environmentalists. You become a generalist, with broad areas of expertise. Many tools of the specialist hunter can be readily incorporated into the techniques of the small game hunter. Many times you will find yourself supporting issues and ideas that you would have never even thought about previously. Small game hunting provides a rare opportunity to learn more while actively participating. Small game is the tie that binds many outdoor people.

Small game hunting has its own kind of specialists. The long range shooter going after prairie dogs, woodchucks, and crows with a centerfire rifle is perhaps one of the most specialized hunters of our time. Often outfitted with a fast-stepping cartridge and a rifle topped with a high power scope, these shooters can easily take woodchuck-size targets at 300 or more yards.

The typical varmint specialist is somebody with an intense interest in making hits at long

Each season offers some kind of small game. Rabbits and hares are available throughout the winter, and various varmints are active in the warmer months.

Small game hunters make use of gear used for other hunting.

Small game hunting is characterized by long seasons. In many areas there aren't even any date restrictions on jackrabbits and ground squirrels. The Eastern and Southern states feature long rabbit seasons—as much as five or six times the duration of a regular deer season. In the Western states it's open season on prairie dogs and rockchucks. Badgers are available anytime throughout their range. Many times season dates will overlap with big game, waterfowl, and upland game birds, providing quite a mixed bag of hunting opportunities. Generous seasons are likely to be part of the small game scene for years to come, because populations are high and rebound easily.

The small game approach integrates well with other hunting. For example, you might go after duck and geese in the morning, and rabbits in the afternoon. Or hunt mule deer in the early

range. These shooters master wind, mirage, and distance to connect on targets that only ten years ago would have been out of reach from the fastest travelling bullets around. They are not plinkers—content to take short targets of opportunity, but rather shooters that have become masters at reading field conditions and applying that knowledge to bullet trajectory and rifle accuracy. Hitting at great distance becomes an overriding drive.

These hunters choose the most sophisticated equipment available. Many borrow techniques from both target and bench rest shooters. They adapt some tricks to meet rugged field conditions, and copy others. The result is a new breed of rifleman, often on the cutting edge of shooting-product technology, capable of applying the latest to successful hunting.

Safety is paramount in this specialized brand of shooting. Targets must be positioned to permit precise shooting. Good back-stops of natural vegetation or earth are always necessary. Varmint hunters, as a group, are aware of the need for bullets that fragment on impact, rather than ricochet across the countryside.

Learn the traits of the animals in your area. Study sign carefully and it will soon seem that game is everywhere.

Rifle practice is a must. Long range shooting at small targets is an exacting skill.

The California ground squirrel shows the variation typical of ground squirrels.

The Golden Mantled ground squirrel is another member of a diverse and broad target group.

morning, prairie dogs in the afternoon, and then shift back to mule deer just before evening.

This kind of hunting fits in well with other activities. Since hunting trips are typically short and simple to organize, it's easy to include camping, fishing, and hiking as part of the action. It takes a minimum of creative planning to get a lot of gunning into one season.

A family outing can be the basis of memorable small game hunting. It provides a chance to teach the principles of safe gun handling to younger shooters in a field setting. It's a good opportunity to teach the hunters of tomorrow how to find sign, read tracks, learn game foods—and how to behave in the outdoors.

A sense of the popularity of small game hunting is found in some harvest figures. In Virginia, half of all hunters in the state go after squirrel; over one million rabbits are taken annually. North Carolina's squirrel harvests are just under four million in good years; 700,000 cottontails are taken annually in this state. Even anti-gun

Small game hunting is for everyone—men and women.

Franklin Ground Squirrel is one of the largest ground squirrels in North America. It is a top target.

states like New York show 700,000 to a million squirrels taken each year, and an equal number of hares and rabbits as well. In Massachusetts, rabbits are considered a nuisance species. Iowa harvests over two million cottontails each year; Illinois takes two million squirrels. Missouri takes several million cottontails yearly, making it the champion cottontail state in the Nation.

Attitudes about small game vary across North America. In the provinces of Saskatchewan, Alberta, and Manitoba the badger is still considered a valuable fur bearer. In North Dakota, rabbits are hunted for fur and good fur harvests come out of this state every year. In neighboring South Dakota, rabbits are largely ignored, but prairie dog hunting is growing. Wyoming encourages

Squirrels are top targets throughout their range. Next to cottontails they are our most sought-after small game animal.

prairie dog hunting, and Montana actively promotes it in travel literature.

These statistics give some measure of the depth of interest in small game hunting. Many states and provinces don't bother to keep accurate records on small game harvests. Species like ground squirrels, woodchucks and rockchucks are still considered agricultural pests and open shooting is often encouraged. As for the crow, nobody likes this raucous nest-robber, and statistics on kills are nonexistent.

In summary, there are a wealth of reasons to go after small game. Few other kinds of hunting offer quite the same mix of pleasure and participation, not to mention the easy involvement of younger family members. Costs are not great, and expensive travel is not required.

The small game hunter is constantly offered the opportunity to learn new woodcraft skills. Locating animals, finding sign, and sorting out the animal from the countryside are all new challenges. Each species offers its own unique characteristics. The hunting of each demands a different set of skills. Together these animals are among the most heavily hunted in North America today. They represent a mixed bag of hunting opportunities available to hunters all across North America.

Many of our small game animals share portions of their range. Foods and lifestyles are usually vastly different, but in many areas two and sometimes three species can be hunted at the same time.

Much equipment can be employed in several kinds of hunting. Clothing, vehicles, rifles, cartridges, optical equipment, and other accessories are all interchangeable. Participating in multiple activities lets hunters get extra usage from expensive gear, and provides reasons (excuses!) for acquiring additional equipment. Wives and girlfriends will never be short of gift ideas for the small game hunter in their lives—he always needs something.

And the meat is edible. Interesting recipes are always possible. Correct handling of game, proper aging, and preparation for cooking are important skills the hunter should develop. Many outdoorsmen are surprised by the tastes of rabbit, woodchuck, and squirrel. Our forefathers lived on these meats, and by today's health-conscious diet standards this meat looks even better. It's lean, low in fat, dark and flavorful, and free of chemical additives, presenting the palate with something not available from the supermarket. Home preparation of game meat is fun. It's a major reason for hunting.

Rabbit stew, or Hasenpfeffer, and Brunswick stew are traditional game recipes that have been around for ages. These recipes are easy to learn and modify to suit individual tastes. They give us all a chance to emulate our forefathers. Experimenting with foods has become a pastime for many, and small game hunting fits right in with this activity.

Young rock squirrels are suitable targets in some areas.

Chapter 2

The Small Game Menu

Blacktail Mecca

Heat from the warm sun penetrated my denim jacket. The air was fresh and clear. It was early spring and as yet hunting season hadn't started, but, as I saw it, this presented little problem. I would go after blacktail prairie dogs. At this time of year I feel a strong kinship to the paunchy blacktail. Like the blacktail prairie dog, I'm emerging from something of a hibernation, having survived another cold winter. The bitter cold had put most hunting on the back burner. There had been few opportunities to be outdoors and pursue serious shooting. Now that it was spring I would be sure I got out and did some shooting.

Blacktail prairie dogs make an excellent pre-season hunting target. They are a fine way to bone up on shooting skills that have been shelved over the winter. Besides, they are a worthy target that offers unique challenges to long range shooters. All the skills of hunting and shooting are needed to consistently bag these critters out on the windy prairie they call home.

Blacktails, which are rodents and not really dogs, were once thought to be in serious trouble

when competition from cattle ranching was eliminating their habitat. But the hardy creatures have endured, and they are re-establishing themselves along large parts of their native range.

The blacktail occupies an oval range across the plains states with its tip in southern Canada. The animal is considered a pest in much of its habitat. The plains of Wyoming still teem with thousands of prairie dogs every spring, much as they did in the early 1800's. Montana, South Dakota, and Idaho have similar situations.

In other states the animal is still protected in national parks and private preserves. However, the cattle-grazing belt of America holds blacktail populations that annually cause great loss of grass—grass that would otherwise be converted into beef. For this reason, hunting is encouraged over much of the prairie dog's range.

Throughout the west this has led to a situation unlike that in any other part of the country. Hunters are openly urged to shoot dogs that eat up scarce pasture grasses. Permission to hunt is easy to obtain. Shooting one does the agricultural economy some good—or so it's thought—and puts the hunter on good terms with landowners. Some states, most notably South Dakota, publish

Distribution of the Blacktail Prairie Dog

these animals stand about 11 inches tall, making then an excellent long-range target.

The prairie dog got in man's way when the west was settled. Historian Vernon Bailey described one colony that stretched uninterrupted for over 250 miles and was measured at just under 100 miles wide. Bailey, writing in 1901, estimated that four million animals inhabited the colony. Ernest Thompson Seton determined that early populations were ten times those of the buffalo. These numbers drastically declined as man moved westward and cultivated the land.

For decades prairie dogs were poisoned using strychnine. This threatened to kill off the dogs

pamphlets that help hunters to locate prairie dogs and identify places where hunters are especially welcome to hunt. License fees are nonexistent and most state wildlife officials will gladly direct an inquiring hunter to the nearest dog colony.

With this kind of cooperation it's easy to see why blacktail prairie dog hunting has grown in popularity. In the far west the dog rivals the eastern woodchuck for the amount of ammo expended and the level of shooter interest. Clubs have been formed with the sole purpose of prairie dog busting.

Most hunters are surprised by the size of these animals. They can weigh up to five pounds. At a distance and seen moving around their colony, they appear to be a plump critter with a flattened head, short or low ears, short legs and a very short slender tail.

In the hand their fur appears thin, coarse and close to the body. Claws are well developed and black in color, with some being white tipped. Overall body length is just over 15 inches and shoulder height is nearly five inches. The tail is tipped black for anywhere from one-fifth to one-half of its length. Important for shooters,

Blacktails were once thought to be in serious trouble, but their numbers have rebounded in recent years. They are a plentiful target.

forever, and conservationists became concerned. In 1972 the federal government outlawed poisoning of prairie dogs on lands controlled by the Bureau of Land Management. Limited controls were also put in place regulating dog poisoning on private lands. Widespread poisoning stopped.

The results were dramatic. Dog populations soared. In Montana there were accounts of colonies growing from 10,000 individuals to 50,000 within three years. Colorado populations increased twenty-fold. Politically active cattlemen lobbied for reinstated poisoning. Today, limited poisoning has returned to private lands and over-population is kept in check. Yet, for the hunter, dog populations today are better than at any time in modern shooting history.

Prairie dogs are big eaters. Some scientists estimate that 32 of them can consume as much forage as one cow. They do compete directly with cattle, eating a diet that is 98 percent grass. In many areas it's the same grass that cattle prefer. The dogs eat everything—leaf, stem, roots and seeds. Grasslands around dens are bared to the earth. The rest of the diet is composed of bugs. It's very easy for an alert hunter to see prairie dogs hopping about the colony, snapping their pint-sized jaws at grasshoppers, blue bottle flies and mosquitoes.

It is important for hunters to know that the blacktail has a cousin known as the white-tailed prairie dog, which differs only slightly from the blacktail. The most obvious difference is seen on the tail, the tip of which is white rather than black. Also, the animal is slightly smaller and less gregarious than its cousin. In many areas, including Utah and California, it is completely protected from hunting.

The blacktail prairie dog is easy to find. The animals live in colonies on the vast stretches of prairie grass comprising their native habitat. Finding one prairie dog usually means more are around. Deserted burrows or unused mounds do not necessarily mean there are no animals in the area. Colonies can range in size from a few dozen individuals to tens of thousands spread over dozens of square miles of ranch land.

These animals clean off an area about 70 to 100 feet in diameter around their individual burrows. This is their signature. The vegetation is kept down in all seasons to prevent predators from sneaking close under cover. The area is also used for loafing—something prairie dogs love to do. The ground becomes hard, baked, and compacted around the burrow entrance, providing a good running pad to escape predators from either the air or land. Few colonial living animals have as many escape mechanisms available to them.

Locating a colony is usually a matter of driving along the myriad prairie back trails that

The well equipped blacktail hunter has a long range rifle and cartridge combination, and also carries adequate optical equipment.

Who's more plump? Blacktails are often described as plump rodents. They can eat a lot of grass, and this brings them into conflict with man.

crisscross the west until a colony turns up. Talking with local ranchers works well, too. In ranch country near small towns and cities the locations of colonies, especially large ones, are frequently well known. Undisturbed colonies attain a great deal of stability.

The colonies are easy to recognize. Many times the hunter will be greeted by the sharp piercing calls of individual dogs acting as sentinels along the outskirts of the colony. When the animals are not actually seen or heard, their dens will be a quick indication of their presence. Unlike the prairie gophers that share large parts of their

range with the dogs, the blacktail constructs a large circular dike around the entrance to its burrow.

These mounds are easy to spot. Scat is in abundance around mounds and across any part of the colony. It is best described as short, chunky pieces about one inch long, normally black or brown. Typically, broken scat fragments are found at the base of any sagebrush plant or other vegetation that survives the feeding habit of the dog. Finally, the surrounding landscape has such an over-grazed look that even inexperienced eyes can see the strain these rodents place on the range.

Many colonies go undisturbed by man and are only briefly visited by predators. The result is that the mounds become a distinct part of the landscape, and serve as dikes to prevent the occasional prairie rains that often turn into flash floods from washing down into the burrow.

Most burrows have only one entrance, although I have seen dozens that clearly sported a second sneaky entrance. These are usually located on the edge of the colony where, perhaps, predator pressure makes this behavior necessary.

Burrows on the edge of the colony provide

The tail is black tipped and about two and one-half inches long.

excellent rifle rests for hunters. They are high enough up from the surrounding land to give a good view of the colony from the prone position, and their gentle slope makes a nice incline on which to belly down.

Happily for the hunter, the mounds are usually free of that pesky cactus known as prickly pear. The brittle lobes of this cactus seem to break off and leave their sharp needles around, lying in wait for the unsuspecting hunter to plant his derriere on just as he is concentrating on a dog a couple of hundred yards away. This cactus, while common on the land found in the colony, is rarely present on the mounds.

Once a colony is discovered, a set pattern of shooting seems to occur. As most varmint hunters know, animals closest to the hunter represent the easy shots. At first, ranges can be as little as 25 yards, but as the varmint becomes familiar with hunters and the report of a rifle, these close-in animals soon disappear. The same is true with gophers and woodchucks. With blacktails the ranges become extreme and soon the hunter finds himself involved in long-range shooting.

It is now a standard procedure for me and my shooting friends to lay a mat over the edge of a suitable mound or on a cactus-free piece of ground. From this mat we can take care of most of our shooting quite comfortably. It sidesteps the cactus problem and also helps us keep track

Shooting from a mat helps prone shooting. Here the author takes a few minutes for lunch with the prairie dog colony in the background.

Dog colonies offer many kinds of interesting sign. This hunter examines a skull from a blacktail prairie dog.

Scat is often found spread throughout active colonies.

of ejected cases for future reloading, as well keeping the cases clean. We never walk out into the colony until our shooting session is completed

Prairie dog colonies are always alive with activity. Except for the hottest two hours in early afternoon, the dogs are constantly on the move, either feeding or loafing in their little territories. The animals are up shortly after sunrise—also an excellent time to be out hunting—and remain active until well after dark. Their foraging trips can take two to three hours and individual dogs can be found over 100 yards from their dens. Young dogs are active and nearly always around the mouth of the den during warm periods of the day.

Dogs are very subject to predation. They are banquet fare for coyotes, foxes, badgers, owls, eagles and hawks. The young are readily taken by rattlesnakes that slither stealthily down into a burrow and ambush unsuspecting young at sunrise. Sometimes snakes become trapped in a den and, unable to climb out, they remain, cleaning out an entire family and taking up residence. Winter usually brings vengeance of a sort as the trapped snake freezes.

With the mat in place the most productive shooting positions are prone and sitting. Sometimes an offhand shot can be tried, just to keep in shape for the approaching deer season. These rarely connect, although I have been pleasantly surprised on occasion. One of my all-time favorite shots was made from the offhand position at a South Dakota prairie dog standing in a wheel rut some 350 yards away. Bob Elman, the well known outdoor writer and editor, bore witness as the dog dropped back into the wheel track and the bullet kicked up dust behind.

A rest is a must in this kind of hunting. Sometimes the hood of a vehicle can be used, but the ubiquitous prairie wind usually rocks the vehicle enough that really accurate shooting is difficult. Bipods that fit onto the front sling swivel are excellent for long-range shooting. Those with extendable legs can be raised for use in a kind of cross-legged sitting position. This is useful when vegetation or the mound obscures the prairie dog. Another method, borrowed from the buffalo hunter of old, is the use of two sticks tied with leather thongs. These are set up in the form of a bipod, but usually the hunter shoots from the kneeling position behind these. The ends of the sticks are sharpened and pushed lightly into the ground.

A good military type sling, correctly fitted to the arm, will go a long way to stabilizing the shooter. In the sitting position a fitted sling is

Dog, den, and rifle. Shots are typically 200 yards long.

almost a must. It should be mentioned here that correct length in a military type sling may be hard to find. One cheap brand that I've seen is too short in the forward part of the sling. It's not possible to get the upper arm into correct position with enough sling left over to bring the rifle to the shoulder.

A rucksack, used for carrying shooting accessories, can double as a good rest. It's very solid as well as being soft enough that no jump is imparted to the rifle. Those hunters who set their rifles directly across the truck box or car hood are usually contributing to about three inches of rise in point-of-impact at 100 yards. Any rest should be well padded to prevent throwing shots high.

Aside from a good rest, there are other pieces of equipment vital to successful dog shooting. Paramount among these are good binoculars and a spotting scope. Binoculars that resolve well and are of reasonably high power are a good choice. Most hunters carry the binoculars they use for deer hunting. Those who are looking to more specialized equipment might consider 10-power lightweight style glasses.

A spotting scope is something the more casual hunter will probably not own. However, for dog shooting at long ranges, it can't be beaten. Scopes of about 40 to 45 power are best. When placed on a tripod they are excellent for discerning dogs from mounds at long range.

One of the handiest rigs designed for spotting scopes is a clamp that fastens onto the glass of a partially rolled-down vehicle window. Once the scope is mounted on the clamp it can be easily focused while sitting in the vehicle. Also, the door can be opened so the scope can be used in other directions. But you have to sit very still for this to work well.

If a fellow does a lot of hunting he will probably acquire quite a bag of equipment. Prairie dog hunting gives the winter-weary shooter an opportunity to use all his hard-earned equipment, as well as the chance to dust off his hunting skills.

Along with specialized equipment, hunters need an adequate rifle and load combination. In truth, prairie dogs are taken with just about any type of rifle and cartridge. Using .22 rimfires, hundreds of ranch boys and girls still annually reduce resident blacktail populations during Saturday afternoon plinking sessions. The casual hunter can use his own deer rifle, but his success may not be great on distant dogs.

Really successful prairie dog hunting demands a modern, high intensity rifle of mild trajectory, and cartridges with good wind-bucking bullets. In the specialized varmint class, the .22/250 is king. The moribund Winchester .225, available only in those awful-looking post-1964 Model 70's, was also a great dog combination. The smaller, less potent .222 Remington and the .223 Remington cartridges are good for dogs up to intermediate ranges.

Moving up into the .25 calibers, the .25-06 is considered the masterpiece of dog cartridges, and the .257 Roberts, slowly returning via the new Model 70 Featherweight, is also highly regarded as a classic prairie dog combination. One of the old-timers that is still a consistent performer is the .250/3000, but it is now available only in the Savage Model 99 offered in classic version. I still have a Model 54 Winchester in .250/3000, outfitted with a factory target stock and heavy barrel. Although it was manufactured in 1936, it is still very deadly on prairie dogs.

Perhaps the most popular cartridge for dog shooting can be found among the 6mm's. The .243 Winchester, long known for its multipurpose role on anything from antelope to deer, is a favorite among western sportsmen who like mild shooting cartridges capable of long range performance. The 6mm Remington, often considered to be slightly more versatile for handloading than its Winchester counterpart, is also a preferred cartridge. The recent commercialization of the 6 PPC offers great potential.

When it comes to rifles, any one of the wide assortment of American-made sporters will work

Coyotes are major predators of the prairie dog. They often roam the edges of the colony looking for young dogs who stray from safety.

on prairie dogs. For the more serious type, target models carrying heavy barrels and full-size stocks are a tremendous aid in extended shooting sessions. They are also more accurate than the standard sporter models.

Adjustable triggers are a great thing on any rifle, but are particularly useful for the serious dog shooter. Trigger weights that come in around 18 ounces are fine for those who know a gunsmith who can safely work this reduced weight out. For most hunters, a two- to three-pound trigger pull is possible on the better quality sporters equipped with adjustable triggers.

Although specialized equipment greatly increases the chances for consistent hits on prairie dogs, it is not impossible to make routine 200-yard shots at standing prairie dogs using everyday, off-the-shelf sporters. Many will perform this well right out of the box. However, what does hinder long-range shooting is the ever-present wind. Target shooters know well that wind effect can have a far greater influence on bullet placement than bullet drop.

For example, a 10 mph wind across the bullet's flight path from either the three or nine o'clock position will drift an 87 grain .243 bullet 10 inches off the center of the target at 300 yards. Unfortunately, wind does not always come at right angles to the shooter, especially on open prairie dog colonies. For ease of figuring, wind coming across the line of sight at the one, five, seven and eleven o'clock positions is about 50 percent of the three and nine o'clock angles. For the remaining angles, wind effect is 87 percent of the right angle positions.

Since the prairie dog presents a target only about three and one-half inches wide and 11 inches tall, wind plays a major role in determining success. After some trial and error, as well as some Kentucky windage, a hunter will be able to second-guess the wind about 60 percent of the time. Ultimately, nothing beats learning by experience, and the abundant prairie dog targets allow for much hands-on practice.

Varmint type bullets are the rule for this kind of hunting. Fortunately, there are dozens around to choose from. In the .25 caliber line I have had good success with the Sierra hollow point, boat tailed, 90 grain bullet. In the .257 Roberts and the .25-06, this is a devastating varmint bullet and has a very favorable ballistic coefficient. In windy country this helps at long ranges, and the greater bullet weight also retains down-range velocity better than lighter .25 caliber bullets. It also does well in my .250/3000.

In the 6mm's, the Hornady 75 grain hollow point is well known for its good performance. This bullet expands rapidly due to its light construction. Perhaps one of the most versatile hunting handloads incorporates this bullet and 40 grains of IMR 4320 in a Winchester case. This travels at about 3250 feet per second and, with a one-inch-above-the-bull placement, will deliver hits on prairie dogs out to 275 yards with a dead-on hold. The same bullet in the 6mm

Adult dogs are capable of denuding large areas around their burrows.

Remington case will develop about 200 fps more with two grains increase over the .243 load.

Some purists argue that the 87 grain .243 bullets and heavier versions are the better prairie dog choice due to the greater ballistic coefficient of these bullets. Theoretically, there is logic to this. However, my experience has shown little improvement in bullet drift by the additional 12 or more grains of lead. It may become significant with 100 grains, but bullets around this weight are poor for prairie dogs as expansion is slower. These heavier bullets are really made for deer and antelope, and should not be used on prairie dogs.

The blacktail prairie dog's super abundance out on the plains means it's an easy target to find. For most hunters, little specialized equipment is needed that is not already on hand for big game trips. Those hunters who do take blacktail hunting seriously will find them a challenging target. Over the years most of my outstanding long-distance rifle shots have been made at blacktails that were standing on the opposite side of their colonies.

Most hunters will, after a few tries, be able to connect on the average dog. By far the biggest advantage to hunting these pesty rodents is the workout both the hunter and his equipment get early in the year. Spring or summer target practice of this kind is hard to find in many parts of the country, and the practice means better shooting during the much shorter big game seasons later in the year.

If it is at all possible, I thank the landowner when I leave. Many times such courtesy is followed by an invitation to come back again to take on more blacktails. Sometimes it has opened up land to me that was otherwise closed or on which stiff trespass fees were charged. Jerome Knap, Canadian Editor for *Field and Stream*, and I met a rancher who told us to shoot all the prairie dogs on his place, and then to cross the fence into his neighbor's place. The old salt promised to phone his neighbor and tell him he had sent prairie dog hunters onto his place. That kind of reception is rare, but for the winter-weary rifleman, it's a welcome part of prairie dog hunting.

Rockchucks and woodchucks

When scribes of future ages look back on our society's hunting practices, they will surely conclude that the woodchuck started it all. Indeed, the animal that gave us Groundhog Day was also the reason varmint hunting evolved into the sport it is today. While the west was replete with small game animals ranging from ground squirrels to rabbits, it was the woodchuck that first caught the attention of riflemen in the east. Eastern riflemen, hankering for something to shoot, and with little big game left, switched to the one animal, a member of the squirrel family, that had actually *grown* in numbers as land was brought under cultivation.

Since World War II the woodchuck has actually expanded its range. In the northeastern USA 'chucks occupied marginal farm country since the beginning of time. However, as pastures became permanent, 'chucks adapted and moved to a field-type environment from the small, open, marginal clearings in woodlands that had previously characterized their habitat.

Traditionally, they prospered anywhere that dry woodlands abutted open fields. But the modern agricultural practice of breaking sod and reseeding with domestic grasses, clover and alfalfa gave the 'chuck an extra boost. As new varieties of alfalfa and clover developed and were successful in different parts of North America, the woodchuck simply followed the fodder across the continent.

Over the last 40 years, man's influence moved woodchuck abundance up one step. Where it was rare, it became frequent; where it was common, it became abundant. Hay or fodder fields, providing food and protection, have become home to woodchucks all over North America.

The woodchuck must not be confused with its

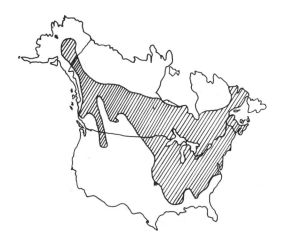

Distribution of the Woodchuck

Distribution of the Rockchuck

close cousin, the yellow-bellied marmot. Gunners know it as the rockchuck, and it's a well known piece of modern shooting lore that Fred Huntington, founder of RCBS loading equipment, named his first successful press after the little rockchuck. RCBS was the abbreviation for Rockchuck Bullet System.

There are some distinct differences between the two animals that might as well be cleared up now. First, and most important to the field shooter, are the ranges occupied by the two species. Rockchucks are found in the west, while woodchucks are found throughout the east and into the North.

Nature has seen to it that there are far more woodchucks than rockchucks. Local hunters refer to each kind as 'chucks, while scientists call both marmots. An alfalfa- and barley-fattened woodchuck outweighs the average rockchuck by two to five pounds, and this was part of the reason eastern shooters continued to develop high-intensity cartridges capable of knocking down an animal that could weigh as much as 14 pounds.

Another difference is coat color. Woodchucks are generally darker and can range from a mealy yellowish-brown in the South to very dark

brown in more northern areas. A woodchuck's underfur is light brown, while a rockchuck will have a yellow belly, hence the name yellow-bellied marmot. Other differences include the feet—always dark brown or black on a woodchuck and *never* dark brown on the rockchuck. Finally, the ranges of the two animals never cross. Unlike prairie dogs and ground squirrels, the various 'chuck species are not found together.

Most hunting literature says all 'chucks can be hunted the same way. It's not true. Rockchucks occupy slightly higher elevations than their eastern cousins, and frequently live in much more remote countryside. This means longer-range shots, often at odd angles, are necessary on rockchucks.

While not a certainty, rockchucks tend to be less wary of man. Any attempt to stalk closer, however, is often frustrated by rocky slopes, open country and stalking noise. Rockchucks got their name from their habit of burrowing near a large boulder and using this as a lookout or hiding post. This makes rockchucks more difficult to find than woodchucks.

Woodchucks have become associated with an interesting legend. On February 2nd of each year

'Chucks have moved to a field or pasture environment from an open woodland habitat during the past 40 years or so.

the lowly 'chuck (or groundhog, as he's called by most Americans), represented as Punxsutawney Phil from Punxsutawney, Pennsylvania, is said to roust himself from his winter's sleep and sally forth to the mouth of his den. There, the animal cautiously pokes his nose into the air and examines the weather. If he sees his shadow, we are supposed to be in for six more weeks of winter. If Phil can't find a shadow, spring will arrive in two weeks.

There are other, less famous ground hogs that also attempt to predict the weather. Wiarton Willie plies his art near the town of Wiarton, Ontario and Madoc Mike works the Belleville, Ontario, countryside. Interestingly, these far-flung groundhogs rarely disagree, and their predictions are eagerly awaited every year.

The idea of groundhogs being reliable weather forecasters on February 2 dates back to the Christian festival commemorating the purification of the Virgin Mary. It is the day on which candles are blessed and is known as Candlemas or Candlmas. An early pope set the day aside to correspond with the pagan festival of *Februa*. Early peoples thought that the weather on this day was a reverse indicator of things to come. Good weather meant a long, cold winter, while an overcast day indicated an early spring.

Woodchucks got their name from the early Cree word *wuchak* or *otchock*. The animal was considered emergency food by eastern forest-dwelling Indians. It's unlikely that plains Indians ever saw a woodchuck in early times.

'Chucks that are up early in February are really staking out territory for the upcoming season. The females emerge as much as three weeks later, and by this time the males have established their territories. So there is at least some biological logic behind the 'chuck's wintery emergence.

The average female 'chuck will have one litter of two to six young per year—varying with range conditions—following a gestation period of 31 to 33 days. The females breed at two years of age, and when food supplies are good many one-year-old females also breed. Depending on location, the young are born between the first week of May and mid-June. Blind, helpless and totally dependent on its mother's milk, a newborn 'chuck weighs less than two ounces.

'Chucks go into hibernation loaded with brown fat. Their heart rate slows to five beats per minute, evidence of a slow metabolism of the stored food. By spring, staying alive over the winter has consumed this fat. As much as half of the animal's body weight may have been lost and must be replaced. When food supplies have been insufficient to prepare the 'chuck for the entire winter, the animal will rise in October or November and scamper about for more food. Without good supplies of brown fat, a 'chuck simply starves.

Inside the hibernation chamber the woodchuck curls into a tight ball with its head beneath its tail. The animal's body temperature drops to that of the surrounding burrow, typically between 40 and 45 degrees Fahrenheit. Woodchucks can survive temperatures as low as 35 degrees F. Their nerve tissue continues to operate at temperatures colder than other mammals could tolerate. Essentially, the woodchuck is deaf and blind during hibernation.

The period of arousal is interesting, and although described here for the woodchuck, it applies somewhat to all rodent species. These animals actually wake very quickly, often over an eight- or nine-hour period. The head area warms first, and then the tail end. This is why it's possible to see a woodchuck dragging his hind end as he moves around the den entrance. The head can be as much as 30 degrees warmer than the hind feet. Heart rate and blood pressure increase rapidly during the waking process. The animal's metabolic rate quickly goes back to normal.

Eventually the animal emerges from its burrow and becomes fully active. During hibernation, woodchucks routinely awake two or three times per week and shift their position in the burrow. As spring approaches these quickening periods increase in duration.

Woodchucks can be found by driving back roads and checking likely areas.

Woodchucks are protected from freezing to death in their sleep. If the den temperature drops too drastically—something that could occur when a hungry badger opens a den but does not find the occupant—the little 'chuck will awake and reseal the burrow.

Both kinds of 'chucks are detested by farmers. They dig holes in gardens, hay fields and corn patches. Alfalfa seems to be their favorite food, and these animals are particularly disliked by ranchers and stockmen. Field crops are not safe either, and virtually any succulent new growth is eagerly gobbled up by foraging woodchucks. Hay fields provide cover as well as food, and over 90 percent of the 'chuck's food is grass and grass-like plants.

'Chucks occupy the open fields next to fence lines and pasture boundaries—the same countryside that is home to pheasants and numerous upland game birds. Many hunters have learned that offering to shoot 'chucks on farm land can make it harder to find the birds. When looking for 'chucks, begin in the same way you would as if seeking upland game. Once in good upland

'Chuck hunting is usually successful. Field borders are often productive.

country, look around the edges of the fields rather than into the center of bluffs and hedgerows. Wise old 'chucks will hide den entrances in shrubs and nearby rocks.

Woodchucks build several doorways into their burrow system. Three or four holes could belong to the same animal. The main entrance is about 12 inches across. Inside, the shaft narrows to about six inches and can run from a few to 40 feet. Like a mine shaft, the tunnel's depth depends on the soil. It can plummet anywhere from two feet in rocky ground to six or seven in softer, more easily worked soils. The straight-down nature of the 'chuck hole helps the animal escape danger quickly. It hangs on the side of its burrow and, if unsafe to exit, needs only to let go and fall back into the hole. The burrow systems can be extensive, with forked side passages and up to three bedrooms. A grass-lined nest serves as sleeping quarters.

The numerous entrances and deep holes, along with voracious food habits, puts the 'chuck at odds with farmers and ranchers. The holes are a danger to man and machinery. In the rock-chuck's high country home, fewer holes are produced; many are simply cracks in the surface rock or passages hollowed out between rocks. Generally 'chucks attack hay crops and, while much of this goes unnoticed, it's a source of irritation when top-quality fodder destined for dairy barns is damaged.

Woodchucks and their cousins are efficient miners. Outfitted with strong digging muscles, strong and sharp claws, and chisel-like teeth, they are capable of digging through most any soil. They can excavate small rocks that get in the way as they tunnel through the soil. They cut through tree and plant roots with ease. With their flat body they shove freshly dug soil ahead of their chest and out of the tunnel.

In an active colony, tunnels are constantly being redesigned by their occupants. Bathroom and bedroom chambers are frequently cleaned. This material can be found at the mouth of the den. Scats look like short pieces of dry ropes,

Woodchucks build several doorways or entrances to their burrow system. Close checking with binoculars turns up these sites along edges of fields and bush borders.

and bedding is made up of locally abundant grasses. Hunters checking out 'chuck dens for recent activity will find this sign near woodland edges and field margins. In 'chuck hunting this kind of sign is more reliable than tracks.

The woodchuck has a habit of moving its burrows as the season progresses. The spring burrow is usually along the edge of woodland or a field. But where old fields are broken and await new seeding, 'chucks will move dens closer to existing, undisturbed fields. For hunters after 'chucks this doesn't mean all the animals have been shot. They have only adjusted their territories to accommodate changes in food habits.

Some don't need *any* reason to move. They will dwell in an alfalfa field during the early spring and summer and move into the woodlands as fall approaches. For the hunter this means whole colonies can give the appearance of having disappeared, when in reality the animals have only made a seasonal shift in residences.

In many areas these shifts produce so many burrows that it can look like a burgeoning population. It's not true, and hunters simply have to be diligent in finding out where the animals are now located. Just as a tip, these moves often provide more opportunity for young animals to be recruited into the breeding population. This is good for the hunter—an increased breeding population usually means more targets in the future.

There are really three ways to find 'chucks. One is to ask local farmers. The 'chuck's bad reputation makes this an effective method. The second, and most common, is to drive the back country, scouting for active burrows along field margins and wastelands. Dens spotted this way will, upon close examination, invariably turn up other closely associated burrows.

Another method that works well in areas where 'chucks are not common is to walk fencelines between bush and pasture. Checking freshly disturbed soil will usually turn up a burrow. The pathways the chuck uses for moving to feeding areas will be readily visible. Remember, most burrows are used year after year at roughly the same time, and this means there are good odds that animals will be available in the area for years into the future.

The commonality of 'chucks has given rise to a couple of hunting myths. Foremost among these is that 'chucks are everywhere. On the contrary, where 'chucks are low in numbers, they can be quite difficult to find. It is not uncommon for only one or two 'chucks to be found in an area with no neighbors for miles in any direction. This is the case especially at the extreme northern edge of the species's range.

The other myth is the animal's lack of intelligence. These animals very quickly learn to associate gun noise with danger. Like predators, these animals can sense when man might be a threat. Any farmer will tell you that while they are doing farm work, the foraging woodchuck can be brazen, almost tame. But let that farmer pay closer attention and the 'chuck is gone. The rockchuck is equally wary.

Anytime is a good time to hunt the 'chuck species. Their sharp whistle can be heard for some distance, and sometimes a scared 'chuck will whistle several times from inside its burrow. That's often a sign the animal plans to re-emerge shortly and offer a shot to the quick-thinking hunter. 'Chucks are active at all times. Early morning and evening are best, but even at midday—especially on a warm afternoon—they will be up and about, actively eating.

Chucks are best caught off guard in the early morning. Just after sunrise a camouflaged hunter who's set up in a nearby bush will easily pick off foraging 'chucks at distances from 50 to 300 yards.

'Chucks are so intent on their morning feeding period that a well concealed hunter can take several shots before they become disturbed by the shooting. Those retreating to the safety of their burrows will shortly re-emerge to resume feeding and again offer the positioned hunter good opportunities. This morning feeding period, lasting about two hours, will provide even the most jaded shooters with some fast action and reason enough to return.

In many top quality 'chuck hunting areas the tall luxuriant vegetation prevents shooting prone, though alfalfa fields that have been hayed allow some prone shooting. The best advice is to go high—find a knoll and shoot down into the 'chucks. Shooting upright, using a tree as a rest, works well, but long range shots are possible only from highly stable shooting positions. Shooters bringing portable benches will find long range 'chuck shooting far easier.

The 'chuck is tenacious, requiring good solid

'Chucks are best caught off guard during the early morning foraging period.

hits to knock the animal over. Those wounded will readily escape down the nearest hole, never to be found. Top cartridges and accurate rifles are a must. Body hits by today's centerfire cartridges will take out most small ground squirrels, but 'chucks require well placed hits, either along the spine, head, or heart-lungs area. Shots placed elsewhere almost assure that the 'chuck will escape.

Some hunters like to know the age of the chucks they have taken in a day's shoot. In the early summer it's easy enough: small 'chucks are the young of the year. 'Chucks begin life weighing an ounce or two, and by the time they are weaned will tip the scales at one to one and a half pounds. By the end of June, a healthy young 'chuck will weigh three pounds. A yearling 'chuck, one born the previous year, comes in at around four pounds.

Age can also be determined by looking at the 'chuck's incisor teeth. Young 'chucks have narrow, pointed white incisors. Yearling 'chucks will have some stain if taken in spring, and light browning when shot during late summer. Adult animals have broad, well developed incisors with distinct staining. Keep in mind that 'chucks belong to the rodent family, and this means their teeth continue to grow for their entire lifetime. Staining is part of the natural aging process.

'Chucks blend into their environment amazingly well, especially if there are some nearby trees to create shadows. Frequently, only their head pokes above the burrow entrance and does not offer much of a target. A shooter needs a good scope and binoculars for hunting to be successful.

Sunup is the best time to go after these animals. They keep nearly the same hours as humans and sleep during the night. Activity periods can vary with weather. Exceedingly hot weather keeps them holed up. Bright, cloudy days are ideal for spotting and shooting 'chucks. Optics work best on this kind of day, and 'chucks are most active. Shoot from sunup until mid-morning, then again from mid-afternoon until

half an hour before sundown.

The animal stands as high as 18 inches. This plus the mound, normally higher than the surrounding land, make the 'chuck a good long range target. Foraging 'chucks, moving on all four legs, present a lower profile. An adult 'chuck stands about six to eight inches at the shoulder.

While 'chucks are no friend of the farmer, they do benefit the landscape. Abandoned dens become home to rabbits and other small game. In addition, their soil churning capability helps spread minerals that would otherwise remain root-bound. Currently, poisons are more of a threat to sustained populations of groundhogs and rockchucks than any hunter's bullet. The drive to squeeze ever more dollars out of agricultural pursuits ultimately represents the 'chuck's biggest danger.

'Chucks have a real role to play in the predator-prey cycle. Coyotes, foxes, and in the far North, wolves and Arctic foxes, as well as various hawks and owls, are all willing to take 'chucks whenever the opportunity presents.

'Chuck behavior patterns are broken only by weather. Wind and rain cause all 'chucks to delay feeding periods until later in the day. For some reason these animals are bothered by wet belly fur, and they'll delay leaving the den after heavy rains have soaked the surrounding vegetation. Mud, easily made around den mouths, keeps the animals in their burrow. Wind, too, keeps 'chucks holed up, probably because their whistling defense mechanism is not effective in strong wind. Bad weather is not the time to be out hunting these furry critters.

'Chucks are most difficult to find late in the summer. Most hunters know that burrowing rodents prepare themselves for winter very early in the summer. In most areas mid-summer sees adult rodents turning fat and heading for their winter den.

This applies to 'chucks, too. Rockchucks disappear from sight by mid August. In the North woodchucks have acquired heavy layers of brown fat and are snug in their winter chamber by the last week of July. Hunters should know that there is much local variation in the onset of winter. It's important to keep in touch with local conditions and sort out the hunting opportunities accordingly.

Spring Jackrabbits

The warm spring winds had done their job. Back trails were dry, making cross-country travel easier than usual in springtime. New plant growth was everywhere. Field borders and ditches sported succulent vegetation; cultivated open headlands still held residues from previous crops. Having thrown off winter once more, the land was slowly coming alive. The prairie air smelled clean, and sounds carried as if nature's acoustic dampers had not been put in place.

Overhead, coursing crows checked for winter-killed carcasses exposed by the warm winds. It was an inviting combination—warm weather, easy access, and abundant new growth. For us it meant only one thing—a spring jackrabbit hunt.

Jackrabbits are rarely considered a source of good spring gunning. That's because nobody thinks these animals are interesting targets, capable of providing a challenge for the hunter. Nothing could be further from the truth: jacks are quick, hard to spot and demand the shooter do his part. In fact, I'll stick my neck out and say spring jackrabbit hunting is a close kin to white-tailed deer hunting in the fall. You hunt jacks the same way you would deer, but you get to do it in the spring.

Although the jackrabbit is a hare, over the years the term *jackrabbit* has become a generic name for any large rabbit or hare. Outdoorsmen have always been satisfied to call any sizeable rabbit or hare a *jack*, but scientists separate hares and rabbits into very distinct groups.

The difference is based on the young. A hare leveret is born fully furred, eyes open, and ready to hop about within a few minutes after birth. Scientists describe this birth habit as precocious,

which really means maturing quickly. Rabbit young develop more slowly, being born blind, furless, helpless, and requiring three weeks before they move on their own.

Hares are known for one other feature. They reproduce wildly, quickly reaching large numbers throughout the northeastern United States and southern Canada. Then, over large portions of their range, populations crash, usually following an eight to 11 year cycle. Why this happens has scientists baffled. But hunters can find proof, and take advantage of this biological phenomenon, by watching these animals in all their

Hares reproduce wildly, reaching large numbers throughout the northeastern United States and southern Canada.

Hares change their coats—thus the name *varying hare*—to blend into the surrounding environment.

traditional ranges as well as in areas peripheral to the normal range. New generations push the animal to find new habitats.

There is one more feature important to hunters. Hares change their coat colors—thus the common term *varying hare*—to help blend into the environment. Their snow-white fur makes jackrabbits a good fur take during northern winters when hides are prime.

The rabbit is taken both for hides and as sport. However, toward spring, long after hides have lost their prime, the animals remain white, especially during years when spring arrives early. For hunters, the animal is thus easier to distinguish from its surroundings.

Jackrabbits are one of our most neglected species. Hunters seem to think hounds are needed to pursue the animal. Dogs are not necessary, and all jacks can be hunted on foot with good chances for success.

In the open west, limited winter hunting of jacks has developed, but the animals are still passed over in favor of blacktail prairie dogs or ground squirrels during the spring. Jacks are worthy targets, and spring efforts are very rewarding.

These animals have herbacious diets. During spring and summer, they'll content themselves with a belly-full of locally available grass. They shift to bark as fall and winter approach. During

Jackrabbits are one of our most neglected species. Hunters seem to think hounds are needed to pursue the animal. Dogs are not necessary, and all jacks can be hunted on foot.

Distribution of the Whitetail Jackrabbit

the coldest part of winter, especially when snow is piled deep, they feed on bark. It is common to find young trees girdled two or three feet above ground, leaving the outdoorsman wondering how this happened. This "tree" diet does not endear jacks to orchard owners, foresters, or homeowners trying to improve their yards with a bit of landscaping. In fact, such destructive habits can often produce an invitation to hunt from one of these folks.

Rabbit populations can change drastically, and appear to vary with food supplies. Foxes, coyotes, snakes, badgers, weasles, hawks, and owls all eagerly devour any kind of rabbit meat, but predation rarely eliminates a population. Diseases can be a factor, but it is good food supplies that allow jacks to realize their unique biological potential.

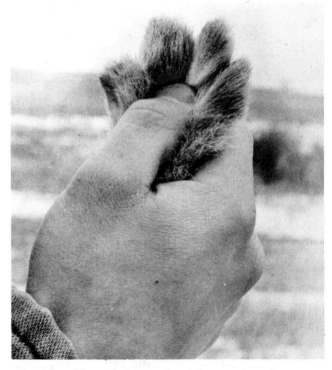

Equipped for winter and cold, snowy springs, the jackrabbit has a foot that is large and well haired.

Each female can breed as early as six months, and is capable of producing between eight and 18 leverets every five weeks. Females remate within minutes of giving birth, so they're capable of five litters per season. Given adequate food, this biological machine cranks out an enormous population of rabbits and hares.

Traditionally, jacks have been hunted with .22 caliber rimfire rifles or shotguns. However, during the spring, hunting on foot with medium-powered rifles is the best way to go. First, the extra power lets the hunter take longer shots, and big jacks, weighing as much as 15 pounds, require solid hits. Second, in open country, wind drift is reduced, producing more and better hits. Third, this shooting prepares the hunter for later whitetail hunting.

Indian tribes used rabbit skins to make winter robes. The skins were not sewn together, as you might expect, but dried and cut into long strips. The rabbit strips were wrapped around sinew from buffalo or deer to form long strands of fur rope. The ropes were then loosely woven together to produce a tight, thick blanket. Rabbit hair robes were a cherished source of pride for their owners, and made cold winter nights tolerable for the rugged tribesman of yesteryear.

Crop residues like broken straw, partially rotted chaff piles, shattered corn leaves, missed hay or sheared cotton stalks are important to jacks. From this material the animal creates a secluded resting spot called a form. The rabbit backs into some trash vegetation and digs into the material with his hind feet and nose. During

Jackrabbits make distinct trails as they move from one part of their home range to another.

the spring these forms are usually found along field borders, but can occur anywhere jacks are abundant. Forms provide limited shelter, but more importantly, camouflage. Jacks eagerly seek and readily use field trash cover.

Hunt these animals by walking field borders and checking for sign. An empty form means a jack is foraging nearby. Scat, tracks, and obvious runways are other good signs. Jacks spend hours clipping back the vegetation along their paths, yielding well defined trails that are easy to find and positive indicators of jack rabbit home range. Bits of hair along fencelines, under logs, beside bush piles, and near field corners are also good.

However, don't be fooled by chewed bark well up on saplings and shrubs. This means only that jacks were there in the winter; it's no indication of where the animal might be now.

Jacks break from their form with great speed. The rifle gunner has to be quick if shots are to count. He must be familiar with his rifle and how it shoots. Many jacks will only run within the confines of their own home range, tending to circle within a small area of about 20 acres. The alert rifleman will use this knowledge to his benefit by remaining motionless, watching and waiting for the jack to slow down. As the animal slows, shoulder the rifle carefully, chose the best

Jacks are top targets for quick-thinking riflemen. This late winter jackrabbit has been stopped by a sharp whistle.

Check the backside and heavily muscled areas for signs of blister disease.

lead and look for any opening in the cover.

Many jacks break cover, and then stop 40 or 50 yards from their form. Here's why: the rabbit has hit an invisible boundary between home ranges, and nature has programmed these animals to respect territorial boundaries. The brakes go on, sometimes with such force that bits of dirt and vegetation are kicked up. This gives the hunter a valuable second chance, and while the animal sorts out its predicament the hunter can shoulder his rifle and pick a clear shot.

Cartridges for this type of hunting must be chosen from the .22 centerfire group. Right now our pick is the .223 Remington. The .222 is good, too. There are many hunters, myself included, who use older centerfire .22's to take jacks for sport or just to work out the old rifle. These fill the bill just fine, no matter what bench rest shooters say.

Many older hunters have taken their share of rabbits with the .22 Hornet, .22K Hornet, .218 Bee, and the .219 Zipper, not to mention the .222

The winter white of snow came too early for this white-tailed jackrabbit, catching him in contrasting colors. Note how his high-set eyes enable him to scan 360 degrees around the horizon while still hiding in his form.

Remington Magnum. Many shooters like the added power offered by the .22-250. I confess to having taken my share of jacks with an aging .225 Winchester. Others use the .220 Swift or the .224 Weatherby. Although really uncommon today, the .25-20 and .32-20 were probably the best jack rabbit cartridges ever designed, and fortunately many of these are still in the hands of trappers and other backwoods types.

Rabbits can suffer from a disease called "blisters." While not an important disease, infected rabbits should not be eaten. The disease is more common during population surges; some scientists have attributed cyclical population crashes to the spread of this infection. For the hunter, diseased animals are easy to spot. Sick jacks are slow to move, many will not bother to build a form, and they appear emaciated. Blister-like abscesses develop under the skin. These can be seen around the neck, head, and along the back. A quick field check can be done by pulling off the hide and examining the skin. Very simply, if there are any blister-like signs appearing anywhere on the animal's body, leave the rabbit behind, preferably burying the carcass. This disease rarely occurs in the spring, as most infected animals have died during the stressful winter months. The disease is not transferred to man.

The spring rabbit offers a unique opportunity for the hunter and shooter. Jackrabbits are interesting animals, and there are plenty to provide challenging targets throughout North America. Near the bottom of the carnivore food chain, nature has blessed them with a means of ensuring survival of the species. However, these animals compel the shooter to be quick and know how to take advantage of his opportunities. Medium-powered rifles in .22 centerfire calibers are the best jack medicine currently available. Yet it takes the combination of good shooting, knowing where to look, and how to put it all together before jacks become regular fare.

Author holds a snowshoe hare, also known as the varying hare, taken during the early part of the winter.

Our Most Prolific Species—the Cottontail

The surrounding countryside was a patchwork of small cattle pastures, interspersed with brushy fence-rows, woodlots, and open areas. The country was grazed lightly—cattle prices were down. As a result, thick undergrowth stretched out from the woodlots and fingered its way along numerous water runs that led toward a nearby creek. Grasses were cured, but bare goldenrod stems stood erect and poked through the light snow cover. Although it was winter, the sun shone warmly and penetrated the thick cover. It was picture-perfect cottontail country on a picture-perfect day.

Eddie von Haufen released his pride-and-joy beagle, Bushwhacker, from his travel box. The dog wasted no time in zipping into the dense undergrowth, chopping through the soft, chest-deep snow, and stopping to test dozens of old trails for fresh scent. Before long, the beagle, programmed by generations of breeding and selection, let out a piercing wail. Our hunt was on.

The cottontail rabbit is our most abundant game animal. It outranks squirrels, woodchucks, and jackrabbits. More cottontails are taken in the eastern seaboard states than white-tailed deer in the entire continental United States and Canada. Everybody hunts the cottontail.

Throughout southern North America, cottontails spend their lives next to cropland and marginal bush pastures. They don't like winter, which limits their range in northern Canada. Nevertheless, you can just about pick any habitat, from hot deserts to open grasslands, including the urban fringe, and cottontails are capable of surviving in it. Few other small game species have done as well living in close contact with man, his dogs, and agriculture.

There are eight species of this versatile little animal. The most familiar is the Eastern cottontail. The next most common is called the Mountain cottontail, although it's at home on the open prairies as well. Where I live it's called Nuttall's

Distribution of Eastern Cottontails

cottontail, after the scientist who discovered and named the little rabbit. Both types can live on winter-cured roughage and come out tasting sweet and delicious.

The third most widely abundant is the Desert cottontail, found throughout the arid lands of the south and southwest. The New England cottontail occupies the low pasture lands of the east. Next in line is the sage-and-chaparral-living Brush rabbit of the drier parts of the west coast.

The Marsh cottontail lives along the southeast coastline in swamps, marshes, and bottomlands of this region; the closely related Swamp cottontail lives slightly farther south. This critter shows a willingness rare among rabbits to swim when nature demands. It is also called the ''cane cutter because of the damage it does to planted crops.

Last is the Pygmy cottontail, which some biologists feel is a separate species. It is, as its name implies, the smallest of the cottontails. Restricted to the backwaters of Idaho, Nevada, and Oregon, it also has the smallest population of all cottontails.

Bushwhacker was making a circle about 125

Some hunters prefer long-legged dogs for cottontail hunting.

yards off my right. It was a natural set up. A little-used trail that led to a well site passed through a 15 acre bush. The dog jumped into the bush at Eddie's command and moved quickly through the tangle of undergrowth and snow. Bushwhacker let out a howl, and the rabbit streaked from cover and into the track along the trail, with the eager Bushwhacker in hot pursuit.

Beagle owners have a language of their own. To Eddie, Bushwhacker was a ''bawler.'' Bawlers, also called ''bawl mouths,'' have characteristic long, loud, pitching voices that pene-

trate the countryside. These dogs leave no question when they're on the trail of a rabbit.

Bushwhacker had no formal training. Unlike security or police dogs, there is no training course for cottontail-chasing beagles. This dog simply did what came naturally and did it well. He trailed rabbits the old-fashioned way—by following the faint scent left by cottontail footprints. Most beagles have no trouble picking a scent and sticking with it, even when dozens of other cottontail trails crisscross the original.

The major reason cottontail hunting with dogs

works well is that the animal does not move far from its home range. Rabbits respect territorial boundaries as if they were made from bricks. The cottontail will simply circle and try to move only within the area it has claimed for itself. When pressed, it will cross into other home ranges, but this occurs only when danger is imminent.

Bushwhacker now pushed the cottontail along the open trail. At only 60 yards I led the straight-moving rabbit by half a length and squeezed the trigger on my .225 Model 70. The cottontail

flattened, and Bushwhacker stopped short. The entire process hadn't taken 15 minutes.

The cottontail is the major prey species for an array of predators. Foxes, coyotes, bobcats, hawks, and owls line up to dine on cottontails that make mistakes in their habitat. Snakes, badgers, and eagles also rely on small rabbits. Even weasles will attack a cottontail, and often come out the victor. There are also recorded instances of Red squirrels taking young cottontails in a grizzly prey-on-prey fight to the death.

Hunting cottontails with a dog greatly increases the number of animals taken.

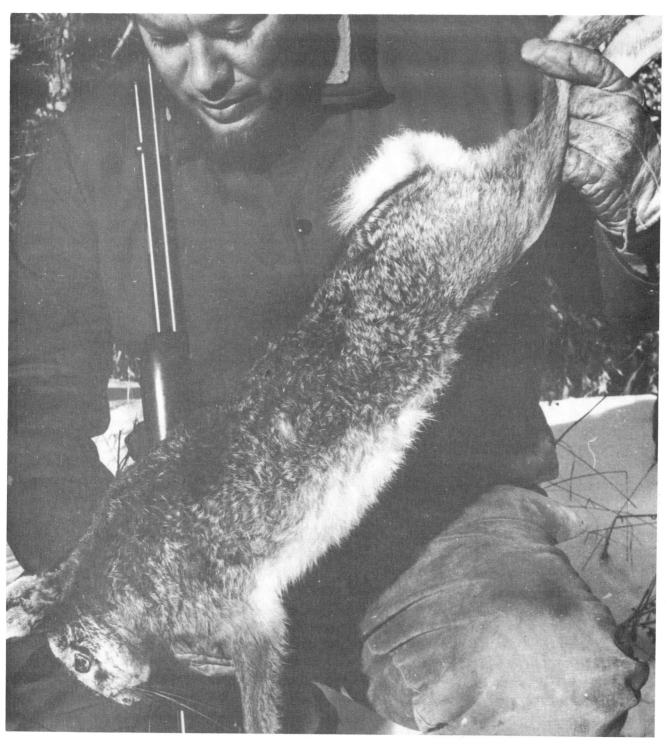

Cottontails are not particularly big rabbits, but their long legs let them move fast through the underbrush.

Beagles are the dog of choice for cottontail hunting.

Turnover in the population is high and most cottontails never see two years, although the odd female has lived five years in the wild. These little rabbits can't be confused with others. As mentioned previously, jackrabbits are large—about 18 to 22 inches long—and can weigh from five to 12 pounds. The snowshoe hare is more medium-sized and rangier, with longer legs than the cottontail, but weighs about the same. They are 13 to 18 inches overall and tip the scales at two to five pounds. Cottontails range from 12 to 17 inches in size and weigh less than four pounds.

Rabbit availability boils down to a very·simple rule. Most hunters have one kind of hare and one kind of cottontail from which to choose. Some of us are luckier: in my home area we hunt Jackrabbits, Snowshoe rabbits and Mountain or Nuttall's cottontail.

Hunters in Colorado may have the best of all worlds—Snowshoe rabbits, blacktailed jackrabbits, Eastern cottontails, Mountain cottontails, and Desert cottontails are all within the boundaries of that state. My cousins living in the Texas panhandle get to go after Blacktailed jackrabbits and Eastern cottontails.

Cottontails never turn white for the winter.

Even those on the cold plains of Saskatchewan never adopt a white camouflage coat for the winter. Some do acquire a sprinkled white appearance—like the New England cottontail that moves from a summer reddish color to a salt-and-pepper look for the winter. Turning completely white with the winter season is left to the hares.

Before long Bushwhacker was at it again. Breaking to the right of the little-used trail, the beagle crashed his way into the underbrush. Not 30 yards away, a bunny flicked its tail and moved deeper into the scrub bush. The howling reached a crescendo as the cottontail circled within the bush and crossed the trail. A few minutes later the bunny reappeared 50 yards further up the trail, moving toward Eddie's stand on top of a brush pile.

Eddie brought his lightweight, aging Model 12 shotgun to his shoulder. He hesitated as the bunny moved toward him, then shot. Jumping down from the bush pile, he ran toward his downed rabbit, stopping only to give Bushwhacker a few quick pats on the back. A moment later Eddie was holding a fine fat Eastern cottontail.

Not all beagles will perform as well as Bushwhacker did that day. Some will only run hot trails; then it's necessary for hunters to put up rabbits by walking and kicking bush piles, checking heavy vegetation, or looking behind fallen logs and the like. The hunter and dog cover the countryside as a team until a bunny is flushed. The dog sticks to the trail until the hunter can catch up or the bunny circles into view.

There are those who claim other breeds of dog are useful for this type of rabbit hunting, too. These hunters feel the bigger hounds—Blueticks, Redbones, Walkers, and various grade hounds of mixed ancestry—are better for deep snow conditions. These observations may be true, but for now, beagles are the dog of choice for most houndmen for this special type of hunting.

Weather plays a big role in determining how cottontails move. In very cold conditions the

Cottontails do not turn white for the winter.

animals sink further into their forms. The hunter or the hound must practically step on the bunny before it breaks from cover. Bunnies are alert to noise, and any movement through crusted snow or undergrowth will warn a rabbit to hold still.

Weather also influences the way dogs react to scent. In extremely dry and cold weather, all dogs have trouble keeping on the scent. Hot trails crisscrossing in the underbrush, something that wouldn't normally confuse a good dog, will do so on cold mornings. Moderately warm, humid days are best for any tracking. Deep snow also tires a dog, as does the cold. Rest periods are important for a dog working under tough conditions.

In heavy cover one dog may not be enough. A wise old cottontail will circle tightly within dense cover. From the rabbit's point of view, it makes good sense. A mish-mash of crisscrossed trails will easily mask the noises of most animals. Coyotes and foxes don't trail cottontails unless there is recent activity; a hot trail is imperative.

Not so with the beagle, who has a superior nose for this type of trailing. It's often the cover that slows the dog, not the scent, and two dogs work heavy cover better than one.

One key in hunting cottontails with a dog is to shake the rabbit's confidence. The rabbit is in its own territory; it's at home. Dog and hunter are visitors. An approaching dog or hunter crashing through the underbrush puts the rabbit on alert. But that doesn't mean the animal will move into view. At the last possible moment a dog triggers the cottontail's flight response. The animal moves, and it comes into view.

Picking a stand is an important consideration in rabbit hunting. Cottontails develop runs and pathways and use them daily to forage and travel, and these will frequently cross man-made back country trails and pathways. Finding a crossing spot is easy—look for tiny trails or paw marks in the snow leading onto the man-made trail. Sometimes scat will be present, or a poorly defined form will be found on the trail's edge.

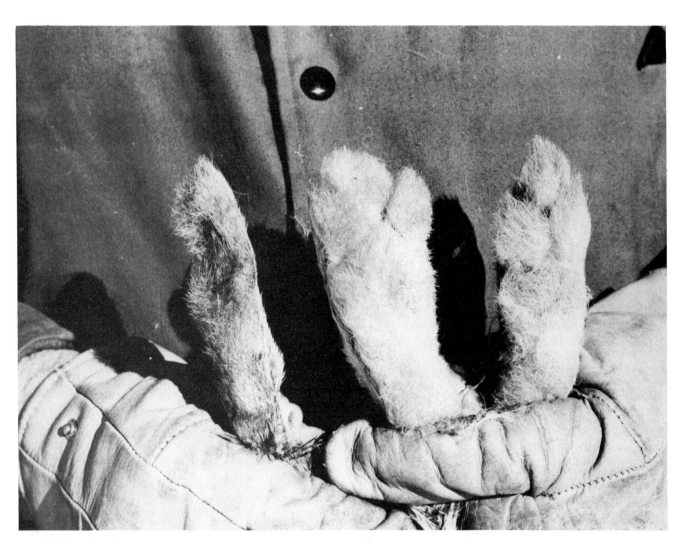

In my home area we hunt three kinds of rabbits. Each is easily identified by their paw. On the left is a Nuttal's cottontail, in the middle a white-tailed jackrabbit, and on the right a snowshoe rabbit.

A white hunting jacket is a good idea for winter cottontail hunting. Cover shoulder straps, ammo pouches, or wide belts with white shoe polish. Carry the rifle low. Cottontails tend to spot the upper body first.

Beagles are carried to the hunting area in specially designed travel boxes.

Cottontails will hunker down into their trail-side form and wait before crossing the trail.

Choose a stand near one of the crossing sites, just inside the cover the dog is working. Cottontails usually run 100 to 200 yards ahead of the dog, and will eventually reach their crossing site. Their goal is to shake the pursuer by reaching larger and denser growth. Usually a cottontail exhausts the trails within the current cover, and, as the dog presses on, the rabbit tries to find different cover and a new set of trails. Stands chosen with these factors in mind rarely fail to produce shooting opportunities.

Be sure to remain still when you are on the stand. Sometimes that's a tall order on a cold winter day, but remember, cottontails have large, well-developed eyes, designed to pick up the slightest movement, even from above. A fidgeting hunter or one jumping and waving his arms to keep warm will telegraph danger to an alert bunny long before the animal comes into rifle range.

Camouflage is a good idea. In the winter white is the obvious choice. Gear like haversacks, ammo pouches, straps, and belts can be tinted with white liquid shoe polish to avoid the contrast between dark gear and white camo. A white jacket is necessary, but white pants are optional. It is the top half of the body that is visible to a scampering rabbit. Upper body movement is

Some hunters feel that bigger hounds, Blueticks, Redbones, and Walkers are better dogs for rabbit hunting.

Any hunter would have to call this a successful day afield.

what the rabbit sees looking up at the world from its position four or five inches above the ground.

Sometimes cottontails that are not being chased by the dogs will be spotted moving out from cover. These are all viable targets. The animals are alerted, and have decided to leave for quieter country. These rabbits move slowly and in short walks, stopping and standing erect, sniffing the air for humans or dogs, and visually checking the countryside. A hunter blending with the background and remaining still will have plenty of time to score. I have shot dozens of rabbits this way and on some days two or three can be added to the pot. You just have to be reasonably still, quiet, slightly camouflaged, and observant.

Strangely, cottontails will sometimes leave a bush and simply stand on the open trail. Some say the rabbits are curious and are really only sorting out the location of the dogs. Others claim this behavior takes place when the rabbit has hit the edge of its territory. It doesn't matter what the real reason is; the secluded hunter has a rare opportunity for an easy shot. Usually, though, cottontails just burst across the trail and disappear quickly into the habitat. A hunter has to be fast to collect on these bunnies, and good shooting skills are a must.

Cottontails are not big animals. A fully grown adult weighs four pounds, though a really big animal might hit five pounds. They reach their full growth potential in less than a year. These little animals don't require a large home range. A breeding male needs only about 100 acres to meet all his needs. In the winter this home range is reduced.

For the hunter, this means there are often many rabbits in a small area. While conditions vary greatly across North America today, it should still be possible to take two or three rabbits out of good hunting country. A dog or pair of dogs will improve the odds perhaps twofold. In many areas there is no limit on the number of cottontails that can be taken, and little or no wildlife management practiced. Where I

live, wildlife biologists don't even bother to estimate the population.

Nearly any rifle or shotgun is suitable for hunting cottontails. Many young shooters begin with a .22 rimfire, but a low-power centerfire is better. Other hunters prefer a shotgun because most cottontails are taken at short range and on the move. That also gives the shooter an opportunity for shotgun practice in the off season. My personal preference is a high-power .22 caliber centerfire, like a .22/250. The .223 is also good. Perhaps the perfect rabbit cartridge available today is the 6mm PPC, available only in the Sako Hunter sporting rifle. At just over 3000 feet per second, pushing a 75 grain bullet, this little cartridge offers a lot of power in a small package.

Shotgun choke is important in cottontail hunt-

Snowshoe hare (left), and cottontail.

ing. Improved cylinder is recommended for all-around rabbit shooting over the full choke, because a more open pattern is required on moving rabbits. Lead becomes more critical with the full choke. Shot size is important, too. Many hunters use the No. 4's left over from duck hunting season, but No. 6's are recommended for small cottontails.

Eddie and I met back at the truck. We hunted most of the morning, stopping for coffee and talking about dogs, guns, and cottontails. As usually happens, I was drawn into explaining why I continue to hunt with a .225 Winchester Model 70. My comment is that the game never seems to mind.

My wife's uncle claims that all my years of shooting the .225 have made me a better conservationist, a pointed reference to some long-forgotten misses at distant cottontails. But I get in my share of comments on Eddie's aging Model 12—I speculate about which might be older, shotgun or shooter.

There is, in fact, a real advantage to a pair of hunters being outfitted with both a centerfire rifle and a shotgun. In more open country, where cottontails flush some distance ahead of the dog, there's often time for a quick rifle shot. Close range shots can be handled with the shotgun. The rifle also works well on standing intermediate range shots. Hunters can trade firearms between hits. This gives hunters the opportunity to shoot with both firearms in one trip.

Bushwhacker had done his job well. For a young dog he was particularly enthusiastic and it was clear Eddie would have a top-notch hunting partner for many years to come. Cottontails were plentiful, and Bushwhacker would be working out over the coming months. Beagles and cottontails are made for one another. The dog is easy to train and handle and provides good companionship afield.

Can't beat those squirrels

There are places that are considered to be the tops in one kind of hunting. For example, New York is said to produce the best woodchucks, Montana the biggest prairie dogs, the Carolinas the greatest cottontails, Wyoming the largest jackrabbits, California the finest rockchucks and Saskatchewan the fattest ground squirrels. These reputations stem from both the number of animals available and the level of hunter interest. Squirrels are a good example. Kentucky is considered the classic gray squirrel hunting territory in North America.

Kentucky has been described as a state of contrasts, with much land scarred by strip mining and poor lumbering practices, but also with many fine farms and estates. The state is certainly one of the finest squirrel hunting areas in the country. Squirrel hunting, no matter what kind, ranks almost as a national pastime, particularly in Kentucky. There may be more squirrel hunters than white-tailed deer hunters in this state.

The season here opens about the third week of August and lasts all fall. In comparing kill data from the 15 or so states with a squirrel season, Kentucky leads by almost two to one over the runner-up. The long season, excellent habitat, and fine fall weather all contribute to the popularity of squirrel hunting.

Gray squirrels far outnumber the larger fox squirrels, and the gray receives most of the hunting pressure. The gray differs considerably from the fox. Grays tend to be mottled or peppery in color. Their hair is multicolored, between light and dark gray, with white thrown in. Fox squirrels, on the other hand, are russet in color, but can also run to shades of grey.

In Kentucky, grays range throughout the state except in what is called the bluegrass region. The bluegrass area supports a better population of fox-type squirrels. However, the ranges of the two animals do overlap; it is possible to find a hillside that harbors both squirrels. That, of course, makes for more interesting hunting.

Distribution of the Gray Squirrel

Distribution of the Fox Squirrel

Although fox squirrels and grays will be found together, they have very different habitat preferences. Fox squirrels will usually be found in small woodlots adjacent to farms and small buildings. The gray squirrel prefers the more densely forested areas that have an abundance of nut bearing trees, such as oak, hickory, and hazel.

A thick undergrowth is needed to provide cover and protection during ground movements. Areas of flowering dogwood, blackberry, and other fruit-producing shrubs often support squirrels in abundance.

My most recent trip into this state resulted from some correspondence with my old friend and native Kentuckian, Chuck Veuillier. Out of our exchange of letters came an invitation to try my hand at squirrel hunting near his home town. I wasted no time in making the necessary preparations.

Chuck and I were armed with black powder guzzling shotguns. However, that was just our particular preference. The next day we switched briefly to .22 rimfire repeating rifles and had just as much success. The shotguns were stoked with number six shot and about seven-eighths dram of black powder. For the .22 rifles, we used a long rifle cartridge with mushroom points. These provided good one-shot stopping power on most grays. I've often thought that a .22 magnum would make a good squirreling round, but have not had a chance to test this out.

Our .22s were equipped only with iron sights; scope-sighted rifles would have been better. Actually, any cartridge could be used on squirrels and I think light loads with home-cast lead bullets in the larger calibers would be great squirrel medicine. These would also allow the hunter to extend the use of his big game rifle into the squirrel season rather than restricting it to the brief white-tailed deer season.

There is a real place for centerfire rifles in this kind of hunting. While the .22 has a role here, it is not my preference. Bottom end reloads in the .222 Remington, .223 Remington, and .222 Remington Magnum are best. Squirrels give the rifleman a real workout. Rigorous practice with a full-weight hunting rifle pays dividends later in the season when big game becomes the target.

Caution is the by-word of the squirrel hunter. The gray's exceptional hearing and keen eyesight make it difficult to spot. Squirrels can resolve detail much finer than the human eye can discern. Their eyes move much faster than human eyes. Also, the bushy tail's eye is equipped with a filter that reduces glare and grades contrast. This all means that a squirrel can perceive movement very easily and quickly. The hunter has to be careful not to create sudden movement and has to maneuver slowly if he wants a shot.

A foot carelessly placed on the forest floor can send your potential squirrel target scurrying; a twig broken at the wrong instant can cause a gray to freeze, usually on the opposite side of the tree where you are standing. I found that short, carefully placed steps keep squirrels from hightailing. I walked half crouched, using my free hand to help pass through blackberry and dogwood patches, picking each footstep.

A short pause every few steps appears to help the stalking effort. Squirrels seem to get nervous as they listen first to noises coming from the moving hunter, followed by a stretch of silence. Often during the silent pause the squirrel will also remain motionless. It is at this time that a careful shot can be made.

Actually, the squirrel makes his share of noise, too. This helps the still hunter. In one good squirrel patch I sat quietly on a fallen oak. From this low vantage I was able to spot four squirrels, each having made some noise. A squirrel would leap from one tree to another and, on landing, create a rustling in the leaves. A second squirrel caught my attention when passing among some dead witch hazel. Others chattered among them-

Typical squirrel sign, left to right: pine cone used by squirrels, cuttings left by a squirrel after eating, scat samples found near cuttings.

Tree nests are frequently used by gray squirrels. Watch nests closely, as there are several entrance ways.

Squirrel foods vary greatly across North America, but acorns are the favorite.

selves. One squirrel misjudged slightly, and had to claw himself back onto the branch he was jumping to. His scratching and scrambling were enough noise to attract the most preoccupied hunter.

When hunting alone, the walk-and-pause method is the most productive. Squirrels would move when I was quiet, and I would either spot the movement or be attracted by the noise. Walking on further, I would turn up more squirrels every time. The walk-and-pause method is the traditional squirrel hunting method. For young shooters, it promotes an awareness of movement that will prove valuable in all types of hunting. It teaches excellent still hunting techniques that are readily transferable to other kinds of hunting, in particular, deer.

Squirrels rarely range beyond a good leap and bound from a den. Either tree dens or nests made from a conglomeration of twigs, grasses, and leaves will provide the hideout. It seems useless for a hunter to wait for a squirrel to exit from his den once it has escaped to safety. However, on a couple of occasions, Chuck and I have played the patience game and were duly re-

warded. Any hunter trying this technique has to keep a keen eye on the den opening; these grays can exit on the sly, leaving the hunter sitting totally dumbfounded.

Often a family will occupy a single den for the entire season. Leaf nests can have several openings, each facing different directions and providing access to many escape routes. Tree dens are usually made by other animals and then taken over by squirrels. They then expand and modify these homes to suit their needs. Often an old tree will be the home of a woodpecker, and then squirrels move in, clearing out the rotted heartwood of the tree to make a nest. They usually add a second exit too.

Nests in good condition indicate good squirrel

Squirrels are important prey species for a number of predators.

territory. Squirrels like to have close neighbors, so several nests will usually be found on one wooded hillside or along a single forest bottom. Old nests quickly deteriorate from lack of upkeep, or are used temporarily by other forest creatures. Birds find old squirrel nests excellent sources of material for their own nest repair and construction. Squirrels also use old nests as sites from which to forage for food, or as vantage points for safety.

Nests are usually found in any of the hardwood tree species such as walnut, beech, maple, or oak. A nest in good condition will be about one or two feet in diameter and at least 10 to 12 feet high. If nests are not present the hunter

should check closely for shell fragments or other debris left behind by feeding squirrels. It is common to find piles of material that, at first, looks like shavings. These shavings, or cuttings as they are called, are the result of feeding activity.

In some areas squirrels form distinct piles of cuttings and droppings. These are called middens, which is really another way of saying refuse heap. These are a classic sign of squirrel activity and should be part of what the hunter looks for when afield. In the north middens can be quite large and prominent. It's an excellent field sign. It's also a quick way to determine what local squirrels have been eating and the kind of habitat to position yourself in for good gunning. This kind of sign invariably leads to a squirrel or two.

It's wise to become familiar with the food habits of resident squirrels. The grays in my area live almost exclusively on oak mast. Others live on pine cone seeds. Food habits vary greatly and can include nuts, berries, fruit, seeds, buds, new growth twigs, bark, eggs, fungi, and insects.

Squirrels do not hibernate, so their food habits shift somewhat with the season. In spring, they prefer new growth, and any green material becomes the food staple during the summer. As fall and winter approach, seeds, nuts, bark and twigs figure more prominently in the diet.

Squirrels are particular about when they eat. During the summer, most feeding occurs in the early morning, just after sunrise. In fall, when mornings are on the nippy side, squirrels shift their feeding toward midday.

Chuck told me that squirrels hate the cold, and any inclement weather, including rain, sends the bushy-tail to his nest. During extended wet periods squirrels delay their movements until mid-morning. Hunters have to keep the weather in mind when picking squirrel-hunting times.

While I like to shoot at moving targets, squirrels have proved particularly difficult. They have an uncanny ability to dodge and change directions, although they really don't seem to be travelling all that fast. Waiting until a squirrel has cleared the underbrush and stopped makes it easier to score. Usually with running shots, the surrounding vegetation and underbrush get in

Squirrels make noise when foraging through oak leaves looking for acorns. Listen carefully for these sounds.

Some squirrel species are protected from all hunting. Check game laws closely and learn to distinguish the various species. This Bryant fox squirrel is considered a rare and endangered species.

the way.

The best targets are squirrels silhouetted against the sky. That can happen when a squirrel on a large limb decides to hold his position. I have to take my shots quickly: that squirrel won't stay around for a second try.

Gray squirrels are not as large as other small game. An adult will grow to a length of ten inches. Squirrels are, of course, well known for their tail—often another ten inches long. This helps the animal keep its balance.

A full-grown gray squirrel could weigh just under two pounds but much over this would indeed be rare. Although the animal is small it can build up layers of fat in years when food is plentiful. Squirrels doing their foraging from nearby corn fields are fat and good-tasting. Kentucky has a good number of squirrels that live in this lush manner. The result is fine eating.

Most squirrels, once they have spotted a hunter, play a hide-and-seek game, with the hunter doing all the seeking. In large trees a squirrel merely keeps the tree between himself and the hunter. This keeps the lone hunter from getting a shot. Most squirrels are so adept at this that once a squirrel has spotted me, there's no way I can get a shot. I have to spot the squirrel before he sees me.

The hide-and-seek game proves frustrating. My host suggested we hunt together, rather than alone. We hadn't travelled far when a large gray made a leap from a pile of fresh cuttings and headed up the nearest oak. Chuck got close to the base of the tree and started to circle slowly. Each footstep broke twigs or shuffled freshly fallen leaves, and the squirrel nervously clung to the large oak. Chuck finally was about to face the squirrel when it scampered to my side and stopped. I was able to make a quick, clean shot with the .22 and the squirrel plummeted to the ground.

Chuck told me that today's Kentucky squirrel is much warier than his cousins of even a decade ago. Hunting pressure, in the form of more skilled hunters and stalkers, has made old tricks

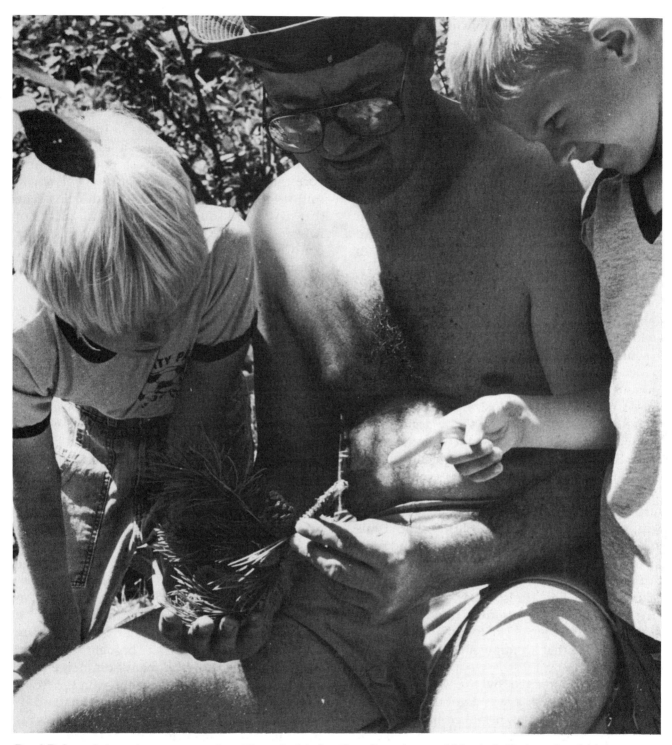

Brad Pyle points out some recent cuttings to his brother Brendan and his dad. Early natural history lessons are an important part of the hunting experience.

used by squirrels common knowledge. The squirrel has adapted by holding tighter and moving less frequently during the daytime. Squirrels are also more alert to distant sounds, like voices and slamming car doors. Hunters have to use care and be alert in the field.

Camouflage, especially in bush patterns, is wise for modern day squirrel hunting. Most hunters are now aware of this, but camo must be combined with good woodsmanship and stalking skills. The approach to squirrel hunting has to be more holistic—to take into account all aspects of the environment, as well as the kind of rifle and load, and all gear from boots to hunting jacket.

Next time I get the opportunity to hunt grays, I will use a scope-mounted rifle. A scope gathers light and gives a brighter picture under the trees. Light-gathering ability is an important feature on a squirreling scope. Due to their size, scopes made for high power rifles would look ridiculous mounted on my small Mossberg .22, and equally out of place on other full-size .22s. A compact scope for high power use is the logical choice. Leupold offers a compact or shorty model scope for rimfire mounting or for any of the short, light rifles that are now commonplace.

I picked up my downed squirrel, and was surprised at the thin coat. Unlike squirrels in my area, these squirrel skins have little value, I was told, and it was not difficult to understand why. In the north, squirrel skins are a regular fur commodity, and in some areas are accorded fur bearer status. The Hudson Bay Company still buys gray squirrel skins. But those hides are superior to the thin kind found in Kentucky. Chuck told me that it's impossible to sell squirrel hides from this area

I was also surprised by the weight of the animal. The one I shot was a good pound, but with the large bushy tail it looked like it should have weighed more. Later I learned that one of the heaviest gray squirrels ever taken weighed in at one pound, eight ounces. Since mine broke the one pound mark, you can imagine I was quite

proud; this was only my fourth Kentucky gray squirrel. Northern members of the species tend to be at the heavy end of the weight scale, but their population numbers don't hold a candle to those in Kentucky.

Gray squirrels are a great target, and Kentucky has them in abundance. I was in that state for a week and travelled through a lot of squirrel country, including the Daniel Boone National Forest. Remember, squirrel hunting is where you find it; there are many areas besides this state that have good squirrel hunting. With plenty of habitat, and a great squirrel population, it's not hard to see why squirrel shooting is a popular pastime.

By any other name: Ground Squirrels

The shrill whistle caught my attention. Placing the binoculars to my eyes I searched the nearby hay field. The alfalfa was growing well at this time of year, and the green background would make spotting easy—or so I thought. A gust of wind blew across the open field and the whistle seemed to waver and disappear. I looked closely. The wind carried the fresh scent of new alfalfa blooms across the field. Bees visiting the pale blue flowers buzzed in the background.

Gophers like this type of habitat. I spotted one no more than 80 yards from the rise where I lay. Again the gopher gave out with that familiar piercing whistle and stood erect near the edge of his hole. Each time he called, his chest contracted as the critter summoned the energy to send high-pitched notes across the prairie.

It was early summer and prairie gophers were abundant. The warm sun had brought them from their damp burrows, and many scampered from den to den. Others fed voraciously on the fresh, succulent new-grown alfalfa. Some, unafraid of predator or rifleman, stood on their hind legs and pulled over mature alfalfa plants to nibble the preferred leaves at the top of the plant. My hunting partners and I nodded to each other. This would make an ideal spot for an afternoon

In the early summer gophers are unafraid of either predators or riflemen. They will stand erect around the mouth of their burrows. They seem to enjoy the fine weather.

gopher shoot.

The term *ground squirrel* is understood to include prairie dogs and woodchucks. However, for hunting purposes, we'll refer to that group of ground-living mammals, always smaller than blacktails and 'chucks, and generally living in colonial burrows. Well-known proper names include Richardson's ground squirrel, Washington ground squirrel, Idaho ground squirrel, Uinta ground squirrel, Belding ground squirrel, Columbian ground squirrel and Mexican ground squirrel.

In one area they are called picket pins and in a different region, gophers. Their lifestyles are similar, and any hunter understanding the behavior of one can readily transfer this knowledge to the others. Perhaps the best example of the group is the Richardson's ground squirrel.

Ground squirrels are widely distributed. They can be found in nearly every habitat in North America except along the eastern seaboard. From the cold reaches of Canada and Alaska, south to Guerro and the Valley of Mexico, from the Pacific Ocean and the Bering Sea over to Hudson Bay, Lake Michigan, Indiana and eastern Texas, these animals can be prolific under the right conditions.

The gopher provides an interesting target for the rifleman recovering from the inactivity of winter. It gives an opportunity to improve marksmanship and allows the hunter to become familiar with his rifle. The farmer often benefits from the reduction of this rodent, especially around hay meadows and along the edges of sprouting grain fields. The damage done by the gopher is immense and many farmers carry out poisoning programs in an attempt to reduce losses.

Finding a place to hunt gophers is usually no problem. The abundance and daytime activity of the animals allows even the casual shooter to plink away. The burrows are found along field edges and undisturbed islands of native grass habitat, as well as hay fields. The entrance burrows vary greatly in size, depending on soil

Ground squirrels are very curious. Beware—some become camp robbers.

Ground Squirrels will readily dig into any earth structure. Dams are very vulnerable to their damage.

conditions and population size.

Most entrances are about three inches across, but some expand to as much as 15 inches when large families use the burrow system in the spring. New burrows are small. Mounds of fresh earth seen at the entrance indicate active holes and mean that somebody is home. Some holes, probably escape exits, are dug from the inside.

In large colonies, burrows are about ten feet apart, but some species build solitary burrows on rocky shale slopes or other rough ground far from their nearest neighbor. Mounds are not diked like those of the prairie dog, but some become large. Gophers sit on these, keeping an eye out for predators.

Unlike other rodents, gopher scat is rarely found. It is usually buried in an underground chamber and breaks down quickly. Likewise, tracks are rarely seen except in the freshest soil. Gophers graze away an area around the den mouth, but never to the degree found with prairie dogs. Sometimes ground squirrels of all species occupy abandoned holes in dry stream banks, road cuts or slope slips. Badger sign is common around active burrows.

Water is not important to these animals. Their well developed gut extracts the last drop of water from the vegetation they eat. Ground squirrels rarely construct dens where there is any danger of flooding. Excessive heat does bother them, though, and they will retreat to the ten- and 15-foot depths of their dens.

It is always wise to request permission to hunt any type of game, and this applies to shooting gophers. Few farmers say no, and many enjoy talking with a hunter who stops to explain what he is doing. Farmers often welcome someone willing to spend a couple of hours reducing the pest problem, and the farmer-hunter contact can often lead to permission for hunting upland game birds or deer later in the season. It is important to encourage this type of landowner contact for the future of sport hunting as we know it today.

We had found our place and arranged permis-sion from the landowner. Since there were no cattle nearby we were allowed free run on a section of land with a great variety of suitable shooting sites. Not only was there the hay meadow, there was a large grain field that bordered a natural pasture. A rock-strewn valley ran through the west side of the pasture and emptied into a large native grass glen. It all combined to provide a gopher paradise and varmint-hunter's dream.

From our perch on the eroded knoll, the 80-yard-distant gopher looked like an easy shot. I eased myself into the sitting position and shouldered my .243 Winchester. I selected a center point on the gopher's chest and squeezed the trigger. The 75-grain hollow point Hornady bullet smacked home and the gopher slumped to the left of his mound.

My partners and I are all veteran deer hunters, and we find the practice gained from gopher shooting to be invaluable. When deer hunting season opens, we have confidence in our shoot-ing ability. We know that we have practiced at varying yardages and have refined our range-esti-mating ability. Our ability to discern game from foliage has also received a workout. The result is that gopher shooting has made us keener and more familiar with our guns. This is valuable when the crucial once-a-season shot at the tro-phy whitetail comes along.

Gophers can be taken at almost any range from ten yards out to 300 yards. Long range shots are difficult, of course; usually the vegetation or the topography of the area obscures the largest part of the animal. The animals don't make the shooting easy, either. They have a habit of duck-ing down into their burrows at the crack of a rifle. Then they cautiously poke only their head above the lip of the burrow.

None of the various ground squirrels are big targets. The gopher presents a target only about nine and a half inches high by three inches wide. Even in sparse vegetation part of the gopher is likely to be hidden in the cover. The average shot is about 80 yards; as the shooting continues the

Picket pins are cannibalistic. They will readily eat the dead of their own kind.

range increases to 150 yards. All the short-range shots are used up in the first few minutes of shooting at a particular colony. The more frequently a colony is hunted, the greater the range at which shots must be taken. These little critters soon learn when they are being shot at and adapt accordingly. Beyond 200 yards, unless the situation is perfect, it becomes very difficult to spot gophers and then place yourself for a good shot.

Running gophers provide excellent targets, but the hunter needs quick reflexes as well as a good sighting eye. As the season progresses, ground squirrels graze further from their burrows. They may forage as far as 60 or 70 yards from home. A rifle outfitted with a scope is best in this situation. The scope's magnification provides a clear picture of the action and helps eliminate any sighting error as the gopher scampers for home.

The most critical element in gopher shooting is getting to know your gun. You should know where it shoots, its trajectory, energy, and effective range. These factors are especially important if the shooter uses homemade loads. It is good business to record the results of different loads and the degree of success with various combinations of powder, bullets, and primers. Naturally, the best way to get familiar with your gun is to use it frequently. Try to be more than a once-a-year gopher shooter, and the results of the effort will be rewarding.

When shooting gophers, try to use the same shooting positions you would use in deer hunting. Drop to the kneeling position and squeeze off a few shots at nearby gophers, holding the rifle as you would when deer hunting. Use the same sighting picture and become familiar with what this picture should look like under different light conditions. Then try placing yourself in the sitting position to fire a few shots at those gophers a little further out that require a steadier hold.

Once you feel familiar with the gun and confident in these shooting positions, progress to off-hand shooting at intermediate ranges. At first you should expect a lot of misses at the greater range. But continued shooting from these positions, under outdoor conditions, can only improve the deer hunter's ability. Wind and mirage are factors constantly influencing shooting, and they'll test your confidence with rifle and scope. Ground squirrels demand good shooting.

On the other hand, greater accuracy in gopher shooting can be obtained from the prone. This position permits shots at the farthest range possible, and while rarely used in the deer range, it does work well for accurately taking ground squirrels under a variety of conditions. Hair-splitting accuracy is possible with a rest or a tripod to support the rifle on. In this way, pin-point placement of each shot is possible. That's what is often required at longer ranges, since the gopher provides such a small, obscure target. For the hunter who delights in varmint shooting, the prone position is the easy route to successful long range shots.

There is no particular rifle and cartridge combination that is designed only for gopher shooting. Any caliber and rifle can be used, from the lowly .22 caliber rimfire up to the center fire magnums. It does not require a lot of energy to humanely dispatch the prairie gopher. In the midwest more gophers are probably taken with .22 caliber rimfire rifles than the total of all other calibers. However, there are those who enjoy taking gophers with the higher performance and flatter-shooting varmint cartridges, and this must be encouraged.

Ground squirrels are perhaps the only small game species that can still be hunted with the less powerful .22 rimfire cartridge. Rimfire ranges are restricted to 75 yards. In the past these cartridges were used by many because of the low price. Today that is not a consideration; anyone who reloads can easily brew up cartridges that surpass the rimfires at low cost.

Gopher shooting seems to follow a pattern. It starts with a few hits, then several misses, back to a few hits, followed by a return to a few misses. Why this occurs is difficult to say. It may be related to range estimation ability and the fact that one shoots downhill toward a gopher. The problem is compounded by the tremendous variation in range and the manner in which the target presents itself. Hunters should be alert to this pattern and not become frustrated when they find themselves in the missing phase. It will pass.

Once a colony is found, the rifleman has to know how best to work it. No two will be alike. All require that cover and approach be watched very carefully. This is particularly true on frequently hunted colonies or those disturbed by vehicular traffic. Hunters should practice good sneaking techniques. Always hide the vehicle, walk in from some distance and use camouflage clothing. Don't slam car doors or create a din finding equipment, and keep voices down. Watch the wind, as it can carry noise and scent for quite some distance.

Patience is important, too. After some initial shooting, all species of ground squirrels head underground. Hold your position and wait for the animals to return. Scan the colony closely with binoculars, watching for telltale movements as the animals venture to the lip of their burrows. Shots will have to be taken at increasing ranges as the shooting progresses, but long range shooting is what this kind of hunting is all about.

Gopher hunting is a good place to learn shooting fundamentals. Since targets are so plentiful, the misses incurred while learning proper technique are excusable. No other hunting in the world provides this chance. Young shooters can begin at short range and work up to long shots as skills develop. Old hands can pick a range at which to shoot. Learning field shooting skills on live game is rare today. Our ground squirrels provide the last opportunity for this kind of learning and training.

All ground squirrels share fundamental elements of lifestyle. They are all prolific, having up to two litters of eight to twelve young, depending on conditions and location. No official population estimates exist for this rodent, and it's no wonder, since there are probably more ground squirrels than any other mammal.

The gestation period is around 28 to 30 days. The large litter size and short gestation are biologically designed to keep lots of rodents populating the earth. Under good conditions, survival is high, and it's very easy for a small colony to expand within one or two years.

Their pest status is well established, and each year ambitious poisoning campaigns are undertaken across the U.S. and Canada. There are no laws restricting poisoning where agricultural crops or products are endangered. Poison is available through most supply stores, and some rural counties provide the stuff at nominal cost to anyone who wants to reduce pest numbers. Mixed with grains and spread as bait, poisons exact a great toll, but the rodents soon learn to avoid the mixtures, and the campaigns falter.

Ground squirrels are cannibalistic, a behavior more pronounced in the spring than during other seasons, but no ground squirrel will turn down a meal of one cousin or another. Hunters may see this habit displayed along roadways and highways. Dead ground squirrels are quickly consumed by all scavengers, but it's common to see two or three squirrel carcasses together on the road. What has happened is that one unfor-

The Franklin Ground Squirrel is just one of many ground-living squirrels that provide interesting targets for riflemen.

tunate squirrel has been killed crossing the roadway or foraging along the shoulder. Other squirrels have spotted the warm carcass and rushed forward to take on a meal. In the process, they've failed to notice the traffic and have themselves become casualties.

Squirrels, believe it or not, actually benefit from this behavior. When they eat the intestinal tract they take in a food supply that is already partly broken down and rich in vitamins. It's a valuable food source.

This behavior can also be seen out on the colony. It's not uncommon to see a freshly killed squirrel carcass being dragged by another ground squirrel toward the safety of its burrow. This action should not be interpreted as one squirrel helping another. It is cannibalism, plain and simple. Often two or three squirrels will fight over the carcasses, and this provides an opportunity for more targets. So intent are these animals that they scarcely notice the shooter.

Forty gophers can eat as much forage as an adult cow. The result is a loss in grazing capacity or a reduction in crop yield. The bad effects of the gopher's food habits are most evident in years when the lack of moisture reduces the overall vegetation. The competition from the gopher against other grazing animals becomes really critical when there is less available forage.

Digging causes problems. The easiest way to gain hunting permission around irrigation dikes and structures is to tell the landowner you want to shoot ground squirrels along the margins of irrigation works. Head ditches, panel dikes and sometimes the actual field provide excellent homes for these animals, and populations concentrate around such areas. Even a single gopher hole and mound in a field served by flood irrigation changes the drainage. This is a source of frustration to irrigators. Damage done to dams and structures is often not evident for years. Then, as water seeps and penetration patterns change, there is suddenly a leak along a dam. Knowing these things can help you to gain access to areas closed to other hunters.

There is a positive side to ground squirrels that is often forgotten: their extensive burrow systems allow water to enter the deeper layers of soil, and their constant digging mixes, churns, and aerates the soil. There is some benefit to agriculture from destroying insects by foraging squirrels, and digging roots up destroys buried insect eggs. Their role as prey keeps predators diverted from farm animals and poultry.

All ground squirrel species have one peculiarity with which few hunters are familiar. The adults go below ground in midsummer and don't usually return until the following spring. With the adults going into dormancy, only the young are left above ground. This means any gopher shot, poisoned, or taken by a predator after that time is a young of that year. The breeding population is safe underground. This mechanism reduces competition for food among the gophers, and is the reason large breeding populations are present and a source of plentiful targets for eager riflemen the following spring. More important, it's the reason squirrel targets dry up as the summer progresses. There are fewer targets, and those available are smaller and don't whistle as frequently.

This biological fact also means it's impossible to completely clear out a colony, even by extensive shooting. This is especially true in mid-to late-summer after the breeding portion of the population has gone underground.

Wise female adults are especially alert for predators and hunters during the spring because the animals are out, far from their den, eating voraciously to supply milk for the young. These animals are very wary, and hunters have to be sharp to score consistently.

Modern farming practices have helped stabilize ground squirrel populations across North America. Grain lost during harvesting makes up much of the fall food. The edges of cultivated fields provide the best habitat for these animals, while old hay pastures offer great food supplies and cover.

Rugged open prairies are home to the Richardson Ground Squirrel. Dens are visible from the air.

Intense agriculture seems to have created a ground squirrel niche. Large modern machinery has left field corners, bush edges, and rocky or hilly land undisturbed. In many farming areas these islands of habitat remain in whatever native vegetation is common to the region. This means big populations of picket pins and gophers. In this way the farmer gets his land, and the gopher gets his share. The overall result is less pressure on gopher populations and, of course, less perception of the gopher as an economic threat.

The ground squirrel has no easy time of it.

Aside from the activities of man, there are several predators that consider the gopher a fair banquet. Hawks, foxes, coyotes, and snakes all prey on the gopher. Badgers thrive on gophers. The young gopher is fairly dumb, and provides easy eating for these predators. Nevertheless, ground squirrel populations continue to grow, and their range keeps expanding.

The best time to hunt the gopher is during the spring. The animals are extremely active after emerging from their winter dormancy. They breed almost immediately, and the young are soon seen around the den mouth. They grow all summer, then follow their parents into dormancy in late August and early September, depending on latitude.

The gopher is most active during the early morning, but many individuals remain active all day long, especially if it is warm and dry. Rainy weather bothers them most and will keep them holed up, interfering with their daily activity patterns until the fields dry. The result in that any time is a good time to go gopher hunting.

Calling a gopher does not always work, but in the spring, when the animals are first out, the call works about 80 percent of the time. It's easy; starving Indians are said to have used this trick when other game food was unavailable. A sharp squeaking whistle works best. At first the gopher will respond by repeating the whistle noise, and then slowly emerge from its burrow. Nearly all types can be whistled up. Late in the season, though, the gopher starts to wise up, and the success of calling decreases markedly.

Gophers can be hunted for hours and still present plentiful targets. The supply seems endless. The hunter taking a position overlooking a large colony will have targets enough for a day's shoot. In the springtime incredible takes are possible—50 to 60 animals are common. The prime method for centerfire shooters is to set up on the edge of a colony and shoot down into the group. Approach a colony from cover, and set up in a nearby bush. The shooting will be fast and long lasting.

These animals readily occupy waste lands around abandoned farm yards. There is frequently good cover, and it's easy to work into a hidden shooting position and still have a good view of the colony. Some hunters have shot from the second-story open windows of deserted farm houses or barns. It's a good opportunity that many hunters don't think of. Obtain permission to do this, and the rewards are yours.

Hunting ground squirrels is a great way to be in the outdoors, sharpen your shooting skills, and at the same time develop good relations with landowners. These animals are interesting—for my money, one of the most intriguing of all small game animals. They are probably the easiest for the novice hunter to find, and nearly every part of North America has at least one species of ground squirrel. A hunter going after these animals better take a lot of ammunition, because the shooting opportunities are tremendous. They provide a really good hunt and are a great way to scratch your spring shooting itch. Go for it!

Badger Basics

During the early 1970's, Plymouth sedans were still large, powerful cars. They were big, taking a lot of road as you went by. At that time most other car manufacturers were well into downsizing their models. Leg room, comfort, and speed were giving way to products that were smaller, more gas efficient, and better built. The Plymouth remained big and powerful. Yet I felt these cars were stable, fast, reliable, and able to take rough use.

In 1975 I had one of those cars. The government agency I worked for at the time supplied its field men with a new Plymouth or Dodge about every two or three years. I was in my third year with this particular car. Given the tough use this vehicle received, it was still working surprisingly well. Most of my driving was on rough, remote backroads or trails. Many were dusty and deeply rutted. I covered many miles on rock-strewn, hard, natural prairie with no roads or trails to follow. Any roads that I did use were apt to be harsh, potholed gravel roads that led from small towns to farms and ranches and then into back country.

The country I drove this car through was unique. Frequently dry, it was mostly open range country, the type seen in old western movies. Sagebrush covered the deep valleys, while productive cool season grasses grew in abundance on miles of uplands. Hot dry winds blew constantly across a seemingly endless prairie resembling a sea that held healthy grass instead of salt water. Barbed wire fences, strung tight as a fiddle

Distribution of the Badger

string, ran straight and stretched for miles, dividing the land into an unnatural patchwork of small and large fields.

Native grass dominated the landscape, but many areas held large alfalfa and crested wheat grass stands. In some places, sprawling grain fields abruptly began where the grass stopped. Barbed wire gates and Texas Gates allowed movement from field to field. Water was sparse.

My job was to establish stocking rates on large tracts of these rangelands. It meant hours of tedious driving, often many miles from the nearest town, working alone, and putting in long days during the hot summer months. The Plymouth functioned perfectly in this kind of terrain.

The grasses growing here were the source of life, making the land what it was. Ranchers grazed thousands of cattle throughout this expanse. Big and small game were everywhere. Antelope grazed the sagebrush and mule deer lived in the coulees. Coyotes and foxes thrived, feeding on plentiful rabbits, bountiful field mice, and scavenged remains. Remnant pockets of prairie dogs could be found. However, without doubt it was the ground squirrel, a.k.a.gopher,

that was most abundant. It lived out its entire life in this area where grass supported all life.

Living in colonies burrowed into the tough soil, gopher populations exist intermittently across the entire central plains region of North America. Small colonies of a few hundred individuals to larger aggregations of one or two thousand are common. Field edges, fence corners, overgrazed pastures, and rough coulee walls provide home to these animals. Out on the prairie rangelands they exist anywhere, living on vitamin-rich grasses and protein-laced seeds.

Badgers thrive here, too. A tough, tenacious animal outfitted with a muscular body, powerful jaws, long claws, and the ability to dig quickly, badgers prey directly on gophers. Where gophers are in abundance, badgers will be found as well. The relationship between badgers and gophers is purely one of predator and prey. It is more direct than with other predator-prey relationships, because when gophers die out badgers die, too. While badgers will take other game, gophers are what they prefer, and other prey, like rabbits, is strictly second choice.

Badgers are efficient predators. Their muscular neck moves a large powerful head that acts like a scoop shovel, pushing loose dirt away from the fast-moving front claws. But gophers, too, are pretty good burrowers. The badger must be fast to dig out a thoroughly scared gopher that has dammed itself behind several feet of dirt as it hears the badger scratching its way toward a potential meal.

Fierce on the attack, this chunky, bowlegged predator fears little on the open prairie. Even rattlesnake venom is largely ineffective against this animal. The thick coat, long hair, and deep subcutaneous fat layers protect the badger from snake bites that would be fatal to any other animal.

Badgers and man have never gotten along well. A cornered badger will fight any animal that comes too close, including a man. They can quickly dig themselves into the ground, but when caught in the open will run from danger at speeds upwards of 25 miles per hour. They are a dominant force on the prairie, capable of keeping young coyotes at bay and opportunistically harvesting game bird eggs, young hatchlings, toads, and the newborn of prairie dogs, rabbits, kangaroo rats, and almost anything else.

It's their burrowing habit that brings badgers most into conflict with man. Unfortunately, not every hole yields a gopher, and those that do pop out often escape. Adult badgers dig an average of three dry holes for every gopher that they catch and eat. For this reason, badgers are sometimes called "prairie prospectors. Many times holes cave in during the digging or do so after some weathering. The result is that large open pits— some as big as 20 inches across—dot the landscape. Many are partially hidden by an existing gopher hole. Holes are dangerous to men on horseback, to grazing horses, and to cattle. Stepping in a badger hole often means a broken leg. On fodder land, hidden holes play havoc with haying machinery. A wheel that falls into one of these excavations can result in a broken running gear, or at least a scared operator. All of this has done nothing to endear the badger to agricultural folk.

For small game hunters, badgers are easy to find. They are likely to be near gopher colonies, so the trick is to scout the colonies, and keep a sharp eye for moving badgers. Badgers can be found any time of the day, although they are most active in early morning and evening. They are bold, often showing no fear of man, and will move among the gopher mounds with unbridled cockiness. Many will barely look up from their digging to check out a hunter.

For me, my Plymouth was the key to much successful badger hunting. In the country, surrounded by prime gopher habitat, I needed only to look and I would see a badger. My intrepid car also got me back into remote areas where many gopher populations were undisturbed by man's activities. The same applied to the badger.

The old car had a nasty tendency to suck in dust while driving the dry back roads. Fine, light brown dust settled over the interior, making it difficult to see the actual colors. Yet the dust was indirectly a boon. It made me stop every few miles to brush off my clothing and hair. During these stops, I checked the countryside with ten-power binoculars and invariably turned up a prize badger.

Badger activity is easy to identify. Freshly exposed earth thrown back from a hole in a fan shaped pattern indicates an adult is near. A spurt of dirt being tossed into the air is a sure sign of a badger caught in the act of digging out a frantic gopher. Badger scat, dry tapered rolls about one and a half inches long, is found at just about any gopher colony.

The real key to badger presence, however, is the obvious digging activity around gopher mounds. Badgers tend to start with mounds at the outside edge of a colony; it's here that several prospecting holes can be found. Gopher patches on knolls are another good spot to begin looking. A hardy badger will mine these areas first. Finally, activity is also common along fence lines and field borders, where gopher colonies are thin and elongated.

When first spotted, badgers react by stopping their activity and focusing on the hunter. Some stand nearly upright at first, but most crouch low to the ground raising their heads, sniffing and looking toward the intruder. Eyes are well developed, and the nose is also keen.

Both are features of the burrowing lifestyle. Large eyes are needed to see in the scant light of deep tunnels and burrows, and a good nose is required to tell if anybody is home. Some badgers react to hunters by diving immediately into the hole they are working. Others will dig deeper into the ground, quickly covering themselves with large amounts of dirt. A number will run toward a familiar burrow.

Badgers are fairly good-sized, and make attractive targets for riflemen. From head to toe the average adult badger stretches 30 inches. Add to this a tail that can be five or six inches, and it's easy to see that this member of the weasle family

The badger is characterized by large, powerful legs equipped with long, strong claws used for digging.

and direct cousin of the wolverine is a prize target.

A northern badger, well fattened in August, can tip the scales at 30 pounds—more than any of our other small game animals. Most adults will weigh around 20 pounds, with northern specimens being slightly heavier than their southern counterparts.

Badgers are showy and colorful. Their digging lifestyle polishes their long guard hairs, so that throughout the summer months their yellowish-

grey coats are sleek and the median white stripe that passes over the head and nose is sharp and distinct. The feet are prominently black, and the long claws shiny with pearl-like tips. No other animal in North America has this combination of features; a badger can't be mistaken for anything other than a badger.

Most states have open seasons on badgers. Recognized as both an agricultural pest and rodent population control monitor, the badger occupies an ambivalent position in the minds of game managers and hunters. Some Canadian provinces perceive the badger as a worthwhile furbearer, and it is"both a trapline and rifle species. In the south the hide is of little value because the animal does not develop the luxurious guard hairs and underfur demanded by the fur trade. The badger is not managed for any particular goal across North America, and indeed, most hunters are not familiar with the animal. It is surely the most underrated small game species in North America today.

The best opportunities for taking a quick badger are when the animal is first spotted. The advice, therefore, is to waste no time. Usually, when seen at some distance—say 300 yards—there is ample time to get ready, perform a mini stalk, and shoot. However, roadside badgers, frequently at the 60-to 100-yard mark, must be reacted to quickly. Wind-blown scent will alert a badger, and their sharp eyes can easily detect the hunter's movements at this distance. A badger will check out a standing hunter, and this gives about three or four seconds to get into position, get a sight picture, and shoot. When a badger breaks into a lumbering run, be prepared to shoot fast and hard. Clean misses will usually kick up dust and an alert shooter can quickly correct his follow up shot.

In situations where a badger is moving too quickly, a quick squeak on a dying-rabbit predator call will stop him in his tracks. Since they, too, are flesh-eating predators—actually preferring their food alive and kicking—the prospect of rabbit meat can override their natural caution. Remember, too, that badgers have little fear and, in many parts of North America, little experience with being targets. But these animals learn quickly and become familiar with the telltale crack of a rifle very soon. If you miss, don't expect to get that badger easily the next time.

Badgers are rugged animals requiring good solid hits in the front end of the body. Shots placed too far back or in the paunch will barely slow the animal down. And approaching a wounded badger can be outright dangerous. The west is full of stories of cowboys who have had holes bitten in their boots by wounded badgers as they attempted to kick what they thought was a limp carcass. Wounded badgers can also dig themselves into a hole very quickly, so good hits are mandatory to prevent an animal from escaping.

As a farm kid, I shot countless badgers with a .22 rimfire, at close range and at long range—it made no difference. In those days everybody in the rural back waters—especially in southern Canada where I grew up—was a crack .22 rifle shot. We all shot frequently, and guns were considered tools the same as a pair of fence pliers.

I confess today to being a poorer offhand shot with a .22 than in my preteen years. Good marksmanship, ample woodcraft skills, and youthful bravado made up for many deficiencies in equipment. Today I wouldn't recommend that any shooter go after a badger with a .22 rimfire.

The strong musculature, thick fat, and heavy bones of the badger call for the use of adequate small game cartridges. Often a badger will peek out from the safety of his excavation offering only that thick, flat head as target for a well placed shot. A precision shooting rifle and accurate cartridge are a must. A good scope helps to sort out that dark skull from the surrounding mound.

Badger hunters are welcomed all over North America. The bad reputation of this animal is as powerful today as ever. Farmers and ranchers still appreciate this category of hunter, and wise hunters can use off-season badger hunting as a foot in the door for in-season hunting. Furthermore, hunters living in the northern part of the species's range should consider the hide a potential source of income. Prime badger trades well in world fur auctions. Hunters and badgers are made for each other.

Badgers are available throughout the year. Only in the far reaches of northern Canada do the animals truly hibernate. In other parts of the range, the animal goes into torpor during the

Badgers can be found at all times of the year. Here an active burrow is checked out closely. Badgers are usually very near when fresh sign is found.

winter months. Buried deep in one of its many dens, it awakes during warm weather breaks long enough to roust some gopher from its deep sleep, then devours it with zeal. Sometimes a lucky badger will find a den of sleeping skunks, thereby ensuring a winter's supply of food.

Nature helps the badger by reducing its caloric demands during the winter, leaving the animal listless and drowsy. Late summer sees the badger voraciously consuming prey and developing heavy layers of brown fat along the back and sides of its body. During warm spells in winter, the badger tunnels out of its loosely sealed den and hunts with only slightly less vigor than in the summer. It is during these periods that hides

are best and the animal most easily taken with trap or rifle. In southern areas, badgers remain active all winter long.

Not enough has been done with the badger as an animal to be called. Under correct conditions the animal responds well to the dying rabbit predator call. Hidden in shrubs or sagebrush along the edge of a picket pin patch or prairie dog town, any hunter can bring a badger to the alert with a few squeaks on a quality predator call. It makes sense—badgers are predators eating the same foods as coyotes and foxes. They have a taste for rabbit, so it's natural they'd be interested in the sound of a dying rabbit. Like other predatory species, the young are less inhibited in their reaction to call sounds.

In most parts of the west, nearly every gopher colony has at least one resident family. A female badger typically rears two young, although when food conditions are good, three are raised. The male doesn't stay with the female, but instead pursues a solitary life nearby. This means good opportunities to use calling, and good odds for success.

For calling to succeed, badgers have to be in the immediate area, either holed up somewhere in a burrow out on the colony or digging out a nearby rodent. They don't move far the way a coyote or fox might. The animals, obviously, must be within earshot of the call, but even deep in the ground the animals seem to pick up the calling noise. They are cautious about leaving the den, and may dally around the entrance before moving toward the sounds.

Once in the open, adult badgers respond aggressively to the calling sound, but tend not to travel far in response to it. If they are going to appear, they tend to do so within ten minutes of the beginning of the calling session. Standing near their den entrance, they test the wind as if checking for the smell of fresh blood. Some will run toward the caller, stop abruptly, raise and lower their head as if trying to spot the distressed animal. Others will hiss loudly and chop their jaws, flashing large white teeth. Badgers are voracious flesh eaters; many of these motions are food-and prey-related behaviors that are interesting for the hunter to watch.

Badgers, for their large size, move incredibly close to the ground. Finding a clear shot is sometimes difficult. Vegetation and topography obscure their movement. Sometimes a hunter has to pop up from his hidden position and shoot quickly. Ranges aren't usually excessive, averaging around 120 yards.

If the hunter can stand the tension, though, waiting for a moving badger to stop and stand on his hind legs affords the best shot. Moving badgers are challenging, especially when using a lever action rifle. In the open they are alert and fearful of man, and if pursued will usually run for the nearest familiar burrow. Their fat bodies, thick skins, and long hair give them a space-invader look, a digging machine out of place on the plains as they waddle along.

I took many of my badgers with a .32-20 Model 92 and a Model 53 Winchester. Any bullet would work, but my preference was a 111 grain, cast, hollow-point bullet with a gas check thrown from an ancient Lyman 311316 mold. Sure it was old, yet it's still one of the slickest molds that company ever produced. Loaded with twelve grains of 2400 powder, the cartridge was as powerful as the .32-20 could be made without causing extraction difficulties in old lever guns.

I had a large supply of hoarded .32-20, 115 grain, jacketed bullets of various manufacture that worked particularly well when loaded with 13 or 14 grains of 2400. These loads were accurate, and made the old Winchesters speak with an authority their designers never imagined. Zipping out of my Model 53 at 1875 fps with the lead bullet and 1975 with the jacketed, they were devastating to badgers at any range.

Head shots are best on badgers, simply because many times that's all the target you'll see above the mound. Badgers in the open present the same target opportunities as other animals, with one important difference. Since badgers are large and

flat, and hug the ground closely, shots into the back and side areas are often required. The fur and flap-like skin can fool the shooter into thinking the back is extremely large. In reality, a badger's back is about eleven inches long, but only the first four to five inches of this contains the rib cage with the lungs and heart. The bullet must hit a target roughly five by four inches, and penetrate this critical area.

At 70 to 80 yards, a running badger is a challenging shot. Misses with the big lead bullets of the .32-20 would kick up lots of dust, providing an opportunity to apply some Kentucky windage to the follow-up shots possible with a lever rifle. Both rifles, equipped only with iron sights, are excellent for rapid firing without removing the rifle from the shoulder. Badgers brought closer by calling, or surprised some distance from their burrows, make excellent targets.

Calling during open winters, when the animal remains active, can also be productive. Hide hunters will find this an interesting adjunct, especially when combined with other hunting. Hunters should experiment with this in their areas. Moving animals will stop at the sound of a dying rabbit, bird, or mouse. More work needs to be done in this area. A quick toot on a predator call out of the truck window may stop a badger for one last investigative stare.

Many hunters first encounter a badger while hunting other species. Their pervasive distribution almost assures that sooner or later an alert hunter will catch one of these critters away from its den. Prairie dog and ground squirrel shooters routinely see the animal. Hunters should use these opportunities to become more familiar with the badger. After taking a few badgers, it's very easy to become hooked on this kind of shooting and begin specializing in badger hunting.

Bow hunters are becoming interested in these squarish animals. For them, badgers are good targets—relatively small, but demanding, and they can be taken at bow ranges. Bowmen

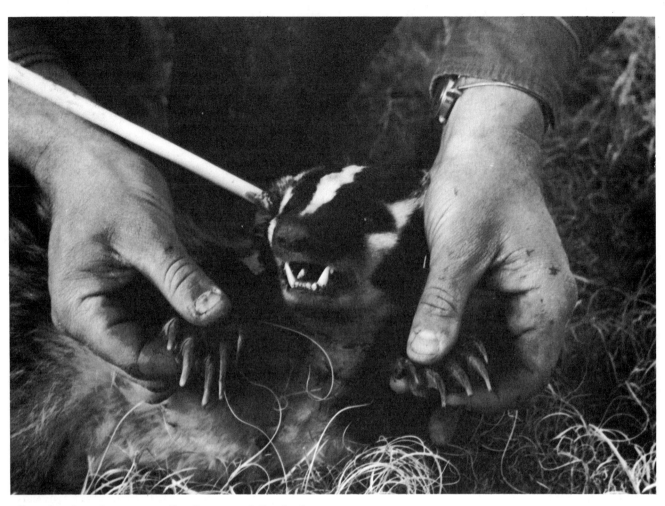

Bow hunters have recently discovered the badger.

particularly like the tenacious character of the prairie prospector, because it provides a good test of killing effectiveness, especially when testing new equipment and custom designed arrows. Indeed, bow hunters have found something that rifle hunters are only beginning to learn—badgers are top notch small game.

One of the first bow hunters I knew to vigorously pursue badgers was Brett Arneson. He would build a blind where he had observed badger activity, or close to the mouth of an active den. He'd get himself into position before daylight. At dawn badgers are most active, and he would invariably turn up one or two every other

morning for most of June and July. The demand for good shooting skills, whether with bow or rifle, in combination with no-limit, wide open seasons and broad distribution, puts badgers on top of the list for small game hunters.

Badgers are unique, offering riflemen a scrappy target that is challenging to find and requires good outdoor skills to turn up again. Few small game animals have given their name to several sports teams, stand as a state animal, and have colored our language by adding a verb. Here is an animal that has earned our respect in the past, and perhaps now is the time to pay attention to it as an excellent huntable small game animal of the present.

My old Dodge car was responsible for getting me back into a lot of undisturbed back country. The car helped me discover badgers, and while its front wheels dropped into more than a few badger mines over the course of many summers, its open window was my favorite rifle rest for all kinds of small game. Perhaps I owe that car something. Badgers and Dodge cars are, no doubt in my mind, symbolic of the fun and adventure I experienced in some of the prettiest country created on earth. Anybody taking on badgers today will share part of that experience.

Crows at a Distance

Anyone reading natural history books written around the time of World War I will find crows dismissed as large, all black, and too familiar to need further description. Man has never had much of a love affair with the crow. The crow has been associated with the raven, a bird of ill omen, dismal in voice, solitary and lumbering in flight, and filling the role of northern vulture. Nevertheless, the crow, unlike the raven, has thrived and learned to live next to man. The raven is today what it was millions of years ago—a bird of the deep wilderness, while the crow has prospered as man cleared, broke, and cultivated the land. The crow today flourishes in agricultural North America.

The crow is an open country bird living an omnivorous lifestyle, eating anything from carrion to newly planted corn. In the west where prairies and open country once prevailed, the crow was probably always around, but it has increased greatly with cultivation. Farming brought with it an abundance of new habitat opportunities, and the crow was there to capitalize on them. Few birds have been as successful at filling the niches created by modern farming practices.

The crow has occupied an ambivalent position among farmers and stockmen for nearly a century. In 1895 the first government report on the crow's economic status was released. Titled the "American Crow In Relation to Agriculture" and offered to the public as U.S. Department of Agriculture Bulletin No. 6, it was based on stomach examinations of over 2000 crows and long-winded testimony from across agricultural North America. Again in 1918, as the world marched home from war, a second major report on the crow was produced. The new findings were based on more stomach samples and 3000 personal accounts of crow behavior. The reports showed that crows eat lots of insects, and the crow received guarded approval.

On the other hand, biologists were not convinced, and as the fledgling science of wildlife biology grew, evidence of crow depredations on important game species became increasingly apparent. Stomach and scat analysis had failed to show the great numbers of eggs crows were stealing every year. Throughout the spring and summer, before grasshoppers are out in abundance, crows destroy a large portion of waterfowl and upland game bird eggs. Field biologists reported that only one in four eggs is brought to hatching, and the losses were blamed squarely on crows.

The crow's reputation as a crafty predator grew as field biologists recorded observation after observation of crows flushing nesting prairie chickens and returning moments later to prey on vacated nests. During the nesting season crows were observed to hunt indefatigably for eggs, which it seemed to prefer to other foods. In the trade-off between killer of agricultural pests for the benefit of the farmer and wildlife predator, the crow has been judged to take more than it puts back.

All things considered, the crow was an undesirable. Duck losses to crows were reckoned to be greater than those to the two million American and Canadian hunters going afield each year. The crow was painted black, and remains that way to this day. Yet the crow prospers. It is wary, intelligent, and capable of adaptation when necessary. It will eat anything

Author has always preferred to take crows at a long distance using high powered cartridges. Crows can be taken off roost sites or while feeding on fields. The targets have to be diligently sought out.

and live anywhere. It has all the traits of the successful predator.

The crow has now survived endless bounties and campaigns designed to eradicate the bird from the face of the earth. When I was a farm boy, bounties were the rage. In my area, crow bounties were still in effect as late as 1961, and programs were administered through the local school districts designed to encourage young boys to hunt crows for reward. A pair of crow legs would bring five cents when turned into the school principal or teacher assigned to oversee the local program.

My cousin, Clifford Pyle, attended one of the

last schools operating a crow collection program. A young, city-raised, female teacher looked after the paperwork. Although mortified every time she saw a pair of pink and black shrivelled legs with their attached grotesque claws, she dutifully recorded on a special government form the dates and numbers of leg pairs each boy (and sometimes girl) would bring to school. Monday was busiest for her, as most kids could hunt only on weekends. Crow bounties were taken seriously and the crow was under relentless pressure. One of the main reasons for going to school was that crows' legs brought in some spending money.

Collecting crows' legs was strictly business. In the early spring the strategy was to locate as many crow nests as possible. These we checked regularly by standing dead-still at the base of the tree or bush, and listening quietly for the "keep-keep" sound of crow hatchlings calling for food. We checked nests while doing some other farm chore—like getting the cows home for evening milking or looking for some steer that felt pastures were greener somewhere else.

Once the hatch was underway, timing was critical. The hatchlings were the easiest and most profitable to turn in as legs. (Besides, it left the adults to produce a new brood some time later that season or next year.) Crows are faithful to their nests, and return year after year, repairing and adding to the existing nest. Some crows have returned to the same site annually over as many as 15 years. My experience shows three to five is more common.

The way we collected hatchlings was by scaling the tree or scrambling up the bush, always hard on clothes. The birds were thrown down from the nest and clubbed. Legs were removed, tied together with binder twine, and turned into the teacher forthwith.

Some years it wasn't possible to cover all the nests in an area, and in short order hatchlings became fledglings. This was always a source of panic, since the opportunities to harvest crow legs were escaping, and school would soon be out for the summer. It was then that the .22 rimfire rifle came into play. For about a week, crow young go through a period where they learn to fly, and remain very close to the home nest. Although these birds can't fly, they move through the trees with ease. Even today, hopping from tree to tree and hiding in the dense underbrush, they are challenging targets for junior riflemen. Their black color lets them blend into the dark shadows of the poplar and willow bluffs. If a young crow remains motionless against this background, it's nearly always safe.

How successful were these programs? It depends how you measure success. They failed to reduce crow assaults on game birds. By the 1970's it was realized that habitat loss was a larger threat to waterfowl and upland game bird numbers than the crow population. Public bounties came into question across North America. Many felt tax money could be better directed, as it appeared that only hunters benefitted from the bounties. However, in terms of providing excitement and some money for a couple of young farm boys, the bounty programs were an unqualified success. The five cents per pair then would be like having 50 cents a pair today. Back then a box of .22 short hollow point cartridges cost 35 cents, and those 50 cartridges would bring down 30 fledglings and a dozen adults.

What did those poor teachers—like Miss Beckowitz—do with thousands of rotting crow legs? The school my cousin attended had a central wood and coal furnace and all legs, once audited and paid for, would end up in there. However, since it was spring, heat was not needed in the small schoolhouse, so over the weeks prior to summer break, crow legs accumulated at the bottom of the furnace. As the season progressed and crow hunting became increasingly difficult, more than one boy would crawl into the furnace and retrieve some crow legs. How many crow legs were recycled in this way nobody knows, but any government study based on crow leg returns would have some built-in errors.

Strange with all the attention directed toward the crow that it never really attracted much sport hunting interest. Killing a crow remained a service to agriculture and wildlife management. Today seasons remain open and the crow is as abundant as ever. Few hunters bother to actively pursue crows, yet they are readily available throughout North America except for some parts of Texas, New Mexico and southern Arizona. Throughout most of the continental U.S. the crows resides all year. In Canada, it migrates south in the early fall and returns in the spring. Many of these migrating crows don't travel more than four or five hundred miles, and often halt their southward movement where food supplies and weather conditions are favorable.

Mature adult crows are great long range targets for the serious rifleman. They are, of course, wary of man, and as a consequence any shooting opportunities *will* be long range. Using a high powered centerfire rifle, hunters should plan that most of their shooting will be done at ranges around the 300-yard mark. There will be times when shots at 250 yards are available, but any distance less will be a matter of rare luck.

Rifle shooters do best to go after crows during the spring. As they move northward, they are less cautious, and once nest repair gets underway paired crows are easier to home in on than migrating flocks. Resident crows adjust their home ranges prior to nesting, and good opportunities become available.

Crows cling to waterways. Nesting sites are often found along stream beds and in bluffs that develop near lakes and big rivers. Abandoned farm yards are also popular crow nesting sites. Nests, in fact, can be found anywhere there are sufficient trees and bushes.

Life along streams and rivers—near *any* water—is easy for the crow. There is always something to eat along the shores. With a broad diet, crows work the shoreline and move inland to feed on insects and crops when necessary. Major roosts are also found in these areas. Crows will also haunt roadsides, checking for freshly

Crow callers must learn to use camouflage. The head and face area should also be covered. This rig closes around the face leaving only the eyes exposed.

killed game, rodents, or other birds. A road-killed deer will keep a family of crows feeding for days. Farm garbage dumps are frequented by crows, and nobody needs to be told about how crows congregate around the dumps of small towns and cities. Crows love to scavenge.

During any planting season crows can be found on freshly seeded fields, intently looking for worms, insects, and insect eggs exposed by the seeding equipment. They are less alert than normal, and it's a good opportunity for riflemen. Under these conditions, many shots can be taken at 150 to 200 yards. In the north, seeding occurs during the spring, while in the deep south crop seeding is done every ten weeks or so. The southern hunter thus has more frequent chances than his northern cousin.

The long range crow hunter has to be opportunistic and take advantage of any situation. He must understand the animal and its behavior patterns. Crows are most vulnerable when nesting or hunting. Sometimes they will make mistakes when other crows are around. The key is activity. When a crow is occupied it focuses its attention on the activity, forgetting about safety. The hunter can use these opportunities for long range shots.

Crows have to be taken by surprise. Once wise to hunters, they immediately leave the area, often travelling for miles, cawing loudly. In fact, some hunters report instances of crows apparently recognizing their car and quickly departing the area.

Late one summer I got lucky on a crow sitting on a fence post about 350 yards away. As the crow's body was toppled by the .25-06 87-grain bullet, about 200 more birds lifted off the surrounding field. Next day, in the same area, I relocated the flock and repeated my feat at the range of only 275 yards. But that was the last time any crow from that flock would fall to my rifle. The following day a sentinel crow spotted my vehicle. Within seconds the flock was in the air and gone. This happened on three additional occasions until I finally figured out that some alert crow was recognizing the approaching car. Later, while accompanying a shooting friend who drove a truck, we both scored on 200-yard crows from the same flock without difficulty.

An exposed hunter, carrying a gun and obviously looking like someone hunting, does not stand a chance with alert crows. The hunter is quickly recognized as a threat and a whole set of survival behaviors are set in motion. A farmer can drive by roosting crows, passing within a few yards every day, and no evasive action is undertaken. However, put a rifle in that same farmer's hand and have him attempt to stalk within 100 yards of the roost, and every crow will take flight. Like other predators, these animals are capable of discerning when man is a threat.

Crows have well developed eyes and optic nerves. They easily see the glint of rifle barrels or the reflection of other hunting equipment, like pack buckles, binoculars, and knife handles. I believe these animals even react to man's eye movements. Human eyes, the surrounding eye sockets, and the face reflect back an incredible amount of light. It is my personal belief that crows, and all game for that matter, spot this reflected light. They respond to the presence or absence of reflected light to sort out man's intentions.

There are few times when the human species walks with head erect, but when hunting, man carries his head upright to check the countryside and survey the ground ahead. The eyes and head are moved from side to side to give a better view. Not only do animals notice this change in how we hold our heads, but when combined with increased light reflected from white faces it telegraphs our intention to an already alert constituency of small game animals. Our postures, movements, and the way light plays off our bodies and equipment combine to send a strong signal to the animal world—a signal that has conditioned crows and other small game to man's behavior.

This has implications for hunters, not the least of which is the obvious need for camouflage. It also means camouflage must be used wisely. Either concealed in fixed blinds or stalking into range, the hunter must use camouflage clothing when crow hunting. The face and hands must be covered, and gear must be covered or colored to absorb rather than reflect light.

Once crows are paired and nesting, one of the pair, usually the male, acts as a sentinel, sitting some 20 or 30 feet up a tree. He posts himself near the nest, sometimes in the same tree. A crow caught in this situation gives the hunter a rare break. An adult will remain in this position longer than at any other time. In a family group, or when crows are gathering prior to migration, this inactivity would never occur. While it seems the crow easily spots the hunter, it sits tight, apparently thinking it has blended into the surrounding shadows. This gives the alert hunter enough time to choose a rest and snap the rifle to his shoulder or even gain a few yards with a short stalk.

One reason often suggested for the crow's success is the lack of offsetting predators. The crow has only one natural enemy: the great horned owl. Natural history societies describe the great horned owl as the evil genius of the woods. While this large predator controls all it surveys, it has not fared well as a species. In the past, when it was legal game, it was duck soup to knock out of the sky with a shotgun. The bird was also easy to find around abandoned yards and building sites, so for years it fell to short range plinkers. As a poultry killer it was shot on sight, and I can recall my father and uncles shooting them without so much as a shrug of the shoulder. It has also been victimized by pesticide poisoning passed through the food chain.

Crows have one major defense tactic against owls. They put the run on owls by ganging up on the bird and mobbing it. A sharp-eyed crow spots a sleeping owl hugging the trunk of a tree, the crow sounds an alarm, all nearby crows gather quickly, and soon the owl is in flight with black crows dive bombing his head. The crows mean business, and the owl's only defense is to dodge the attackers. They dive and re-dive, rarely making contact with the would-be predator. The chase is kept up until dark, or until the owl gives up and moves away.

When crows roost in the evening, though, the tables turn. The night-hunting owl silently and swiftly takes a roosting crow in a flash. At roost, crows sit tight, cawing nervously, afraid to shift their hard-earned positions on the tree while the owl ruthlessly harvests what it needs. The great horned owl, having knocked its prey from the tree, scoops it up with sharp talons and begins feeding within yards of the roost site.

Nevertheless, crow numbers have increased in spite of this major predator. Game birds, rabbits, and field mice are all easier prey for the owl than crows. Besides, these alternate species carry less risk of injury to the owl. The owl has a large prey menu, and like all predators it takes what comes easiest. Where close encounters of the owl kind become too bothersome, crows simply move out and re-establish in owl-free territory. In this way the crow smartly sidesteps its sole natural enemy.

Roosting, aside from being a crow's major defense strategy, is a behavior significant for all hunters. After the young become able flyers, about mid-July, small flocks composed of two to ten family groups from a common area gather and forage together. They also form nightly roosts in nearby protective shrubbery. The roost, chosen in owl-free bush, usually contains some tall cover and is some distance from man. Sometimes roosts can be as simple as old windbreaks in abandoned yards. There will be some high point for one or two sentinel crows to perch and survey the countryside. Old crows teach young crows where to roost and, providing habitat remains or disturbance factors don't change, roosts become incorporated into the crow's annual cycle of behavior.

Roosts are used for years, offering a ready source of shooting. Hunters can use this knowledge two ways. First, routes can be planned to put the shooter into a hidden position for clear shots at roosting birds. Once the hunter is in place it's possible to get off about half a dozen shots before the crows take wing.

One friend plotted eight crow roosts within a 15-square-mile area, and worked out shooting blinds for each. He knew how to reach each roost without alerting the crows, much the way a prairie duck hunter becomes familiar with how to approach individual swamp bogs over a broad area. Shooting from dense cover at ranges that approached 325 yards, his take of crows with a high power rifle was well above average.

The second hunting method most successfully applied near roosts plays on the crow's hate for

Hunters have to get into position quickly when calling.

the owl. Using a good quality call, the hunter re-creates a crow's distress cry. The call is accompanied by a dummy owl, placed on a post or tree. The approaching crow easily spots the fake owl. The crow, shrieking for help, alerts the roost, and the mobbing instinct takes over. Duped by calling and the sight of the major predator, crows flock to help their cousin. It's then that a well camouflaged shooter gets in some quick shotgunning.

Crow calling is not particularly difficult. Using a high-pitched crow call, held between the thumb and forefinger of the left hand, sounds are produced by growling or grunting through the call. Long drawn out calls are required to attract and hold crows, so take deep breaths, and use the diaphragm to keep call volume high. Calling is done before shooting and continues during shooting.

Simply blowing through a commercial call is not enough. Sound produced this way is too similar to the crow's danger call, and these sounds will scare off wise crows every time. It's important to make your call shriek and moan—almost begging the crows within ear range to come over and provide some assistance to a fellow crow who's alone against the predator.

Traditional advice on crow calling has been to

practice during the spring and early summer. Crows, busy raising young, are not roosting at those times, yet nesting pairs respond well to calling. Once the caller finds individual birds responding to his sounds it's a good indication that technique and cadence are correct. It is also a good opportunity to observe the reactions of small groups and young that have just learned to fly. This can give good information on necessary lead, flight patterns, and habits. Once the black predator is responding in a regular fashion, it's time to set up for a top-notch crow shoot.

Varying somewhat with geographic location, crows band together after harvest or in the fall. In the north groupings begin in late July, while further south they occur in late September. In general, cold weather encourages banding, while warm weather delays the process for a few weeks. The season signals the crow to band and begin some form of migration. Hunters should watch the weather and crow behavior closely before beginning to look for roosts and hunt locations.

The best method for finding roosting sites is to ask neighboring farmers. In most instances landowner permission will be required anyway, so a few minutes spent talking with area farmers can save time. There is still a lot of anti-crow feeling in rural North America, so farmers are very willing to share information on locations and numbers.

Another sure method is by following, from cover, a crow's flight path late in the afternoon. As darkness approaches, all crows within an area move toward their roost. The numbers going to roost can be large, so there are many opportunities to spot groups or individuals moving toward the nightly post. In the southern parts of the range, huge roosts of several thousand crows are possible, while in the north roosts rarely exceed 500.

Once roosts have been located, make plans to appropriately hunt the area. Indiscriminate shooting with shotgun or rifle causes birds to abandon their protective sites. Sometimes roost sites will be moved several miles. Therefore, never shoot directly at a roost unless you are well hidden by cover. Plan how to call sites based on flight paths and the cover that leads to the roost. Never set up closer than 200 yards from the roosting site.

Crow hunting was once far more popular than it is today. A quick survey of outdoor magazines shows little interest in crows and long range shooting, but years ago there were frequent articles. Magazines today carry stories about expensive hunting trips that most readers can never afford. But the broad distribution of the crow means little travel is necessary for any North American hunter to participate in good crow hunting opportunities. It provides top gunning for either long range riflemen or call-using shotgunners.

Chapter 3

Small Game and Varmint Cartridges

Today, hunters can choose from a wide selection of specialized small game ammunition. Years ago, such cartridges were scaled down, and, in many cases, downloaded big game numbers. While they were very effective at short distances, they didn't hit accurately and consistently under long range field conditions.

The behavior of small game also changed. Before small game hunting became popular, these destructive pests grew in number. Poisoning campaigns and shooting were encouraged, and the animals surviving the poisoning became tough targets for hunters using older, slower-moving bullets. Increased demand resulted in improved small game ammunition and a greater selection in bullet weights.

An abundance of game, surplus military guns, and war-trained machinists also led to the redesign of many traditional cartridges. Wildcatting, the process of remaking cartridges to achieve improved performance, grew in popularity and attracted interest. This further increased demand for shooting products, and for cartridges designed for small game shooting.

Varmints brought a new tone to post-World War II shooting. Heavy bullets, travelling in arc-like trajectories, proved ineffective at taking small game at ranges much beyond 200 yards. Varmints are small agricultural pests, destructive to crops, produce, land, and cattle. The economic losses and inconvenience created by these pests made them suitable targets for eager hunters. A new sport—small game hunting—was born.

Varmints remain destructive pests, but they aren't pursued by farmers and ranchers as much as they were in the early 1950's and 1960's. Today, varmint damage is less economically threatening than it was a scant two decades ago. Farming has become more intensive, and the economies of scale applied today are little affected by marauding varmints. However, the sport of shooting remains popular, and varmints easily provide some of the best field shooting opportunities in North America.

While their pest status has somewhat declined, varmints still offer challenge, meat, hides, and family sport. Different cartridges and bullets, and various performance levels, are part of the equation. The hunter also has to factor in wind bucking ability, bullet construction, recoil levels, and noise, not to mention the availability of rifles and rifle styles. If you want to participate in varmint shooting, you must pick the right cartridge.

Picking a cartridge from today's selection of rifle calibers can be a complicated task. There are dozens of cartridges suitable for a variety of game, all ready to be compared, tested, and shot over great distances. Some shooters choose several different cartridges for their small game hunting, while others pick one for all shooting.

Many shooters, yours truly included, end up with a large number of rifles. A few hunters select highly specialized calibers designed to meet one or two strict purposes. Most small game hunting needs, however, can be met with either a general or dual purpose cartridge.

A number of factors influence cartridge choice, aside from personal tastes. From the pipsqueak .17 Remington to the fire-belching .224 Weatherby Magnum, there are several criteria on which to base small game cartridge selection. One is the distance at which game will normally be taken. This factor includes trajectory, power, and accuracy.

The size of the game will also influence the decision. Thick-bodied badgers require more bullet energy than small bush rabbits at similar distances. Finally, the terrain and the conditions under which the hunting will be done are prime concerns. Thick bush calls for different solutions from the windy prairie. These criteria are basic to small game hunting, and a hunter must work these through according to the needs of his area.

Varmint-class shooting places special demands on the cartridge. *Bullet construction* and *accuracy* are prime considerations in this kind of shooting. Bullets must be light, so they expand rapidly upon contact with the animal or, for a miss, go to pieces on the surrounding countryside, reducing the chance for a dangerous ricochet. Good accuracy is obviously important to long range shooting. Bullets that pitch, yaw, or come out of damaged barrels will miss small targets at long ranges. Bullets must travel true and arrive on target with enough energy to humanely kill the animal.

Ranges encountered in varmint hunting are often long. Typically, shots are taken at 300 to 400 yards. At the end of this distance, bullets must still have punch and expand readily. Lightweight bullets excel for this kind of work, because they combine accuracy and knockdown power in one package.

Cartridges chosen from the .17 Remington, .22 Hornet, .222 Remington, .223 Remington, .222 Remington Magnum, .22-250, .243 Winchester, 6 PPC, and 6mm Remington lines are suitable. Older shooters might add the aging .220 Swift, or the moribund .225 Winchester. Other suitable cartridges include .250 Savage, .257 Roberts, .25-06, and the .257 Weatherby Magnum. Some shooters would add the dead .25-20 in this list.

Muzzle velocity is an easy way to compare one cartridge to another. Muzzle velocities anywhere from 2500 fps to 4000 fps are adequate for small game hunters, but it's best to choose something at least 3000 fps. Muzzle velocity is critical because it determines both bullet energy and trajectory. The numbers are easy to understand—the fastest bullet is almost always the best. As a result, great emphasis is placed on this aspect of bullet performance. Manufacturers widely publicize muzzle velocities.

- Hunters spend hours pouring over factory ballistic charts, studying which cartridge is best for their purpose. Sometimes too much faith is put in these numbers. Hunters must learn to sort out the important characteristics from the trivial. Down range performance, consisting of bullet velocity, energy, and trajectory, is more important than muzzle velocity. (Most game is taken well beyond the muzzle.)

Subtle differences between cartridges don't always translate into improved down range performance. Muzzle velocity differs between the .222 Remington Magnum and the .222 Remington by 220 fps with comparable bullet weights.

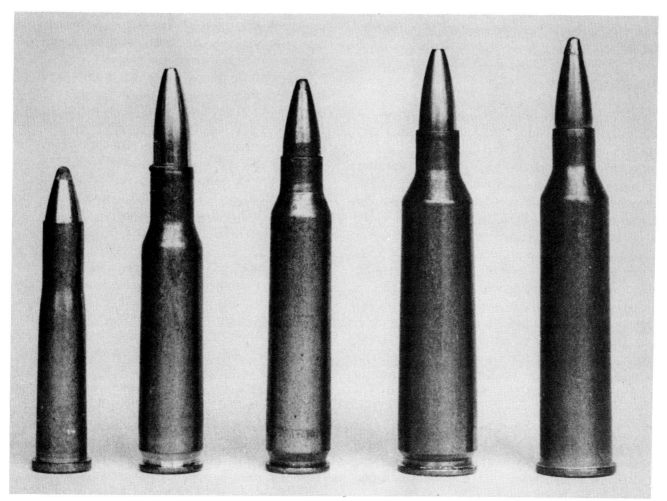

The .22 Centerfires—.22 Hornet, .222 Remington, .223 Remington, .22/250, and the .225 Winchester.

At 300 yards, however, energy differs by only 60 foot-pounds, offering no practical gain for hunters. When sighted to place all bullets dead-on at 200 yards, the non-magnum number arrives on target 10 inches low at 300 yards, while the .222 Remington Magnum is down nine inches at that distance.

Comparisons of two cartridges with muzzle velocity differences as much as 220 fps show no difference in performance. Trajectories are no better and energy differences insignificant. A few more feet of muzzle velocity is not critical to successful hunting.

In addition to ballistic considerations, recoil and report are important to small game hunters.

Many shooters are attracted to small game hunting by the easy shooting characteristics of low powered, small caliber cartridges. Recoil-sensitive shooters and beginners should choose small caliber centerfires over more specialized, high intensity cartridges. Picking a .222 Remington over a .25-06 can transform a beginner into an old hand after just one summer's shooting.

Characteristics of Today's Cartridges:

It's open season on small game cartridges. As this is written, there are four calibers and over 30 cartridge styles suitable for small game in North America. It's easy to become bewildered by the offerings. Sorting this out is the goal of this section.

The .22 Centerfires

The .22 centerfires have a long and glorious history of performance and reliability. Inadvertently, Charles Newton, the great rifle and cartridge inventor, opened the door to varmint hunting cartridges when he created the .22 Hi-Power in 1892. This was marketed by Savage beginning in 1912. Performance of this early cartridge on deer was unspectacular, but on small game it was devastating.

This invention touched off a wave of cartridge wildcatting and development. The original Neidner Magnum came out of the .22 Savage Hi-Power case and later the .25-35 Winchester case. The .25-20 case was redeveloped by Harvey Lovell into the .22-3000 Lovell. Other entries included the .22 Newton-King, the .228 Ackely Magnum, and the .22-250 Mashburn. It was as if everybody wanted a cartridge named after himself.

The .22 Hornet was developed by modernizing the old Winchester. 22WCF. Success was brisk for cartridges like the .218 Bee, .219 Zipper, and the .219 Donaldson Wasp.

There are many choices, with cartridge power running the gamut from those nearly too weak for small game hunting to those seemingly overpowered. The .22 Hornet is still found on manufacturers' price lists, but its day in the sun is over. It's on the underpowered side of the ledger, but was a good performer for many years. The Thompson/Center TCR '87 single shot rifle is one of the last available in this cartridge.

Next in line is the .222 Remington. It was born in 1950 and was first available in the Remington Model 722 bolt gun. Bench rest shooters amassed incredible records with this cartridge, and its accuracy was soon tested in the game fields. It became a favorite of woodchuck shooters because of its low recoil, mild report, and inherently good accuracy. Although considered under-

powered by today's standards, it remains a highly recommended choice, and has broad application in small game hunting.

Factory-available with a 50 grain, pointed, soft-point bullet, the .222 leaves the muzzle at a nominal 3140 fps, and at 300 yards still has 1700 fps and 321 foot-pounds of energy. A heavier 55 grain commercial loading is also available that develops 3020 fps at the muzzle with 1773 fps and 384 foot-pounds of energy at 300 yards. Sighted-in to be dead on at 150 yards, it will be only 2.5 inches low at 200 yards.

The successful performance of the .222 Remington gave rise to other cartridges. These included the .015-inch-longer .222 Remington Magnum. Designed as a semi-automatic military cartridge, it in turn spawned the Viet Nam-famous 5.56mm military round, or .223 Remington. Like the .222 Remington, it performs best around the 200-yard mark, with some shooting extending to 300 yards.

The .222 Remington Magnum first appeared in 1958 and seemed to be rapidly gaining popularity with several manufacturers, most notably Sako, with several top-line rifles in this little cartridge. But the bubble burst when the more versatile 6mm's appeared and the little magnum, one of the nicest shooting cartridges of all times, virtually disappeared from the gun shelf.

The .222 Remington Magnum holds a special place in my heart. I used it on a lot of small game, and it was the first cartridge I ever reloaded. My university roommate, Tom Rycroft of Paris, Ontario, was an avid magnum shooter. I used his Magnum-outfitted Remington Model 722 to dispatch woodchuck and squirrels on his father's 125-acre corn and cattle farm. At the back of the farm gentle slopes gave way to a small creek that crossed the property.

Woodchuck dens covered the slopes, and the split-rail-fenced hedgerows along the farm's perimeter were home to fat squirrels and juicy rabbits. Tom and I frequently took our fill of all three species and returned to the house to reload our empties. At the same time, our field-dressed rabbits and squirrels were taken by Tom's mother, who would prepare them for our Sunday supper. The pleasant weekends spent on that farm hunting small game and reloading Tom's small supply of .222 Remington Magnum cases will live forever in my memory.

The .223 became famous, or perhaps infamous, in Viet Nam. As the military cartridge of choice, called the M193, it fed the M-16's carried in that conflict. There is a history of military cartridges becoming popular as civilian numbers. This has held true for the .45-70 and .30-06, and perhaps less so for the .30-40 Krag and .30M1 cartridges.

And it's fast becoming true for the .223. All gun manufacturers list rifles available for this cartridge. Surplus brass is easily obtained at low prices, and shooter-reloaders have displayed a willingness to use the cartridge. In most gun lines it has already replaced the .222 Remington and the .222 Remington Magnum.

From the factory it comes with a muzzle velocity of 3240 fps, pushing a 55 grain bullet. A 40 grain bullet is available, giving the little .223 a nominal 3620 fps. At 300 yards it offers 1906 fps and a striking energy of 444 foot-pounds with the 55 grain bullet. The 40 grain bullet produces a 300 yard velocity of 1950 fps and gives 340 foot pounds of energy. A 55 grain load zeroed for 150 yards will be just over two inches low at 200 yards.

The rifle should place all shots .80 inch high at 100 yards. It is a very capable performer on prairie dogs, gophers, squirrels, rabbits, and woodchucks out to 225 yards. Like others in its class, it's very pleasant to shoot, and shooters can fire all day without developing sore shoulders or flinching.

The .223 is an excellent intermediate range rabbit cartridge. The heaviest jackrabbit I ever shot was with a Ruger Mini 14 in .223 at about 225 yards one snowy afternoon in 1978. Returning home from a meeting I spotted two jackrabbits in the center of a large grain field. By the time I stopped, loaded, got into position and fired, the first rabbit had moved out of range and stood looking back at his cousin. The other animal, unaware of my presence, didn't move, leaving an opportunity for a clear, safe shot. The jack weighed 15 pounds. I worked up a sweat tramping through the deep-crusted snow to retrieve my prize.

The .220 Swift is next on our survey of .22 centerfires. It has, perhaps, the most colorful history of any cartridge in America today. It is the classic long range round, developed by Winchester and introduced in the mid 1930's. Winchester dropped the cartridge from their rifles in the famous 1964 product purge. Anyway, this is a powerful cartridge, producing 4110 fps, the fastest of any modern cartridge, and it offers small game and varmint hunters unparalleled range. Indeed, it is the first cartridge that shoots farther than the hunter can see. Ruger still chambers rifles for this cartridge.

The cartridge is extremely accurate and flat-shooting in properly bedded rifles. It has a reputation for wearing out barrels, but shooters need not worry until about 3000 rounds have been fired. Allowing time between shots for the barrel to cool greatly prolongs barrel life. Case life is short, but that is a small trade-off for the flattest-shooting cartridge available today.

Report is important when beginning shooters are part of the hunting party.

The Swift produces 3135 fps at 200 yards, the same as the .222 Remington does at the muzzle. It has 800 foot-pounds of energy at 300 yards, and when sighted-in to be dead on at that range is only seven inches low at 400 yards.

The Swift is not a cartridge for beginners, as muzzle blast is high and lightweight rifles will give the shooter a substantial kick. Bystanders several hundred yards away will have no trouble recognizing the sharp crack of the .220 Swift. However, veteran shooters owe it to themselves to try a Swift.

The .22-250 is the current favorite among .22 caliber centerfire shooters. It can do anything within the capabilities of smaller cartridges, but with 400 fps more in muzzle velocity. With factory loads, the .22-250 pushes a 55 grain soft-pointed bullet at 3680 from a 24-inch barrel rifle. The 40 grain factory bullet leaves the muzzle at 4000 fps—ballistically close to the Swift. Down range performance yields energy levels of 603 foot pounds with the heavy bullet; the 40 grain pill produces 430 foot pounds. Both pack lots of punch to take any small game at these ranges.

Trajectories are equally impressive, and a rifle placing bullets two inches high at 100 yards will be dead on at 275. This gives an effective point blank range of 325 yards for the average prairie dog.

This cartridge originated by necking down a .250/3000 case, and was the subject of much experimentation by a number of tinker-gun-smiths for three decades. It was legitimized in 1965 when Remington adopted it for the Model 700 rifle. The .22-250 has evolved into the varmint hunter's duty cartridge.

It can be used for prairie dogs, gophers, squirrels, and rabbits without a hitch. Recoil is not noticeably more than with the smaller .222 Remington and .223 Remington. Long range performance is better because of the increased velocity, but there is also more noise. The cartridge can be downloaded if noise is a problem, a remedy that can be applied to any cartridge.

Many consider the .22-250 the best all-around varmint cartridge available today.

From 1964 to 1972, a cartridge called the .225 Winchester was available in the newly-designed Model 70. Few shooters today are familiar with this cartridge, but at one time it showed some promise. Shooting texts dismiss the cartridge as a mistake, but it once performed as well as the .220 Swift. Later Winchester downloaded the cartridge, and the few boxes around today would probably produce 3500 fps at the muzzle with the factory 55 grain bullet. Trajectories and performance were so similar to the .22-250 that comparison was inevitable. However, the .225 case was semi-rimmed—just like the .220 Swift that it was meant to replace. The long and favorable history of the .22-250 as a wildcat sounded the death knell for the .225.

I have always had a particular interest in this cartridge. It has always performed well for me. The .225 in my gun rack has accounted for many long haired predators and countless prairie dogs, gophers, and rabbits. It has taken its share of badgers at intermediate ranges, and crows at extremely long ranges.

An old friend, wildlife biologist Ted Weins, watched one evening as a crow toppled over at a distance of 475 yards, victim of my careful aim and that gun's performance. Badgers stop dead in their tracks with nearly any shot from this rifle/cartridge combination.

I bought my Model 70 in .225 from an old friend, the late John Zadd, a professional agrologist many years my senior. He was an avid hunter and outdoorsman. One day we talked about rifles and cartridges. He had experimented with the .225 and found it worked fine, but where he lived and worked there was little need for a varmint grade cartridge. He, too, had read the bad press on the .225 and asked if I was interested in this lemon. A deal was struck, and that rifle has not left my side for nearly 15 years.

One proprietary cartridge has to be mentioned in this list. The .224 Weatherby Magnum, available since 1963, ranks ballistically between the

.222 Remington and the .220 Swift, and is very similar to the .22-250 in performance. It comes in a belted case—characteristic of Roy Weatherby's magnums. It's expensive, both to acquire a Weatherby rifle and to purchase the factory cartridges. This has prevented widespread use of the cartridge, and limited the experience shooters have had with the product.

The .224 Weatherby with a 55 grain bullet produces 3650 fps at the muzzle, and at 300 yards retains 68% of its velocity—2403 fps—and 705 foot-pounds of energy. Loadings with 50 grain bullets give 3800 fps at the muzzle. These velocities are for factory Weatherby rifles outfitted with 26 inch barrels. The 200 yard midrange trajectory is 1.7 inches; the cartridge is very flat-shooting. Weatherbys are noisy and famous for their kick. These factors have not endeared the cartridge to the hearts of varmint shooters.

The .22 centerfires have a few disadvantages. The lightweight bullets are highly susceptible to wind. Light breezes blow these bullets off target two inches at 100 yards. Bullets of this caliber have low sectional densities, ranging from .128 to .171. (Sectional density, the ratio of bullet weight in pounds to the square of its diameter in inches, is a good measure of a bullet's wind-bucking ability.)

The .243 as a Small Game Cartridge

Few cartridges have their origins in hunting and game. Most were designed because somebody thought their recipe would work and proceeded to develop it. Others came to life because they performed well on the target range, while still others had military origins. Not so with the .243. It evolved from a successful line of hunting-quality .243 or 6mm wildcats.

Some of these included the .243 Rockchucker, .240 Cobra, .243 Ackley, .240 Kraig, and the .240-250. There were also British production numbers called the .240 Holland & Holland, as well as its counterpart, the .246 Vickers. The

The .243 Winchester and 6mm Remington compared to the .257 Roberts and the .270 Winchester.

6mm Lee Navy has been credited with inspiring the .243, but when the .243 was introduced in 1955 the Navy round was already long dead.

The late Warren Page is responsible for bringing the cartridge to the attention of North American shooters. In a 1954 article in *Field and Stream*, Page urged the firearms establishment to pursue the .243. He considered it the equal of the .220 Swift or the .22-250 wildcat in velocity and flat trajectory to 250 yards, and also superior to the .22 centerfires in retained velocity beyond the 300 yard mark. Page also detailed the superb deer-killing ability of the cartridge. It was Pages's publicity that led to the acceptance of this cartridge.

The .243, or 6mm, is preferred to the .22 centerfires for varmints for two reasons. First, it has more power. The .243 Winchester and the 6mm Remington—once called the .244 Remington—produce 3350 and 3470 fps, respectively, when shooting factory 80 grain bullets. At 300 yards this gives three times the striking power of the little .222 Remington. Trajectories are flat. A .243 sighted-in two inches high at 100 yards will be only four inches low at 300 yards. On standing targets like prairie dogs, this means a point-blank range of 375 yards.

The second reason for the .243's popularity lies with the bullets. All bullets used in these cartridges have high sectional densities—ranging from .169 to .242—which means they perform well in crosswinds that would blow lightweight .22 bullets off narrow targets at 250 yards.

When it comes to varminting, bullet choice is critical. Loaded with 75, 80, or 87 grain bullets, the .243 Winchester and the 6mm Remington are superb choices for varmints as far out as 400 yards. These lightweight factory bullets are specifically designed for varmint shooting by having thin jackets that break up readily when they hit small game flesh or nearby ground. Serious varmint shooters should avoid heavier bullets, since they don't expand on thin skinned varmints.

The .243 is available for a host of rifles and is produced in more factory-made rifles than any other caliber, with the possible exception perhaps the .30-06. It has a good following in Europe as well. Recoil and muzzle blast are low in rifles with 24 inch or longer barrels. Carbine models are a bit heavy on noise, but recoil is still light. These factors have made the .243 Winchester and 6mm Remington popular dual-purpose cartridges, capable of taking varmints and deer under a variety of conditions.

Shooters can spend all day firing one of these mid-sized cartridges without developing flinch or fear of noise. This fact has produced a myth about .243 and 6mm shooters. It is said they tend to be above-average shooters. It's easy to understand. These guys can shoot more without tiring. Their added practice turns them into better game shots. Kills are more sure, and long range shots become the rule. Beginning shooters can pick the .243 or 6mm and know they have in their hands a gun that is easy to control, light on recoil, low on muzzle blast and very accurate. These cartridges inspire shooter confidence.

Differences between the .243 and 6mm are not significant for most hunting purposes. The 6mm Remington holds 54.57 grains of water while the nominal .243 Winchester case holds 52.81. For all practical purposes the two cartridges differ by only 75 to 120 fps, depending on bullet weight, in favor of the Remington.

Full metal-jacketed bullets are available for the .243 Winchester. Hunters have used these on small game, but it's not a recommended practice. Hard-point bullets require head and neck shots to humanely dispatch animals. Some predator hunters routinely use hard points, but the bullet has its problems on all kinds of game. Since the bullet does not expand upon impact, not all the bullet's energy is spent on the animal. Hard points often penetrate soft-bodied animals like rabbits and rodents. This creates an opportunity for the animals to escape, often only to die several yards down the trail, out of the hunter's sight. The use of hard point bullets on small game is inhumane, and can't be justified by thinking sportsmen.

The proprietary .240 Weatherby Magnum holds nearly 20 percent more powder than a 6mm Remington Magnum. Depending on bullet weight, this produces about 200 to 300 fps more velocity. Introduced in 1968, it features a belted case and represents the maximum performance that can be wrung out of a .243 caliber bullet. Ballistically, this cartridge, with an 87 grain bullet, leaves the muzzle at 3500 fps. At 300 yards it still has 76 percent of its bullet velocity—2663 fps—and is capable of producing 1370 foot-pounds of striking energy. Trajectories are very favorable: only 10 inches low at 400 yards when sighted two inches high at 100 yards. The only factory rifle currently chambered for the .240 Weatherby is the Mark V Weatherby Magnum. As is common in dealing with Weatherby products, both rifle and ammunition can be costly.

Coming onto the cartridge scene is the 6 PPC, invented in the mid 70's by the bench-rest shooting duo of Lois Pamisano and Ferris Pindell. Recently, Sako brought out their excellent Hunter Grade sporting rifle in this caliber.

The combination looks bright. With the specifications offered the cartridge has small game emblazoned all over it. Recoil and report are nearly nonexistent, yet velocity figures are high—3085 fps with a 75 grain hollow-pointed bullet—which means good trajectory and long range performance.

The .234 or 6mm class of cartridge is excellent for small game hunting. The differences between the .243 and 6mm are slight, almost not worth mentioning, and the .240 Weatherby doesn't outdo them by much. Both combine flat trajectory, easy recoil, good wind-bucking ability, and tolerable muzzle blast into one compact, accurate package.

There is an incredible number of commercially available firearms for the .243 and 6mm cartridge, and any back-country store carries a couple of boxes of .243 Winchester or 6mm Remington next to the .30-06's and the .22 rimfires. It approaches the ideal in small game cartridges, and remains adequate for deer and antelope. The small game hunter who wants only one cartridge for all his shooting might want to stop here.

The Quarter-Inch Choice

The first .25 caliber to hit the American hunting scene was the little .25-20 single shot. That was in 1882, and while it didn't last long, it kicked off nearly 100 years of interest in other quarter-inch calibers by the American shooting public.

From the start these smaller calibers were associated with varmint and small game shooting, while cartridges like the declining .45-70, new 30-40 Kraig, and the then-radical .30-06 were reserved for big game hunting. Interest in the .25 calibers grew with the introduction of two straight-sided Stevens cartridges called the .25-25 and the .25-21. Although highly accurate, they enjoyed limited popularity.

The first really successful quarter-inch cartridge was the .25-20, a shortened version of the .25-20 single shot. It deserves attention in any discussion of small game .25 caliber cartridges. Introduced in 1893, it had more rifles chambered for it than any other cartridge until the arrival of the .30-06. Winchester, Marlin, Remington, and Stevens all chambered rifles for it.

Shooting a factory-loaded 60 grain hollow point bullet produced a mediocre 2250 fps, while the 86 grain lead load produced 1440 fps. However, the short length of the cartridge permitted generous magazine capacities on the Winchesters and Marlin levers. This boosted popularity of these firearms. Its inherent accuracy and performance on edible small game gave it a fine reputation among farmers, trappers, and others who use firearms. The rifle helped popularize the cartridge, and it became known as the queen of varmint cartridges.

Another reason the .25-20 merits discussion is that its blunt-nosed bullets impart all their power to whatever they strike. Using 86 grain bullets, at 200 yards, this old-timer produces just over 200 foot-pounds of energy—plenty for rabbits, squirrels, and short range gophers. Although Winchester and Marlin quit producing rifles for this cartridge nearly 50 years ago, Kimber Arms of Clackamas, Oregon, still produces a nice single-shot bolt action in this caliber called the Model 82. The .25-20 lives!

Following the early success of the .25-20, in 1895 Marlin offered the .25-36, and Winchester introduced the .25-35. There was little difference between the two, although the Marlin version, at just over 1000 foot-pounds of striking energy at 100 yards, was slightly more powerful than the .25-35. Nevertheless, the .25-36 died

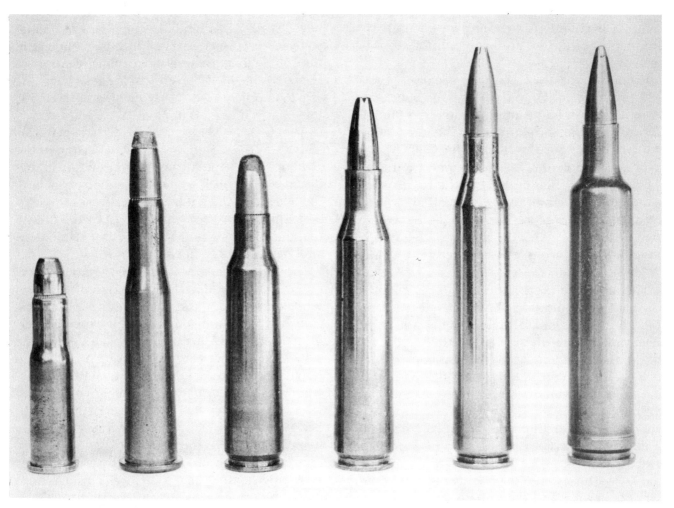

The quarter-inch family: the .25-20, .25-35, .250/3000, .257 Roberts, .25-06, and the .257 Weatherby.

quickly, and the .25-35 prospered as a dual-purpose deer and varmint cartridge. Using the 87 grain bullet, it produced just under 2400 fps at the muzzle. This encouraged the chambering of several single-shot rifles for it. Savage also chambered their Model 99 in .25-35, and this allowed reloaders to use spire-point bullets through its rotary magazine.

Next in line was the short-lived .25 Remington. Introduced in 1906, it was designed around a series of Remington rifles, notably the Model 14 pump, Model 8 semi-automatic, and the Model 30 bolt gun. Stevens also offered their Model 425 lever in this chambering. These rifles achieved

only limited acceptance, and the cartridge withered on the proverbial vine.

The .250/3000, invented by Charles Newton and produced by Savage, gained high regard by shooters and hunters. The story of this cartridge is a classic in firearms lore. Newton originally designed the .250/3000 to shoot a 100 grain bullet, but Savage correctly saw the value of having a lighter bullet that travelled at 3000 feet per second—a new high in commercial cartridge performance—and thus the 3000 in the name. An 87 grain bullet was chosen, and the rest is history.

Flat trajectory, good accuracy, and excellent

killing power firmly established the cartridge with American shooters. It was the first dual-purpose cartridge useful for varmints and deer-sized animals. As it turned out, the .250/3000 was excellent teamed with the Savage Model 99 rifle. Other rifle makers like Winchester and Remington introduced bolt guns in this cartridge. From 1914 to 1960, Savage offered the Model 99 in .250/3000; its withdrawal prompted howls of protest from the gun fraternity, and it was brought back in 1971. For several years after that the Model 99 was offered in a neat little carbine model with a straight grip and plain stock, called the Model 99E. Unfortunately it is no longer listed, but was a fine-shooting little rifle, ahead of its time by 20 years.

In 1953 the published velocity of the 87 grain bullet was boosted slightly to 3030 from 3000 fps, and the official name changed to .250 Savage. Factory 87 grain loads are still available from Remington and Winchester, although recent catalogues don't list them. There is also a 100 grain loading, but the 87 is the one varmint and small game hunters really want. It's a very pleasant cartridge to shoot, with a velocity of 2342 fps at 200 yards, and when sighted in to be on target at 200 yards, will drop eight inches at 300. Not bad performance for an old cartridge with a new name.

For many years the .250 Savage received little attention, and waned under the onslaught of the 6mm and .243. While the cartridge will never set the world on fire, it has received some excellent support in recent years. Ruger created a stir by bringing out the Model 77 International in this cartridge. Winchester then brought the .250 back into the Model 70 lineup by introducing Model 70 XTR Featherweight, and later the Model 70 Lightweight and Winlite rifle in this caliber. Remington had beat Winchester to the mark three years earlier with the Remington Classic in .250 Savage. There are probably more rifles available in .250 Savage today than at any other time.

Newly manufactured rifles address a problem

experienced by many early .250 users. Originally the .250/3000 sported a 1:14 twist, which would not always stabilize bullet weights above 100 grains, especially the round nosed 117 grain bullet commonly used by reloaders for the .25-35.

Modern barrels now feature rifling running one turn in ten inches of barrel, enough to provide stability for all bullet weights. For those hunting small game and using lightweight bullets, it's no big deal, but hunters considering the purchase of secondhand rifles for small and intermediate game, a quick check of the rifling is wise.

The initial popularity of the .250 spurred more research and wildcatting effort into the .25 calibers as a group. However, the powders available at that time were not suited to the .25 caliber

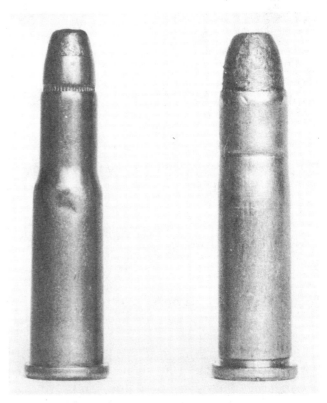

The .25-20 and the .32-20. The author feels these were the greatest short range small game cartridges for many years.

Traditional small game species like this porcupine were taken with the older .22 Hornet, .25-20, and .32-20 cartridges.

bore. One cartridge that did develop and prosper under those conditions was the .257 Roberts. Remington introduced the cartridge in 1934. Its popularity grew and it became known as a well balanced, useful dual-purpose cartridge.

The .257 Roberts had little to offer over other long-time performers. The 1936 Western Cartridge Company *Rifle and Pistol Ammunition Handbook* lists the 100 grain .257 Roberts as leaving the muzzle at 2900 fps. Contrast that with the 2810 fps produced by the .250/3000 carrying the same bullet. It is clear that a discerning gun public would not move to the cartridge

in great numbers.

The .257's troubles were compounded by the short magazines offered in the popular bolt guns of the day. It was necessary to seat the original 117 grain round-nose bullets deeply to allow the cartridge to function through the magazine. This also crowded out powder space, and factory velocities were never what they should have been.

A major blow to the .257 Roberts was the sudden death of its inventor, Ned Roberts. As a gun journalist of considerable repute, he pushed the cartridge in his stories and column for over

One of the best ways of getting around the cartridge selection dilemma is to have several rifles in different calibers. It's expensive, but it sure is fun.

A major advantage of small ammunition is that much can be carried in a small ammo pouch.

20 years. When the advocate for a cartridge passes on, the popularity of the cartridge declines.

For years, however, the .257 Roberts hung on in the hearts of diehard gun enthusiasts. When Ruger made a run of about a thousand Model 77 bolt guns in 1975, the .257 Roberts staged a comeback. In 1982 Winchester Arms metamorphosed into U.S. Repeating Arms, and the new company hung its hat on the Model 70 Featherweight, specifically in several old-style cartridges—one of which was the .257. Remington followed in 1982 with the Model 700 Classic.

The return of the .257 Roberts may be assured, at least for big game hunters. The .257 Roberts Plus P ammunition produced by Winchester adds 100 fps to the 100 grain factory load and 130 fps to the traditional 117 grain round nose loading. They seem to have forgotten the small game shooter, who needs 75, 87, and 90 grain bullets. However, it does let the .25 calibers compete better with the 243's. The 100 grain Plus P load has virtually identical down-range ballistics to the .243.

Today the top .25 caliber is the .25-06. It is the hands-down favorite of deer and woodchuck shooters across North America. All American and several foreign rifle companies feature the cartridge in their lines.

The cartridge came from rather humble beginnings. It's little more than the ancient .30-06 necked down to .25 caliber and given just over 17 degrees of shoulder. In the early years it was not recognized as a good long range varmint cartridge, and never reached its full potential due to the poor powders available during the 1920's. From early on it competed against a bevy of wildcats and its own brothers, the .257 Roberts and the .250 Savage. However, the overall accuracy, and the fact that heavier bullets could be used prompted Remington to bring the cartridge out in 1969 as a commercial offering.

The .25-06 is a top varmint cartridge. It produces 3440 fps at the muzzle with an 87 grain bullet, and still has two thirds of its velocity left at 300 yards. At this distance there is lots of energy—954 foot-pounds to be exact—for long range hits on soft-bodied varmints. Anyone living in the wide open spaces of the west will be impressed with this cartridge's flat trajectory. It's easy to appreciate any rifle that, when printing dead-on at 200 yards, is only six inches low at 300 yards. That eliminates guessing on distant targets. The heavier bullets buck wind and get on target with fewer misses and less need for Kentucky windage.

The .25-06 is flatter shooting than the .220 Swift, about as accurate from good barrels, and, with bullets of good sectional density, much less sensitive to the wind. Factory-available loads are adequate for varmints and deer. As with any dual purpose cartridge, good bullet selection is fundamental to success. When going after varmints, choose only 87 grain weights available from Remington, or 90 grain offerings from Winchester. Leave the heavier bullets for deer hunting.

The most common complaints one hears about the .25-06 are of its magnum-like characteristics: it's loud, and it kicks more than any other .25 caliber. Sharp kicks can lead to flinching, and the loud report leads to irate land owners. The cartridge is known for damaging game meat. These factors mean the .25-06 is not for beginners, and even old hands must master the recoil. Some wonder why the cartridge wasn't named the .25 magnum.

The .257 Weatherby magnum is better than the .25-06 for long range shooting. It tops the .25-06 by about 150 fps with any given bullet weight, making it the hottest commercially available .25 caliber on the market today. This cartridge is based on the shortened, necked-down British 300 Holland and Holland Magnum. First available in 1944, it delivers outstanding performance at velocities that make men shiver. It was the only Weatherby Magnum that Jack O'Conner ever spoke favorably of.

It's a fast, flat shooting cartridge that comes in an excellent selection of commercially availa-

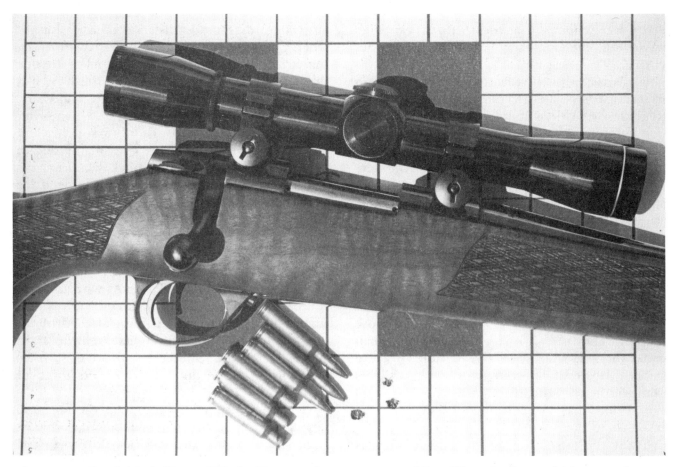

In a correctly sighted rifle, outfitted with a good scope, many of the .22 centerfire cartridges produce excellent accuracy.

ble bullet weights. The 87 grain is of most interest to small game hunters, with anything heavier best left for big game. This bullet is known for its devastating effect on small game, and hunters after rabbit meat might want to select a less destructive cartridge. On the other hand, where edible meat is not the goal, as in prairie dog shooting, this cartridge gets bullets to the far side of a dog town with good accuracy and plenty of punch. The 87 grain bullet is of Nosler manufacture, and is known for explosive expansion and penetration.

Muzzle velocity for the 87 grain bullet is a whopping 3825 fps coming out of a standard Weatherby 26 inch barrel. At 300 yards it still produces 2818 fps and provides 1535 foot-pounds of energy. When sighted-in at 300 yards it will be seven inches low at 400 yards, providing a point blank range of 425 yards on prairie dogs and similar small game. Results are spectacular on stationary game like prairie dogs.

It is probably the best prairie dog cartridge ever invented, but shooters who buy expensive Weatherby rifles and cartridges are hardly ever found out on the prairie dog towns of the open west. Too bad. They're missing out on a grand opportunity to take advantage of their cartridge's performance, and a real opportunity to use their fire-belching magnums.

Aside from the obvious recoil—20 foot-pounds—and prominent muzzle blast from these cartridges, their cost is the main factor the average sportsman has to consider. They are the most expensive commercially available cartridges in the United States today—bar none. The rifles are not cheap either. Cost is clearly a big reason the .257 Weatherby Magnum gun and cartridge are not more popular.

Nevertheless, there is a distinct place for the Weatherby Magnums in the shooting world. They reduce the need for hold-over at great ranges, and they provide the killing power necessary for long ranges. Good shooting is, of course, necessary to correctly place the bullet, and this becomes crucial at longer ranges. It was the .257 Weatherby Magnum that introduced American shooters to the characteristics of light bullets combined with ultra-high velocity. It remains the fastest quarter-incher available today.

The .256 Winchester Magnum was one of the finest short range performers ever. I mention it here because of its similarities to the .25-20, and its value as a cartridge that performs well without destroying meat. The original factory load pushed a 60 grain bullet at 2760 fps, which compared favorably to older cartridges like the .218 Bee and .22 Hornet. First available in 1961, it was intended as a pistol cartridge along the lines of the .22 Remington Jet. The pistol developed for the cartridge showed that extraction would be a problem, and the project was dropped.

Marlin developed a neat rifle for the cartridge,

called the Model 62 Levermatic, available between late 1963 and 1969, but it did not impress the gun buying public of the day. Today the T/C Contender barrels are the only .256 Magnums around.

The .256 was an effective small game cartridge out to 225 yards. When fired from a 24 inch barrel gun, it provided 1015 foot-pounds of muzzle energy, and at 100 yards still produced 586 foot-pounds. Recoil was virtually nonexistent and report light. Why did it fail in the market place? It was promoted as a pistol cartridge and not as the short range small game cartridge it really was. Too bad.

So let's sum up the quarter-inch calibers this way: as a group they are excellent small game performers, offering plenty of velocity, good energy, and impressive accuracy. There is one for every level of shooting skill—from beginners to old hands—and for every application—from short range, close-in type cartridges, to dual purpose kinds and magnum kickers. Most have mild recoil, and many feature easy report. They can be used in a number of shooting categories, from squirrel potting at short ranges, to fast-moving jackrabbits at intermediate distances, to long range varmint shooting in strong cross winds. For our kind of hunting, choose light-weight bullets—generally anything under 100 grains—for all shooting. For the hunter seeking one rifle for small game and varmints, the .25 caliber line meets any hunting situation the North American continent can present.

Chapter 4

Choosing the Rifle and Shotgun

Rifle Actions for Small Game

Who has ever heard of a "small game rifle"? Is this just another marketing technique designed to extract hard-earned dollars from shooters and hunters, who probably already own more rifles than they can shoot well? Is the small game rifle something with which the average hunter can feel comfortable? Is the small game rifle a reality, or can any game gun be called a small game rifle? Are small game rifles the latest rage down at the rifle range? Perhaps this rifle style is just another shooting fad. In short, *is* there such a thing as the perfect small game rifle?

The campfire debating society has raised these questions, and more. A specialized, one-of-a-kind, small game rifle has not traditionally existed. A few years back, most hunters were happy with any rifle. Many of us, previously content with cast-off or crudely modified military types, became the market for books on how to improve upon the remnants of World War II.

We were happy to have a rifle; one that shot well was something that would never leave our grasp. Countless military conversions passed through countless hands, with each shooter adding his, or in some cases her, special modification to the cumbersome military hardware. Many shooters acquired secondhand rifles that became treasures. Lucky was the nimrod stalking the farm country with a brand new Remington or Winchester.

That was then, this is now. Better economies, improved opportunities to shoot and more leisure time have put shooters in a position to go afield with new equipment. Industrial technology made products less expensive, more convenient, and more readily available than ever before. There are now more shooting products than in the heyday of big game hunting in the post-Civil War period. You can now have a big game rifle, a plinking rifle, a mountain rifle, a bush carbine, a target rifle, a varmint rifle, and behold! a small game rifle.

There have been other changes. The phasing out of black powder, with the development of smokeless, for example. Hunting evolved from a daily survival skill, where hunters had to take game or go hungry, to a relaxing outdoor pleasure that put men in touch with nature.

These changes were facilitated by new products, redesigns of established products, and development of North American society.

Over time, specialization has characterized this evolution. From the buffalo hunter's large caliber, heavy barreled rifle to the sleek, smokeless powdered carbines favored in the eastern deer woods of the 1950's, every type of hunting demands its own kind of rifle. The future will produce its own hunting tools—as yet unheard of designs in rifles and support gear—that will meet the requirements of tomorrow.

Today, small game rifles run a broad gamut of action types, designs, features, and styles. For some shooters the tack driving, heavy barreled rifle outfitted with bipod, chambered in a hot .22 centerfire and topped with a wide-angle, high magnification scope represents the ultimate small game gear. Others see a quick shooting, compact, lightweight lever as the best small game rifle. There is growing interest in the use of paramilitary, semi-automatic rifles for small game. And there are still plenty of shooters hunting game with whatever rifle is at hand.

There are six basic action types available to the small game hunter: the famous lever, the popular bolt action, the reborn single shot, the dying pump, the modern semi-automatic, and the

Is there such a thing as the perfect small game rifle?

Many shooters cut their teeth on old military rifles that were modified to accommodate the needs of the varmint and small game hunter.

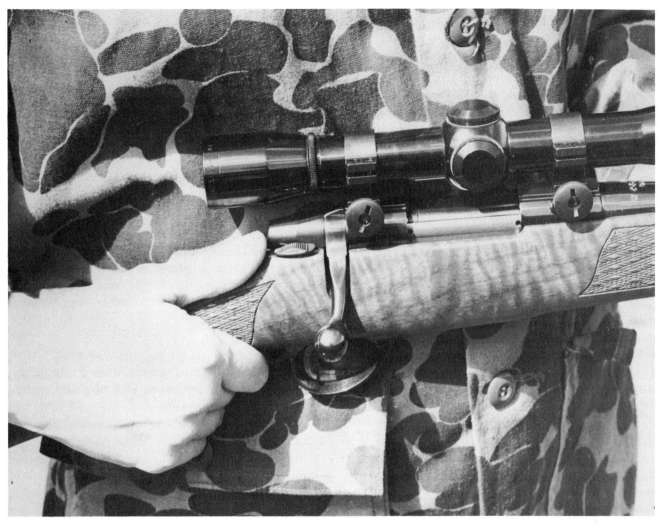

The bolt action rifle is by far the most popular action style available to shooters, and is especially favored by those who reload their own ammunition.

drilling, or combination rifle. Each type has features that make it useful under varying field conditions.

The bolt is the most popular rifle action around. There are good reasons for this. Long range shooting with high intensity cartridges usually requires a bolt gun, because this design gives greater accuracy and camming power, as well as more reliability extracting tight cases. Reloaders generally favor the bolt action for the latter reason, while beginners like bolt guns because of their foolproof nature. Another point

favoring the bolt is the selection of cartridges—better than any of the other action types, except perhaps the single shot.

The availability of many magnum quality cartridges also turns many to the bolt. Although the bolt is slightly slower to operate than other actions, small game hunting often requires accuracy more than fast follow-up shots. For these reasons the bolt continues to grow in popularity, and each year sees new designs and modifications.

A minor factor in action selection is whether

or not the shooter is lefthanded. While there are lefthanded bolt guns—notably the Savage Model 110 DL—right-opening bolt guns are troublesome for southpaw shooters. A lefthanded hunter using a righthanded bolt has to extract a cartridge across his line of vision, as well as cross the hands to work the action. His alternative is to use his less efficient, non-dominant hand. Both interfere with good concentration and accurate shooting.

Levers, though, are great for lefthanded shooters; the cartridge extracts straight up and over the shooter. Levers also allow quick follow-up shots, they often come in light weight, tightly configured packages, and they're easy to carry over rough country. Many make good saddle guns. While cartridge selection is not as broad as with bolts, levers offer real advantages for the small game shooter.

Lever guns are declining in popularity, but they still hold a special place in the hearts and minds of most shooters. Even the most dyed-in-the-wool bolt shooter often has one or two levers stashed in his gun rack. Later in this chapter, we'll take a closer look at the lever, and the many advantages this action type offers field shooters today. Small game hunters should keep the lever in mind.

Single shots frequently give shooters only one chance, but many of the better quality models—like the Ruger No 1 Special Varminter—have excellent triggers, providing better control and let-off than traditional models. Reloading, especially from the prone, is quick and easy, allowing the skillful shooter to get away a repeat shot in short order. Beginners find these rifles easy to use. Another advantage: the short action allows for a longer barrel and greater maximum velocity.

Pump action rifles are in decline, yet Remington produces a line of pumps second to none. Working like a short trombone, these rifles extract, eject a spent cartridge, and reload another round as fast as the hunter can move his arm. The pump gives the hunter a fast second shot without taking his eyes off the target. This has been the major selling feature of these guns for decades. With their shotgun-like configuration and slightly less weight than similar caliber bolt guns, these rifles are fast-handling, and let the shooter get on target quickly. This has given pump guns an excellent field reputation. Lefthanded shooters can use them with no difficulty.

Semi-automatic rifles are growing in popularity. However, models in the military or paramilitary format seem to be gaining at the expense of those in sporting or hunting configurations. Long gone are old favorites like the Winchester Model 100. There are now over three dozen paramilitary models to choose from, but only six sporting versions on the market. That's a sad commentary on shooter interests, but hopefully it is a passing fad. The current success of paramilitary rifles is an embarrassment to the rifle manufacturing establishment. Most paramilitary models are foreign-made copies of existing military kinds.

Military look-alikes are little more than new ''military surplus''. One manufacturer developed a middle-of-the-road semi-auto that was useful for hunting—but then, ignoring hunters' needs for a good autoloader, marketed the weapon for the police and security markets.

There will always be a place in hunting for semi-auto rifles like the Browning BAR and the Remington Model 4. However, paramilitary rifles are nudging their way into this arena by providing models in small game calibers like .223 and .243. Some 9mm's are also adequate small game guns, as are weird concoctions like the .30 Russian. The semi-auto offers real advantages to shooters and hunters. The benefits these rifles offer are discussed in detail later in this chapter.

There are combination guns, but serious American shooters have never favored these firearms, and as a consequence, ''drillings'' have never had their day in the sun. Savage produces an inexpensive, well made, break-action shotgun-rimfire and shotgun-centerfire; Model 24 is among the

In spite of controversy, para-military rifle configurations maintain their popularity.

designations for these rifles. Few other models are worthy of consideration; they are often much too heavy, and offer no real advantage over the Savage.

This gun can be very useful, although it has been largely passed off as a survival or camping gun. It runs into trouble with scopes, and hunters are usually best off using the gun without a scope.

Factoring Field Conditions

While selection of action types is influenced by personal preferences, there are field conditions to factor in to the selection process. It may seem strange, but rifles are designed in laboratories and not in the field. Only recently have designers become aware of the need to build rifles in tune with *where* they are used, rather than *how*.

For the once-a-year shooter, field conditions are secondary in the selection process. However, for the serious hunter, for whom specialization is part of the plan, attention to detail at this level will mean more enjoyment in the field.

One of the most easily understood factors is range. Short distance plinking requires different equipment than long range shooting. At greater ranges, trajectory and wind-bucking ability become very important features of the cartridges and bullets used.

Often these features are emphasized in only a few calibers and rifles. These features are not critical in short range shooting, but rapid bullet expansion and good quality sights *are* important.

It's also important for the hunter to ask himself at what distance his targets will typically appear. Generally, short range means less than 100 yards, intermediate range means between 100 and 200 yards, and long range is anything beyond. Many hunters pick a rifle-cartridge combination based on the longest anticipated shot they might encounter. This system works, though there is risk of being over-gunned at the ranges game is most often encountered. The best advice is to decide on your average range, even if it might mean passing up the occasional 200-yard shot at a rabbit.

Another factor is the kind of terrain where most of your hunting is done. Weight becomes critical when the rifle is going to be carried long distances, especially in mountainous regions or back country. Rifles that are difficult to carry are hard to shoot once the hunter is tired and winded from a steep climb.

Heavily wooded countryside tends to mean short range shooting, but on the open plains, long shots are more likely. Cartridges capable of dealing with this variety of terrain are another part of the equation.

It is important to match the gun to the game. Where targets are small mammals and rodents, sufficient energy and bullet performance are required in order to deliver humane, quick kills at all ranges. Rabbits call for less energy than badgers, and the average hunter will shoot at more rabbits than badgers in a hunting lifetime. This means the hunter has to weigh his options and perhaps pick a rifle-action-cartridge combo that allows both kinds of hunting, while being perfect for neither.

A hunter who wants to retain rabbit pelts might consider using a rifle that shoots a mild cartridge with a hard point bullet. In short, the game we hunt greatly influences the firearms we choose. Make no mistake, this is as important in small game hunting as it is in hunting deer, elk, or dangerous game.

Recoil and muzzle blast should be taken into account when matching the hunter to the gun. This is especially true for young shooters or those of any age just beginning with rifles. Many shooters have become turned off by hard-kicking recoil or ear-piercing muzzle noise. Any 200-pound hunter with some practice shooting can handle a .257 Magnum Weatherby, but a 125-pound novice could be in for some unpleasant surprises. A rifle that weighs six pounds will deliver more apparent recoil than a nine-pound gun firing the same cartridge. Small game guns are shot frequently—both at the target range and

A major consideration, especially for women shooters, is how the gun handles. Rifles with heavy barrels or other weighty features may prove hard to handle for some shooters.

in the field. This makes muzzle blast and recoil top considerations in fitting the gun to the gunner.

Muzzle report is also greater with short barreled rifles than with long barreled rifles using similar cartridges. This has long been the complaint with carbine rifles. Noise is particularly annoying in areas close to habitation. Some of the best small game shooting today is in the heart of farm country, and noise bothers farmers. It scares farm animals and upsets the rural gentry. Hunters shooting in heavily populated rural areas should always be aware of noise from their

rifle, and use cartridges that produce reduced report whenever necessary—even to the point of using down loaded cartridges. Noise will always be a factor in whether or not shooters are to be allowed access. Muzzle blast can determine how welcome you'll be in these areas.

Another consideration is how the gun handles. Rifles with heavy barrels, long barrels, large stocks, and uncomfortable butts do nothing for good shooting. If a gun doesn't feel right, it won't shoot right. Before you buy any rifle, test it for fit by throwing it to your shoulder and lining up the sights on some object in the store (preferably not the owner!). Do this several times, and think about how it would feel with your winter clothes on and full back pack in place.

Weather conditions can also have consequences on rifle and ammunition performance, as well influencing the hunter's attitude. Cold winters, for example, will freeze rifle actions. Moisture is always the rifle shooter's foe because it changes stock density, causing minute shifts in point of impact. Heavy winter clothing changes the way a rifle fits the shooter. Cumbersome gloves and mitts destroy trigger control. Wind makes fools of the best long range shooters, and this is compounded during cold falls and winters. Good weather is fundamental to the enjoyment of small game hunting and the quality performance of firearm and ammunition.

Finally, keep ammo availability in mind. Factory ammunition for the .223 can be found anywhere in the United States, Canada, and Europe, but the story changes when you want .220 Swift or .22-250 ammunition. Old, semi-obsolete, and wildcat cartridges are fun to shoot, but supplies must come from handloading, and handloading requires supplies of components. Nobody wants to run short of ammo miles from home and not be able to find more locally. Yet this happens every year, and many a disappointed hunter has had to quit the field before it should have been necessary.

Outdoor conditions influence our shooting in other ways. On the shooting range, light and wind conditions are controlled, but outdoors these can change quickly, presenting the shooter with a challenge. Lighting influences sighting, even with modern scopes. Shadows produced by trees, changing cloud patterns, and topography make accurate shooting difficult, and produce different shooting conditions from one day to the next. All these factors conspire to make field shooting challenging and significantly different from shooting at the target range.

Shooting psychology also plays a role. On the target range the key is to psych down—to let go

Old or semi-obsolete cartridges are all fun to shoot, but replacing exhausted supplies can be difficult.

of mental tension and fix concentration—from one shot to the other. Consistency is necessary for successful target shooting.

In small game hunting, alertness for game, quickness of sighting, and good reflex action are needed. Perfect balance is rarely obtained when shooting under field conditions. Stances are never perfect, thanks to game catching the gunner off guard or out of position. The shooter has to struggle with these realities, and still make shots that seem impossible.

Different barrel lengths, varying magazine capacities, and larger trigger guards would all be welcome.

It's necessary to know the limits imposed by distance on holdover, trajectory, and bullet performance. Hard to do well, distance estimation is best learned by practice. Skilled hunters memorize the distances to familiar objects, yet range estimation learned in one area rarely applies in another. The quality of light, the accompanying contrasts, different ground cover, and topography all make range estimation inconsistent from one environment to the next.

Nature continuously changes, always playing out that age-old life-and-death struggle with all her living things. It is in this environment that the shooter-turned-hunter finds himself, and he, too, must change. He must adapt quickly, learning and understanding that shooting a rifle under field conditions is not the same as shooting a rifle at the range. The wise hunter exerts control, attempting to move all the factors in his favor.

Few hunters consider the relationship between rifle skills and environment. Most shooting today is done on rifle ranges and not in open fields, deep valleys, or broad plains. Moving and seeking game requires rifle handling skills plus a mix of other abilities applied under constantly changing field conditions. Those skills are different from the skills required on the rifle range. Good field shots are made, not born. They are made by applying the principles learned on the range but mastered in the field.

Rifles have yet to be designed that satisfy all aspects of the hunter's environment. There are more options today than ever before, and perhaps rifle manufacturers are responding somewhat to the needs of riflemen across North America. Nevertheless, there is a long way to go. Hunters need more from manufacturers.

They need rifles with shorter barrels that are more useful in the tight swamplands of the south. Northern hunters need rifles with larger trigger guards and fatter triggers for use with winter gloves. Mountain hunters need short, heavy barrels on carbines in order to preserve accuracy and reduce heat build up during long shooting sessions. Rifles must be-

Unlike the shooting range, where ideal conditions produce a target that is sharp and clear, small game animals rarely present a good target. Large parts of the game are obscured by vegetation, burrow mounds, trees, and shadows. Game survives by being inconspicuous. The variability of the target presented by small game is perhaps the toughest factor facing small game hunters. Conditions are never perfect.

Walking in the outdoors is always different. Nothing is level or flat; nowhere in the biological world is anything perfectly square. The hunter must adapt his body to nature's demands. He must move smoothly and without commotion through countryside that has influenced the design of the animals living there. And, as the hunter walks, he must always be ready.

Range estimation is a critical field skill that shapes and defines many shooting requirements.

Range is one of the many factors influencing the choice of action type.

come less club-like. The rifle must fit the hunter's needs.

Small game hunting stands unique in the demands it makes on the shooter and rifle. The hunter weighing the rifle options before him must consider the factors outlined here. Pick those that are relevant in your particular area. Keep in mind that the perfect rifle, the one designed to meet all shooting and hunting conditions, hasn't been invented yet. Pick those features that will help your shooting under your unique circumstances, and choose the tool that best fits. There are just rifles that better meet our needs, under certain conditions, at certain times.

The Lever vs. the Bolt

A serious shooter in the early Twentieth Century would have been privy to one of the most interesting debates in firearms history. Not since the invention of smokeless powder had anything polarized shooters, hunters, and gun cranks to this degree. The debate pitted the upstart bolt action rifle against the proven lever action. In the shooting press of those early times, the advantages and benefits of first one, then the other, were touted monthly with much fanfare. Some exchanges were downright vitriolic.

Everybody knows that lever action arms were made famous by Winchester. Perhaps the most famous lever is the Model 94 and its variations, but Winchester fame was earned long before the stubby 94 made the scene. The rifle that started it all for Winchester was the Model 73. This was the first mass produced, high volume, repeating action rifle ever offered to American shooters. It was replaced by the Model 76 in much more powerful cartridges like the .45-75 and the .50-95 Winchester. This was, in turn, superseded by the 1886 Winchester, easily the finest repeating rifle ever made. Shooting large caliber, black powder cartridges, it offered accuracy and power in a smooth, fast repeating package. Later, it made the important transition into smokeless powder times with the design of the .33

Winchester. Also, several of the loadings, including the potent .45-70, were refined in smokeless loadings and available for years.

The 1892 Winchester was little more than a scaled down 1886, making use of the same cartridges available in the early 1873 Winchester. The rifle was popularized by Admiral Peary when he carried a short barreled .44-40 Model 92 on his historic trip to the North Pole in 1909. Today the rifle remains popular. Originals are still found in the hands of back country dwellers, and Browning introduced a modern version in 1979. The Model 92 Winchester was probably the best close range, small game rifle ever invented.

It was the Model 94 Winchester, though, that became the standard against which all other rifles would be judged for two generations. Originally offered in black powder .32-40 and .38-55, it hit the jackpot when it was brought out in smokeless powder .30-30 and .25-35. The .30-30 would become the cartridge by which all other cartridges were judged.

There were other early Winchester levers. The model 95 offered the first lever action box magazine, and provided hunters with cartridges that were powerful even by today's standards. It was available in the .30-03, the forerunner to the .30-06, then the .30-06 and the powerful .38-72 Winchester, .303 British, and the .30-40 Krag as well as others.

Other manufacturers produced lever rifles,

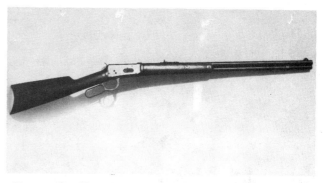

It was the Model 94 lever that became the standard by which all other rifles would be compared.

The debate between the lever and the bolt began many years ago.

One of the first really successful small game rifles was the Winchester lever Model 92. This rifle remains popular, with aging secondhand models bringing top prices at gun shows.

too. Stevens, Colt, and most notably Marlin all joined in the fray. Marlin began production with the Model 1881. Like Winchester's, these were top ejecting models and it wasn't until 1891 that Marlin unveiled a solid top receiver that was to become the hallmark of the firm. Marlin was able to gain a toehold on the repeating rifle marketplace by marketing the .45-70 for some years before Winchester was able to bring out the 1886.

Marlin rifles gained solid reputations. Although slightly more expensive than competitive Winchesters, the rifles claimed safety margins unavailable in other rifles of the day. Simplicity was a feature of these rifles that resulted in great reliability and performance. The company was also highly innovative, being the first to bring lightweight repeaters onto the market. They displayed a willingness to accommodate almost any custom feature to their line of rifle.

However, this early and diverse crop of lever rifles suffered from some faults. Breech blocks did not lock at the front, and this contributed to short case life when reloading was attempted. The two-piece stocks common to the old levers were not conducive to good accuracy. As cartridges developed, levers were unable to handle the greater pressures. Some models lacked sufficient camming power to reliably extract dirty or oversize cases. Others just did not evolve with the demands of the shooting and hunting public.

Against this background the bolt rifle was slowly developing. Beginning in Europe with the needle gun in 1829, the bolt action became a reality with the invention of the Mauser system in the late 1860's. By 1898 the Mauser action was well advanced, and served as the model against which all other bolts would be compared.

The Spanish American War, and in particular the Battle of San Juan Hill, forever changed the direction of rifle design in America. Using the 1893 Model Mauser and the 7 by 57 cartridge, 700 Spanish regulars inflicted 1400 casualties on American troops. This was enough to focus American military attention on an improved bolt action rifle.

The result was the 1903 Springfield and a lasting love affair with modified Mauser designs. After the Krag fell out of military favor and failed to catch on as a sporting arm, a rapid evolution in modified Mauser actions occurred. Out of this came the Model 54 Winchester, the Model 70 Winchester, scores of European imports, the various modern Remington 700's, the Savage 110, and, most recently, the Ruger 77.

A rivalry grew between the lovers of the lever and the bold boys of the bolt. There was little doubt that lever rifles did not stand up to the rigors of military usage, but the lever remained

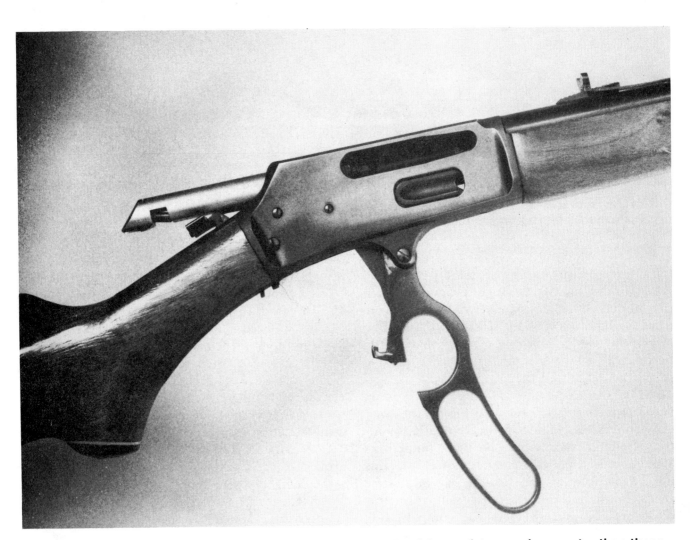

Marlin lever rifles competed against the Winchester. The rifle claims safety margins greater than those of the Winchester.

a preferred hunting rifle. In the hunting fields, wherever big and small game was sought, the lever would remain king for many decades to come.

Knowledgable hunters continued to prefer the lever rifle, especially in the '86 version and the latter '94 Winchesters. The '86 held its esteemed position because it was available in .45-70. Except for a brief period, the cartridge has remained in production to this day. The 94 earned its reputation based on its quick handling and the performance of the .30-30 cartridge. A crop of Western movies and television serials added to the Model 94's fame.

Lever action rifles offer distinct advantages over the bolt. Without a doubt they are faster—at least 50 percent faster—to reload and get back on target than any bolt rifle can ever be. There is economy of motion. The lever movement is simply up and down; the rifle need never leave the shoulder. The bolt, on the other hand, must be worked up, back, forward, and down to complete the reloading cycle. Where the speed of a second, well aimed shot is required, the lever wins, hands down!

The accuracy of the bolt rifle has always been

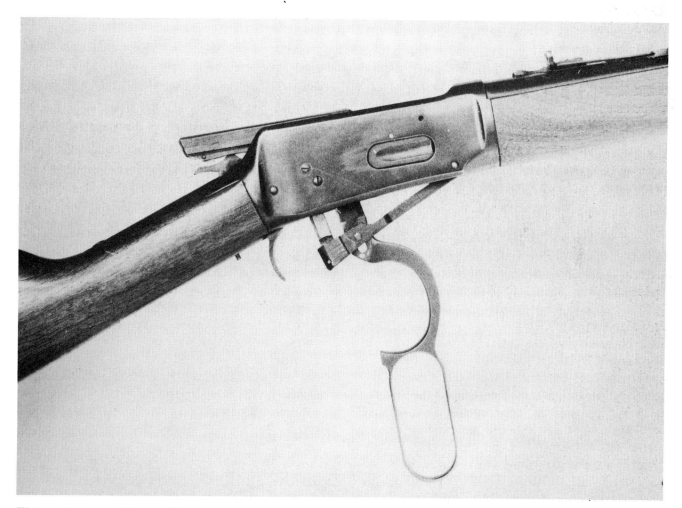

The early crop of lever rifles suffered from some minor faults. Breech blocks did not lock at the front end, shortening case life.

The Browning Lever, called the BLR, in .22/250 probably represents the ultimate lever for small game hunters. In .257 Roberts and .243 Winchester it crosses the line into the dual purpose rifle. In .222 Remington, .223 and 7mm-008 it is ideal for all our small game.

touted as far superior to any lever rifle. Yet any serious student of firearms will admit that a factory original Model 71 .348 Winchester is as accurate as any .30-06 Model 70 fired with open sights at 100 yards. Indeed, there is little difference between the two cartridges, with the .348 developing 2520 fps with its nominal 200 grain factory bullet, compared with the factory 220 grain .30-06 bullet travelling out of the muzzle at 2410 fps. Hunting accuracy and performance would be essentially the same, and any difference would be in the mind of the observer.

Lever action rifles are easier to carry on horseback than bolt outfitted models. The thin profile of the lever gun carries a clear advantage over the bolt; there is just less bulk to ride under the right leg. This makes riding much more pleasant.

As a kid I was fortunate to have an old Model 92 Winchester in .32-20, and an equally aged horse that ate more feed than a pen full of market hogs.

With my thin 92 and my fat horse I logged many miles over freshly broken prairie land and endless summer-fallowed fields. If that had been any other rifle I would have given up horseback hunting. As it turned out, the 92 and the horse became my hunting friends.

Winchester was not the only saddle gun maker. The Savage Model 99 was also nice to carry on horseback. It offered several additional features that made it the top lever rifle for many years. Outfitted with a scope, something not easily done with the Model 94, it was as accurate as any bolt. The action was strong, capable of operating pressures in excess of 50,000 pounds per square-inch. Originally available in the .303 Savage, the rifle was eventually manufactured for nearly every modern cartridge including the .25-35, .32-40, .30-30, .38-55, .300 Savage, .243 Winchester, .308 Winchester, .358 Winchester, and .284 Winchester. As a hunting rifle it earned a good name when teamed up with the .250-3000. Recently the .375 Winchester was added. This Savage rifle continues to be a favored small game gun.

Lever rifles were once criticized by the throng of reloaders as incapable of reaching full accuracy potential, since cartridges were restricted to flat nosed bullets. The Savage changed this, and spire or spitzer pointed bullets could now be used directly through the magazine. Reloaders who bothered to tinker with the .30-30 using pointed bullets were amazed at the accuracy the cartridge was capable of producing.

It has long been held that lever rifles were less

Removable clips make the lever faster loading than most bolts. A second clip, carried in the pocket, can be snapped home faster than filling any magazine rifle.

accurate due to the two-piece stock. This criticism was leveled at both the excellent Model 71 Winchester and the Savage Model 99. Also, the increasing demand for scopes put the Model 71 prematurely into the junk pile, and any new lever coming out of Winchester would be designed with scope users in mind. In 1955 the arrival of the Model 88 Winchester successfully circumvented both problems. It featured the first one-piece stock ever to appear on a modern lever action rifle, and would accept a scope.

The lock-up on the Model 88 was much like a bolt. This effectively quieted complaints, going back to the days of the 1886 Winchester, that lever guns allowed cases to stretch, rendering them difficult to reload and shortening case life. The 88 featured three forward locking lugs that resulted in 30 percent more locking area than a Model 70.

The Model 88 dispelled several other concerns. The action developed some camming power to overcome tight cases. The barrels were the same as used on the Model 70. This was topped off by the introduction of powerful new cartridges like the .308, .243, .358, and the .284 Winchester. Scope mounting was now easy, and the rifles came drilled and taped for a base. For increased speed the lever had 40 percent less travel than the traditional Model 94, and 25 percent less than the competitors' Model 99. Lock time was enhanced by using a hammerless firing pin. Best of all, the rifle came with a removable clip, something no American lever to that point had featured.

The net result was a highly accurate, fast operating rifle in modern day cartridges that could serve both the small and big game hunter.

Serious shooters always knew that lever rifles could not be bench sighted in the same manner as a typical bolt. This had been learned years before when wringing the last bit of grouping ability out of a scope-outfitted Model 99 Savage. With any of the bolt rifles the shooter merely plunked the forend down over the rest and began firing, but, due to the light forend on the Savage,

it was necessary to place the rest under the receiver.

The Model 88 Winchester behaved in nearly the same fashion, except that it was important to place the rest under or just forward of the clip. Using these techniques, accuracy in both rifles is the equal of any factory bolt gun using commercial ammunition.

Until this time gun writers invariably advised hunters to outfit their lever rifles with good quality receiver sights. Improved accuracy and better short range shooting was possible under forest and woods conditions, where lightweight levers proved very successful. Tang sights became immensely popular with lever users, and this spawned much after-market development. Names like Lyman, Marbles, and Williams grew out of this. Small game hunters particularly benefitted from this development period, because these sights greatly improved the shooting characteristics of all levers. Rabbits, squirrels, and pests like skunks and badgers were taken in great numbers with peep sight outfitted rifles.

Although the Model 88 was a capable successor in the Winchester line, it failed in the market place, and was discontinued in 1974. The future of the Model 99 Savage, which has survived competition with bolts, levers, pumps, and semi-autos, is on shaky grounds while Winchester and Savage talk merger. Yet lightweight barrels and tubular magazines, long considered the bane of good accuracy, continue to be offered on the various Marlins.

The issue of stretched cases has been dealt with, but the need to use small base dies continues to haunt the lever scene. These are generally more expensive and not as readily available as standard dies. Small base dies are used exactly the same way as standard dies, so there is no learning process. They are necessary because tolerances are finer in particular lever rifles than in run-of-the-mill bolts. The additional camming power of the bolt removes the need for precise fitting of cartridge to chamber.

The void in modern lever rifles was filled

when Browning began production of their model BLR in 1974. Initially the 20-inch barrel lever was available in .308 and .243; the list has now grown to include .222, .223, .22-250, .257 Roberts, 7mm-08, and .358 Winchester. The rifle is a throwback to the Model 71, with its exposed, two position hammer and two piece stock. However, that is where the similarity ends. The rifle has thoroughly modern appointments, although the rack and pinion mechanism was developed by Bullard a century ago. It has a recessed bolt, seven locking lugs, side ejection, and the shortest lever throw of any lever to date.

As for accuracy, it will hold its own with any factory rifle right out of the box. Like any rifle today, it can use improved trigger pull. It retains all the other features that make a lever rifle the ideal hunting tool. It is lightweight, flat sided for ease of carrying, short, and has a removable clip. True to the form of its generation, sighting must be done by putting the rest under the clip, and small base dies are a must for reloaders.

Lever rifles of all makes and at all stages in firearms history have been excellent choices for the lefthanded shooter. Most bolts are right-handed, but the lever has always performed equally when shot from either side. This was the reason many lefthanded shooters chose a Savage 99. However, this very firm was the first to regularly catalogue a bolt action rifle specifically designed for southpaw shooters. It seems strange that a company would divide a market share in that manner, but it was all to the benefit of the shooter.

Lever rifles are difficult to clean. The rifle must be cleaned from the front end, and care taken to avoid overzealous stroking of the bore. In black powder days, mercury primers ruined bores unless proper scrubbing was undertaken following the day's shooting. But the cleaning equipment available to modern shooters will not damage the bore. Bore cleaning is not the chore of bygone times, nor nearly as critical to maintaining bore condition.

The Winchester Model 70 Featherweight is said to be the ultimate bolt, though there are those who'd disagree.

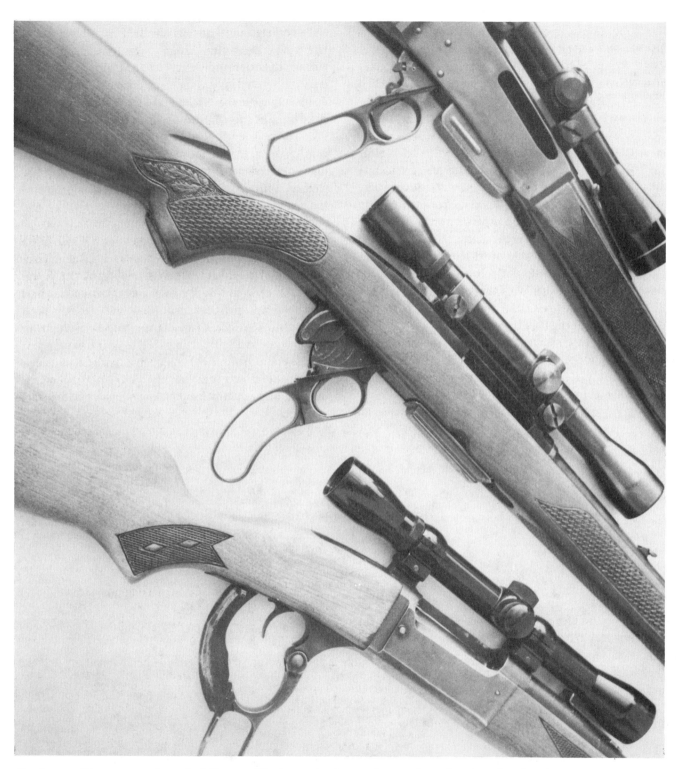

Designs will come and go, but there will always be levers for serious hunters to shoot.

The failure of the Model 88 Winchester (it sold 283,913 copies) was a blow to Winchester. But the company has jumped into the lever foray with both feet. In 1979 the firm experimented with a Model 94 that had thickened receiver walls, and created the Winchester 94 Big Bore. The design of this rifle meant that offset scopes were once again required if the full potential of the cartridge and the rifle were ever to be realized. This was also an effort to cash in on the remaining goodwill of the historic .38-55 by making the .375 closely resemble the obsolete cartridge.

Out of that market testing Winchester went on to develop the Model 94 angle-eject. Introduced in 1983, using the new .307 Winchester, the .356 and .375, it was followed in 1984 by the 7-by-30 Waters in the same model with a slightly longer barrel. Performance of these cartridges is similar to the established models, but it's less powerful than the .348 Winchester and less flexible than the .284 Winchester. The angle-eject is an attempt to upgrade the lever actioned Winchesters for scope use once and for all.

The lever rifle is an integral part of the American shooting scene. Designs may come and go, but there will always be lever rifles for us to shoot. The lever rifle today can compete directly with the average bolt action rifle. There are plenty of reasons for choosing the lever over the bolt.

The lever has not benefitted from the experimentation and development of the bolt. This is especially clear in the area of cartridges and custom bullet designs. There is more to choose from for the bolt gun shooter.

There is one fundamental difference between the two action types. The lever belongs in the game fields and not on the target ranges. The need for a quick follow-up shot, the need for a high capacity firearm of light weight, and the ease with which the rifle mounts to the shoulder are all factors that favor the lever rifle. Camming power, tight extraction, and heavy barrels—the lever's weak points, are target range factors.

Will the lever surpass the bolt's popularity in the years to come? A lever that can handle the 7mm Remington Magnum would be very well received; cartridges like the .300 Winchester Magnum would also attract an immediate following.

Perhaps the Browning BLR represents the pinnacle of lever rifle development. It can hold its own against any bolt and still offer the advantages that have always made the lever a practical hunter's rifle.

Bolt guns have often been referred to as "riflemen's rifles". Well, lever actioned rifles have earned the title of "hunter's rifle". They have helped generations of outdoorsmen and hunters put game on the table and test their shooting skills. In the past these rifles have provided protection of property and life from man and beast.

For the one-rifle hunter going after mostly small game, the lever's advantages far outweigh such esoteric items as camming power and stiffer barrels. Levers have their place where action and travel combine in the outdoors. In the canoe, on horseback, across your arm, over your shoulder, or mounted in the truck cab, a lever rifle is the tried and tested tool of the outdoors. Effective for small game because of their easy handling and quick repeat shots, these rifles, in their countless variations, were made for action, not for the debater's lectern.

Shooting Autoloading Rifles

Hunting with semi-automatic rifles has been a matter of controversy for years. Ever since Bonnie and Clyde were gunned down with a .401 Winchester Model 1910 semi-auto rifle, gun owners have associated auto arms with bad guys and blue coats.

They have endlessly debated the ethics of semi-auto arms in the hunting fields. Some say that rapid fire arms detract from the sporting chance afforded game species, while the opposite argument claims quick follow-up shots reduce opportunities for wounded game to escape and die a lingering death. They argue that hunters armed with autoloaders are the more humane. Gun companies, sensitive to anti-hunting sentiment, have kept the number of auto offerings low. Indeed, most companies promote auto arms as police-only equipment. From time to time this controversy boils over in the shooting press. The loser is the hunter.

Somewhere, someone decided that it would be more dramatic to label these rifles automatic. This incorrect terminology left an impression of machine-gun-toting hunters decimating our game animals, shooting more than they could use as they killed everything in sight. Other terms, including semi-auto, self-loading and autoloading were developed to clarify the connotation, but it was too late.

In truth, the rifles available for hunting purposes are merely self-loading. The cartridge is extracted and ejected, and a new one is placed into the chamber at each pull of the trigger. The term automatic is a misnomer and semi-automatic does nothing to clear the definition. The term *autoloader* is the best descriptive compromise available.

There are many small game hunting scenarios in which the autoloader will shine above all other action types. In heavy cover like cedar swamps, fast moving rabbits can be taken with a quick second shot. Out on the wintery plains, jackrabbits breaking from their forms and streaking across the snow covered prairie are great targets for an autoloader-outfitted hunter. Autoloaders make ground squirrel shooting more challenging as the shooter quickly moves from target to target. An autoloader will fit just about any small game hunting situation.

A word about follow up shots, the unique feature of this action type: autoloaders are the fastest—bar none—at making available a loaded round. Levers are quick, pumps quicker, but the autoloader is king in terms of getting off a second, well-aimed shot. Irrespective of what the hot-stove league might say, no action is faster than the autoloader.

It takes about three seconds to recover from the first shot's recoil and place the sights back on a moving target. This may seem an eternity, but it's half the time needed with a lever or a pump. Third and fourth shots then follow, and within ten to 12 seconds, all shots can be aimed and delivered at a cooperating target. Note the term *aimed*; it requires only three or four seconds to empty the average four shot autoloader, but good aiming takes additional time. But the total time required is small, and no man alive can better this with any other action type currently manufactured.

Historically, autoloaders have not been known for their accuracy, though early autos delivered accuracy sufficient to bring home deer and black bear taken at ranges of less than 150 yards. Today's models give small game hunters all the accuracy necessary to take rabbits, chucks, gophers, prairie dogs, and any similar sized game up to 300 yards. Rifles like the Remington Model Four and the Browning BAR routinely deliver this level of performance with factory cartridges. These rifles can be further improved through handloading, and with today's quality controlled components, the accuracy attainable is better than ever.

For years my Model 100 Winchester in .284 consistently produced two-inch, five-shot groups at 100 yards. This is acceptable shooting even in today's accuracy-conscious world. The load is no secret—51 grains of IMR 4320, thrown from an aging Lyman powder measure into Winchester brass behind a 139-grain flat base Hornady spire point bullet—and has proven itself time and again on black-tailed prairie dogs and big jackrabbits at the 225 yard mark. In short, when it comes to hunting small game, the autoloader accuracy issue is dead.

Weight is always a factor in action selection. Autoloaders do not compare well with the current run of lightweight bolt repeaters. The Remington Model Four weighs 7-1/4 pounds, while the Browning BAR comes in at seven pounds ten ounces. The foreign produced Vorere Model 2185 weighs just over seven pounds.

The long obsolete Winchester Model 1910 weighs a ponderous 8-1/4 pounds and the Model 100 carbine is seven pounds. On the other hand, the Ruger Ranch rifle in 7.62x39 tips the scales at a mere 6-1/2 pounds, making it the lightest sporter weight auto on the market today. There are many rifles of other types that weigh less than the autos mentioned here. Choose other action types when weight is a critical factor in rifle selection.

Sportsmen owe the survivalist fringe a vote of thanks for focusing attention on autoloading rifles. It was the demand from this group that encouraged the proliferation and importation of quasi-military autoloading rifles. Hunting is part of the survival package, and all para-military arms are capable of taking small game animals.

Although other calibers are available, the predominate choice in this rifle group is the .223 Remington. This results from the two lives this cartridge leads, one as a small game sporting round and the other as the major U.S. military cartridge. Survivalists liked the military cartridge, and helped the round move into civilian life. Their demand for military look-alike rifles will eventually pay off in the evolution of improved autoloading sporters.

The great number of rifles with military configurations makes choosing one a problem. No recommendation will be given here as to which might make the best small game choice. Performance is usually perfect in new arms, but maintenance can be a problem. These rifles require care—more care than sporting arms—if they are to function flawlessly.

As a group, they are persnickety in the ammunition they consume. Reloads must be properly constructed, brass correctly undersized, and bullets seated true. Clean ammunition is necessary. The rifle must also be scrupulously clean. No reader of books like this needs to be reminded of the battle difficulties experienced with the M16 in Viet Nam when powder retardant recipes were altered. The M16, manufactured to tight tolerances, malfunctioned due to accumulated residues of the altered powder retardants.

This is the final negative point to be made about military rifles: scopes are now nearly mandatory for most small game shooting, and military-style rifles are difficult to scope, although many models now offer mounts and scopes that fit a particular product. Many of these are expensive and can only be used on one rifle.

All centerfire autoloaders produced today load with a separate clip. This is a great invention, as it makes reloading easier and quicker. Few bolt rifles possess this feature. In the field, clips are remarkably easy to lose, and, for some reason, expensive to replace. A hunter going afield with an autoloader should carry a replacement clip or two, so that a lost clip will not mean a wasted day. Small game hunters should carry their clips in handy belt pouches that keep things organized and clean. Clips are a great invention, and when managed properly help make the autoloader an effective hunting tool.

Overall, cartridge selection is not bad. The Voere offers the greatest current choice of any available selfloader. It comes from the factory in 5.6x50, 5.6x57, .222 Remington, .222 Remington Magnum, .223, 6.5x57, .243 Winchester, 308 Winchester, 7x64, .270, .30-06, and 9.3x62.

Continuing with sporting arms, the Ruger family of autoloaders offers models in .223 and 7.62x39. Marlin produces their camp carbine in 9mm and .45 Auto. The Browning BAR comes in .243, .270, .308, and .30-06, while the Remington Model Four is available in these plus .280 Remington. These cartridges will cover small and big game hunting.

Most of the negatives associated with autoloaders relate directly to cartridge quality and reloading difficulties. Tight cases will not fire in most autoloaders. Sometimes the firing pin will only slightly dent the primers of tight cases. This happens because the firing pin's force is dissipated as it drives the case further into the

The Model 100 Winchester was probably the finest self-loading rifle ever invented. Unfortunately, it's now extinct.

chamber. The result is an unfired cartridge with a small primer dent that must be rebroken into components, resized, and assembled before it can be used again. Undersized cases and special reloading skills are necessary.

For this reason, small and ultra-small base dies are recommended for these reloading tasks. They resize the case smaller than normal dies, but in the process ensure a proper chamber fit. The brass is overworked during small base resizing operations and the shoulder is set further back than normally required. These aren't big problems, but they are considerations that any shooter of self loading rifles has to learn.

Perhaps the autoloader's worst characteristic is the one that makes these rifles most useful to the shooter. During auto ejection, cases are yanked from the chamber with considerable force and thrown some distance. Finding these cases can be difficult; winter shooting can be particularly frustrating. Cases pick up all kinds of dirt, snow, mud, and leaves that must be cleaned off prior to resizing to avoid ruining a good die. Cases can become lost in the ejection process. Retrieval is always time consuming and not always successful. Cases fall down gopher holes, blend into the surrounding vegetation, or deflect off nearby shrubs. While benefitting from the autoloading feature, be prepared for some lost and dirty cases.

Many times cases are damaged along the rim during the extraction and ejection process. Some autoloaders bend the case mouth slightly. Many military rifles dent the case wall. Others, with fluted chambers to aid extraction, leave multiple imprints on the case. These small damages shorten brass life, some more than others. Damaged brass requires more attention during reloading, as some cases must be guided into the sizing die. But if you love shooting an autoloader, you have been taking all this into account for years. The benefits outweigh the difficulties.

In summary, the autoloader action type presents both benefits and problems if chosen as your one small game and varmint rifle. Much of the downside is related to cartridge reloading, so for the hunter counting on factory cartridges (there are a few such rich people left) for all of his shooting, the autoloader is a safe bet. On the other hand, learning additional reloading skills and having the patience to pick up a few brass is a small price to pay for the benefits of quick follow up shots that go out with accuracy.

There is one further point often largely forgotten in the technical discussions involving autoloaders. Autoloaders are fun to shoot. Successive shots delivered quickly and accurately add a great dimension to small game hunting. For many, fun is reason enough to pick an autoloader and keep it in the rifle rack for those times when a good time is the order of the day.

While semi-automatics are rare in centerfire cartridges, they proliferate in .22 rimfires. Small game hunters should not rule out the rimfire as a fun gun that is cheap to shoot and has good short range accuracy. However, the rimfire plays a much different, or at least less serious, role in getting small game at long ranges or putting rabbit meat on the table. Under the right conditions, these guns perform well, but they lack the long range punch necessary for most of the hunting recommended in this book.

A Place for Single-Shots

There is a large group of hunters who firmly believe single-shot rifles put them on equal terms with the game they hunt. They feel that since early hunters had only one shot at their game, they see no reason to afford themselves more. In their minds, any hunter not taking his game with one shot raises doubts about his skill as hunter and outdoorsman. They like hunting this way, and the single-shot helps them relive the early times.

Some will take game only within 100 yards, believing that a greater distance represents a failed stalk. Most of these individuals are dedicated, highly familiar with the areas they work, and knowledgeable about the animals they hunt.

These hunters simply prefer single-shot rifles to all others.

Single-shot rifles had pretty much disappeared from the shooting scene after the second World War. The common Winchester Hi and Low walls were no longer produced, and Remington falling blocks had thankfully disappeared from the shooting scene. Gun cranks, intent on designing new wildcat cartridges, consumed the Winchester low-walls because the action was safe enough to run up new highs in pressure levels. Also, the action needed little modification to accept a host of cartridge heads, and the thick barrels left lots of steel for rechambering projects. These decades of experimentation used up the available single-shots, and soon a market void existed.

As far back as 1966 there were few single-shot choices. A Navy Arms imported Remington-style rolling block, and Savage single-shot break action in .30-30 or .22 Hornet were available. A year later this all changed.

At the peak of the 1960's, the heyday of modern sporting arms, Ruger brought out the first single-shot rifle and forever changed the shooting scene. Today Ruger Number Ones and Threes dominate the single-shot market.

Sharpes pioneered the falling block, external hammer, and breech loading action in 1848. These were large and cumbersome rifles. The design was later modified by Alexander Henry. These early single-shot rifles earned a reputation for accuracy, easy maintenance, and rugged reliability. The long barrels fostered good accuracy, the design let the shooter effortlessly throw the rifle to his shoulder, and many of the early cartridges were good game getters.

The Ruger singles are available in a full range of modern cartridges—the broadest selection of any rifle manufactured today. Many older small game cartridges, considered obsolete, can be found in these rifles. A good example is the .22 Hornet. At one time as many as 22 different calibers were available in the various Ruger singles.

This style of rifle offers several advantages. The short receiver allows 26-inch barrels to be put in place without increasing overall length. This means as much a 100-feet-per-second increase in muzzle velocity from factory loads, so hot reloads can more closely approach their potential. These rifles handle well and line up on target quickly.

The result is a rifle that is carried into the hunting fields and shot more frequently. This, of course, makes the shooter a better shot. These rifles possess the same kind of balance found in the old Winchester and Marlin levers. The combination of these factors gives us a gun that is fun to shoot.

Out-of-the-box accuracy of the single-shots is no different from that of other action types. Ruger accuracy is sufficient for most shooters, but can be improved with glass bedding and some experimentation with forend pressure. Triggers are usually excellent, being externally adjustable for weight of pull and travel. The rifles also come factory equipped with their own scope rings. These accuracy-enhancing features make the Ruger an excellent small game rifle.

Newcomers to small game hunting will appreciate a couple of additional Ruger touches. These are very safe guns. With only one shot to chamber, it's easy to tell the rifle's condition. Leaving the action open following cartridge extraction is good safety training for beginning shooters who might forget such caution during the excitement of the hunt. Also, the safety is conveniently found on the tang. It blocks the hammer and sear, but still allows the action to be opened and loaded or unloaded.

As with the other actions, there are tradeoffs to be made. The only real complaint about the single-shot is its lack of versatility. After all, it *is* a single-shot. Granted, most models can be reloaded quickly when a second cartridge is held in the opposite hand. Still, rapid shooting at numerous targets is fundamental to the style of hunting we're talking about here.

For shooters who take pains to put the odds

Single shot rifles are best represented by the Ruger models. The short receiver allows the use of longer barrels, the rifles line up on target well, and all handle well.

Many hunters feel the single shot puts them on the same terms as the animals they hunt. It doesn't matter whether the targets are winter rabbits or summertime gophers—these hunters take pleasure in connecting on game with one well-placed shot.

in their favor by using cover, a rest, or a good stalk, and feel great pride in hitting game with one well-placed shot, single-shots represent no great handicap. Besides, no action type absolves the hunter from missed shots. The hunter's major challenge lies in connecting on shots at long distances or at moving small game. He does this through good field techniques, not a hail of fire.

What makes a guy hunt with a single-shot? Well, it's usually pride in abilities honed over years. Sometimes it's a longing for easier and simpler times—when one shot would have brought home pot meat. There is also the snob appeal of going afield with a single-shot. The single-shot is often considered a badge of experience, a refutation of newer technology—if you could call a '98 Mauser type new. Hunters with single-shots feel confident as they stride across open fields or push through hardwood forests. It is a feeling well deserved. Anytime you can connect at distant targets with the first and only shot, you can be justifiably proud.

To answer the question, "Is there a place for the single-shot?", it's clear that there will always be a treasured spot for this action type. As long as there are hunters taking intense pride in their woodsmanship and outdoor skills, there will be a demand for the single-shot. Many are works of beauty, have quality features, and a heft that says "shoot me often". Hunters adore these features and as long as this special appeal exists in the hearts and minds of modern hunters, single-shot rifles will have a special niche in any shooter's gun rack.

Lightweight Questions

The shooter's quest to find the best solution to firearms problems is represented by something that has come to be known as the mountain rifle. Lightweight rifles were designed in Europe, and were favored by hunters frequenting such hunting spots as the Black Forest in Germany and the awesome Preipt Marshes in Russia. In these rugged areas, terrain restricted movement and everything had to be carried by horse or man. Under these conditions lightweight rifles proved superior and found favor among generations of hunters or, as they were called, Jaegers.

In America, lightweight rifles failed to evolve. Lever rifles were king and many, except the 1886 Winchester, *were* lightweight, and handy. These were referred to as carbines. However, by the 1920s, attention was being paid to bolt action rifles. Savage is credited with bringing out the first Mauser type bolt action lightweight rifle in America.

At the time, Savage didn't think of their gun as particularly special at five pounds, 14 ounces. A rifle in the then-new .250/3000 and .300 Savage cartridges was just the modernization of their extensive line. It was a graceful, though unpopular, rifle and later versions were actually made heavier by shooter demand.

Lightweight rifle manufacture remained in the dark ages. It was only after years of writing and hunting that Jack O'Connor drew hunter attention to the many advantages of lightweight rifles. In 1952, the Winchester behemoth spit out the first Model 70 Featherweight. Remington had the Model 725, and later the Model 600 carbine, perhaps the best American-made mountain rifle ever. For a while it appeared that lightweight rifles had achieved a foothold with North American hunters.

It didn't last. The Winchester Featherweight was discontinued in 1963. The Model 600 became a controversial rifle, precipitating lawsuits for its company, and was finally dropped from the catalog in 1967. A similar Model 660 merely used up available parts and was discontinued in 1971. All became collector's items, and to this day trade at six and seven times their original price. For a while no lightweights remained.

This all changed when Winchester reintroduced a modernized Featherweight Model 70 in 1981, and the number of lightweight rifles has since proliferated. Now short actions, fiberglass stocks, reduced barrel lengths and lightened

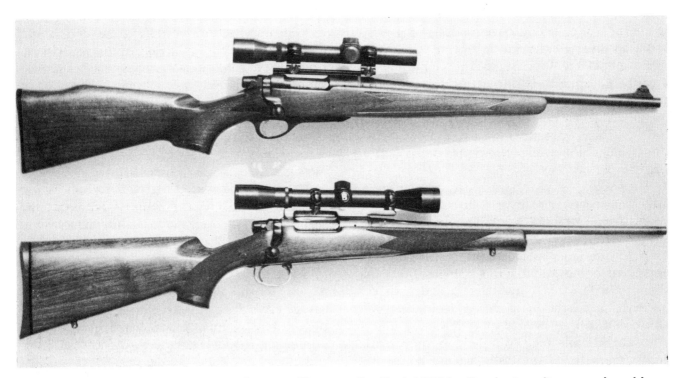

One of the earliest and best mountain-type rifles was the Model 600 by Remington. It was replaced by the Model 660, shown on the left. Later the Model 7 Remington replaced the lightweight series.

barrels characterize all rifle lines.

Full length Mannlicher style stocks have found some takers. Present favorites include the Remington Model 7 bolt action weighing six-and-a-quarter pounds, outfitted with an eighteen-and-a-half-inch barrel; Ruger Model 77 Ultra Light tipping the scales at only six pounds—in 20 and 18-inch barrel lengths; Winchester Lightweight Model 70 at six-and-a-quarter pounds and featuring a 22-inch barrel; and the lightest of the light, the Sako Hunter at five-and-three-quarter pounds.

How useful are these rifles to the small game and varmint shooter? They are a boon. While the reduced weight may not seem great when compared to their sporting cousins, even a few ounces shaved from a rifle that must be carried all day translates into saved energy—energy that may mean the difference between a hit or a miss late in the day. These rifles are excellent on

day-long rabbit hunts, where row upon row of fenceline is scouted on foot for sign. Climbing, carrying, and toting are made a little easier with a lightweight rifle.

Active rifle users also claim a lightweight rifle is not slung over the shoulder as frequently as heavier models. In other words, these rifles tend to remain in your hands—where they should be—letting the hunter get on quick-moving squirrels or mad-dash rabbits with less fumbling and more speed. Some hunters say there is no need for a carrying sling—mountain rifles are so pleasant to carry they have no desire to sling them over the shoulder or under the arm.

Lightweight rifles contribute another way. Hunters outfitted for early fall hunting carry roughly 12 pounds of clothing (including boots), 150 cartridges plus containers totaling two pounds, backpack including water equalling 15 pounds, and various accoutrements (knife, compass, belt, binoculars) coming in at eight pounds. This adds up to 32 pounds of support gear. Now add a 12 pound rifle (rifle, mounts, sling, scope) to reach an equipment total of 44 pounds. All this must be lifted and moved with every step. Any rifle shaving four pounds from this means a significant saving in weight.

Weight reduction is achieved by the use of a reduced action length. This is amply demonstrated in both the Winchester and the Sako. The barrels are also very light. Small caliber rifle barrels need not be as heavy as those on larger caliber rifles, so streamlined barrels are common to the lightweights. Barrel length is also decreased. The shortened action means that pro-

portionately less steel is needed in the floor plate, magazine, follower, and trigger guard, with a further saving in weight. The saving in steel is followed by an equal saving in wood. Stocks are slimmer, lack rollover combs, and have thinned forends. In the end this chopping, slimming, and redesigning results in a rifle as much as 20 percent lighter than the sporting version of the same line.

In mountainous or coulee country, the lightweight rifle really shines. Hunters are welcome to carry as much weight as they like, but only a few trips from the vehicle across a valley or broad plain will convince most of the advantage to lightness.

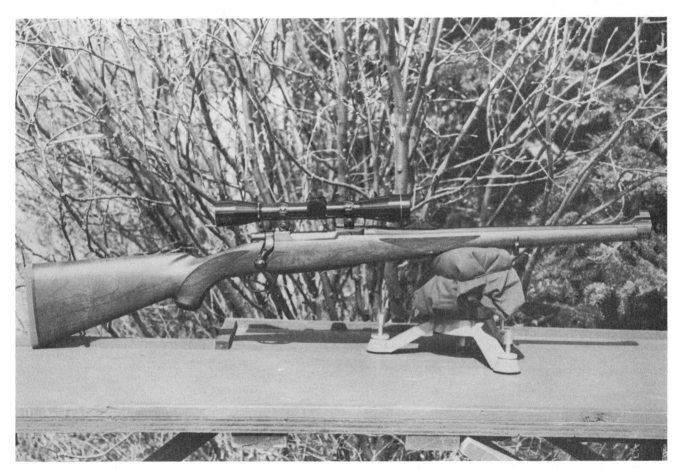

Mannlicher-styled rifles have gained a toehold with the American shooting public. The Ruger 77 in .243 is a fine little rifle for field shooting trips.

Most hunters believe they can shoot better with a heavy rifle. This is true, especially if a natural rest or mechanical device is used. However, rests improve the accuracy of all rifles—light and heavy. Shooting while standing erect, perhaps the silliest thing a hunter can do, wastes the accuracy potential of either heavy or lightweight guns. There is just too much room for shooter error. It doesn't matter that a given rifle can shoot one minute of an angle. Most hunters standing up can't hold a rifle within one minute of an angle. It's surprising that some hunters have yet to learn this fundamental fact of successful rifle shooting. Irrespective of rifle weight, use a rest whenever possible.

Some hunters complain that lightweights are hard to hold steady even from sitting and kneeling positions. These hunters claim the gun does not sit in place when lined on target but tends to wobble from side to side, especially during high mountain or open prairie winds. Shooting from your strongest position is always the best answer to these problems. For most hunters this means prone.

Knowing how to use a sling helps, too. A sling will move shot accuracy up one position. Thus, sitting and using a sling lets the average shooter perform as well as if he were shooting prone; kneeling with the correct sling lets the shooter do as well as sitting; and standing with proper sling will deliver the same accuracy as if kneeling. Correct sling use overcomes the feeling that lightweights don't easily line up on target.

Lightweight rifles have opened doors for younger shooters and those who find handling a heavy rifle difficult. Every rifle on the market except the Model 94 Winchester was too heavy for me as a skinny teenager. Others probably share this experience. Women often have difficulty with so-called man sized rifles. Lightweights cure this and enable girls to be taught safe handling and correct use of centerfire rifles.

The lightweight's major criticism is the tendency for their buggy-whip barrels to overheat quickly during heavy shooting sessions. This changes the point of impact, and at 250 yards can account for mysterious downrange misses. But beware—this potential exists with nearly every rifle—even bull barreled models.

This .303 British was considered "avant garde" in its day because of the extreme weight reduction the design represented.

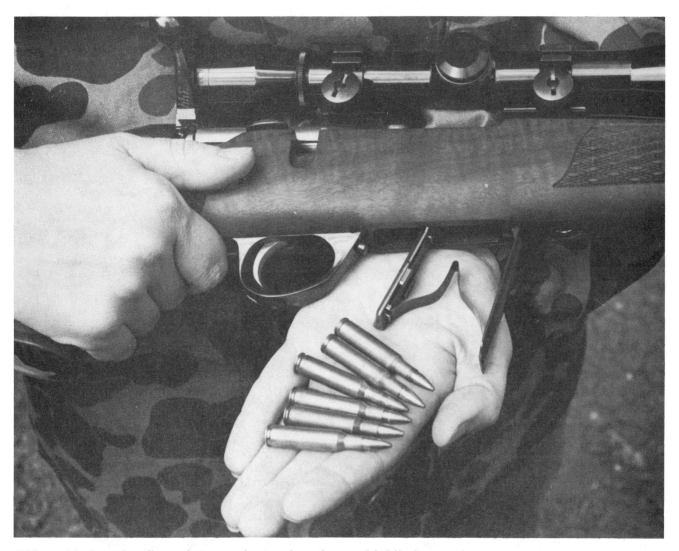

Rifles with dropping floor plates are better than those with blind magazines.

Taking good care of your barrel and controlling the amount of shooting are key elements in keeping light barrels shooting on target. Allowing the barrel to cool after every four shots for three or four minutes reduces shifting and warping.

Pay particular attention on very hot days as barrel steel readily absorbs both ambient and cartridge-produced heat. Free floating barrels help by letting air circulate. Give the barrels a further chance to cool during long shooting sessions by cleaning the bore following every dozen rounds and, on hot days, protect the barrel from the sun.

Those not excited by lightweight rifles point out that human muscles are designed to overcome resistance. A light rifle does not provide enough muscle resistance, and therefore there is a tendency to overthrow when sighting or leading. These shooters say rifles are designed to be shot, not carried, and it is better to walk all day with a heavy rifle that will hold on target than

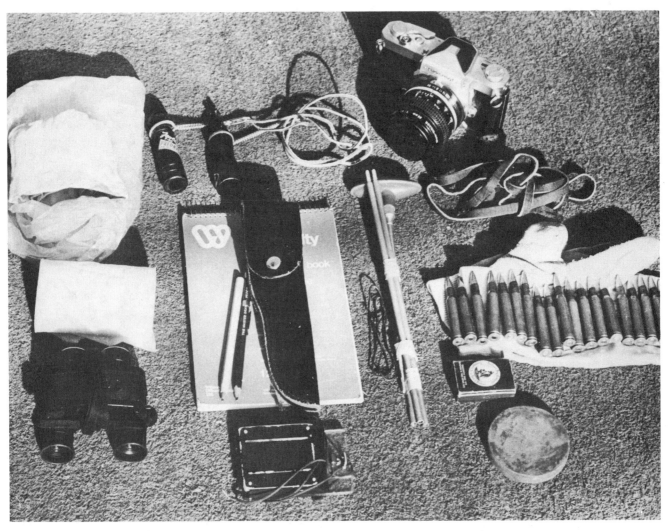

The average hunter will carry about 44 pounds of gear. A lightweight rifle lightens the load.

a lightweight that waves all over the place when sighted. They argue, especially with shotguns, that light guns lose momentum, resulting in poor follow-through on running shots. Some hunters claim it's difficult to hold on target with a lightweight after climbing a mountain.

While the current crop of lightweights is finding much favor with riflemen, there is one point many ignore: scope weight can greatly increase overall weight. It is important, where weight is the major factor in rifle selection, that a scope's contribution be considered. On the other hand,

there are those who want lightweight rifles only so they can mount large objective-diameter scopes in place. This is done to provide a good rig for early morning and late evening shooting. Although total weight approaches that of a sporting rifle, the large objective lens helps gather the light, and a tradeoff is made. Where overall weight is a problem, lightweight scopes have to part of the package.

Present cartridge availability is adequate in most lightweight lines. It would be nice to see older cartridges like the .22 Hornet, .22K Hornet and .222 Remington Magnum brought back. In this author's humble opinion, returning the .32-20 and .25-20 in these modern rifles would greatly benefit all intermediate range shooting and small game hunting in particular. Lightweight rifles combined with "lightweight" cartridges is a concept rifle manufacturers have not yet recognized. Perhaps they will someday.

Perhaps the only complaint of real consequence against the lightweight rifles is their short barrels. This has long been the beef against carbines as well. Historically, .30-30 ballistics were hampered in the Model 94 by its short barrel when compared to the Model 70 in .30-06. Since each inch of barrel provides about 50 to 75 feet per second of muzzle velocity, short barrels do sacrifice some muzzle velocity. However, even a loss of 200 fps over a longer barrel changes little of the bullets' striking energy.

Lightweight rifles need one other refinement. This is the use of a high capacity, detachable clip. Clips serve best in allowing the shooter to remove the cartridges in a neat, compact unit rather than tipping them onto the ground, which now happens with dropped magazine floor plates. It would also spare hunters from running each cartridge through rifle actions without detachable floor plates.

For some reason the clip has not caught on in North America. The only bolt gun ever to feature clip loading was the English manufactured Parker-Hale.

What started as a trickle has turned into a flood. Lightweight or mountain rifles are everywhere. The hunter after small game would do well to select any of the current lot. Don't buy a light, compact rifle on the basis of weight alone. Good quality lightweights must also be well made, correctly finished, and reliable. The cartridges that it's chambered for must deliver acceptable accuracy and ballistics.

In choosing a lightweight, our average hunter might come close to achieving that mythical holy grail of rifle selection—the perfect small game rifle. For the kinds of hunting situations where movement and speed are critical to success, and where the rifle spends more time carried than fired, the lightweights are tops. True, it has its problems. It has its detractors, including some well known gun writers festooning the mastheads of established outdoor magazines—in other words, guys that should know better—but overall, light rifles will meet your needs time and again. Choose them, carry them, and shoot them.

How About Heavy-Barrel Rifles?

How about heavy-barrel rifles? You know, the kind often referred to as varmint, target weight or bull-barreled rifles? Is there a place for these in modern small game hunting? Should the hunter choose one for all of his shooting needs? How real are the benefits this rifle delivers?

Lightweight rifles now dominate the consumer market, and have pretty much pushed heavy-barrel numbers to the back burner. This trend, whether short lived or long term, is due to the changes hunting has undergone over the last 20 years. Yet heavy-barrel rifles offer several advantages.

At one time, when gun steels were soft, heavier barrels were a necessary part of the manufacturing process. Without great gobs of steel, old gun barrels couldn't contain the pressures. Thinner barrels would have burst, so it was necessary to use lots of steel.

When better steels were invented, resulting in lighter barrels, shooters and hunters found the new lightweights were harder to hold steady, and heated up quickly. Both factors contributed to reduced accuracy—at least in the minds of our forefathers—and soon heavy barrels became associated with better accuracy. Demand for heavy barrels returned and found a strong following among dedicated shooters.

The traditional relationship between accuracy and barrel weight exists today. Today, the heavy barrel is chosen by accuracy-conscious shooters who are familiar with their rifles and who routinely fire a lot of ammunition.

Heavy barreled rifles offer some real advantages to the shooter. The Parker-Hale Model 1200V and the Remington Model 700 BDL with heavy 24 inch barrel are both top performers.

However, tradition alone does not account for the continued demand for heavy-barrel rifles. There are some real advantages to rifles outfitted this way. Physically, varmint rifles differ from sporters with longer as well as heavier barrels. Going from breech to muzzle, varmint barrels feature little taper. This gives the barrel extra stiffness and vibration resistance. These physical features are at the heart and sole of the improved accuracy produced by heavy-barrel rifles.

The physical differences do not stop there. Heavy-barrel rifles are offered today without sight dovetails. This, it is thought, contributes to better accuracy as no gadgets interfere with the barrel's sine wave created during firing. Ballisticians and physicists believe the barrel, free to vibrate unencumbered, is more likely to repeat its pattern in the same manner, shot after shot. For the hunter-shooter this translates into tighter groups.

There are five practical advantages for hunters using heavy or target weight barrels. First is the familiarity that develops between shooter and rifle. Heavy-barrel rifles, usually in mild midsized centerfire cartridges, are fun to shoot and therefore tend to be shot more frequently. People owning these kinds of rifles are highly motivated to shoot. They use them all year round, taking whatever small game is available and expending much ammo checking their rifle's zero. Much credit is given to the rifle when indeed it's the constant practice that makes the hunter a better shot. In the end it doesn't matter, as the result is an improved shooter thoroughly familiar with his rifle.

Another advantage lies in the demands made on the shooter's style. If heavy rifles are to be productive tools they must be handled differently from sporting kinds. A heavy rifle demands better muscle control, solid stance and revamped tactics from the shooter. It makes sense that any rifle weighing ten pounds requires good fit and firm support. Thought must be given to stance, as shooting off-hand is more difficult, while shooting from a sitting position is actually easier.

Using a rest is almost always required, except perhaps in the simplest of shots. This all combines to make the hunter careful, more considerate of circumstances, and alert to the potentials and handicaps of his particular rifle. These demands really make the shooter a better hunter.

A third advantage is reduced nervousness. While drawing a bead, everybody shakes. This is because the human body is a quivering mass of flesh with the heart pumping blood through miles of veins and arteries, lungs exchanging air, and the brain consuming energy making thousands of split-second decisions and overseeing other organs. All this activity makes the body shake. Add to this the adrenalin let loose by inexperience or hunt tensions, and it's a physiological wonder that man can stand, let alone execute a clear shot. The solid feel of a heavy-barrel rifle reduces these built-in shooter stresses. It settles into position easier than a lightweight version, and is harder to move off target. In essence, more muscle bundles are utilized holding a heavy gun than a light rifle.

The added weight seems to tell the body it means business, and the body responds by diverting energy into the effort. Nearly every hunter can tell you about this feeling, and indeed, it's a necessity for success with these kinds of rifles.

A major advantage of heavy-barrel rifles is the reduction in felt recoil. Along with this is the near elimination of muzzle jump. These are real aids to shooting and will, quite independent of other factors, have positive influences on accuracy and marksmanship. This fact was well recognized in early military rifles—many weighing in at over nine pounds when fully loaded. Routinely fired from the prone in the field, or from parapet or parados in fixed positions, recoil in powerful cartridges like the .30-06, 8 by 57, or .303 British rarely became a factor in extended shooting sessions.

The same holds true today. Long shooting sessions using heavy-barrel rifles, firing hundreds of rounds at targets like black-tailed

The author with his favorite heavy barreled rifle. This is one of the few Model 54's in .250/3000 with heavyweight barrel.

prairie dogs or various ground squirrels are pleasant, even when done with .25-06's or hot loaded 110 grain bullets stuffed into .30-06's. The effect of recoil is cumulative and even mild jarring firearms like the .22-250 can become disconcerting after several rounds. After all other shooting skills are learned, recoil is the single greatest deterrent to good marksmanship. Heavy barrels reduce apparent recoil and when combined with mild powered cartridges, virtually eliminate the problem, freeing the hunter to concentrate on his shooting. Improved marksmanship soon follows.

Heavy-barrel rifles handle heat better than their lightweight counterparts. Heat generated during firing becomes a shooting problem when several rounds are rapidly fired without leaving time for the barrel to cool. Undissipated heat, both from the sun and shooting, causes a barrel to change point of impact. Heavy barrels are not as susceptible to this because of their rigidity and their ability to transfer heat uniformly along the barrel. Their sheer size and weight allow more heat to be absorbed and redistributed throughout the steel. This not only contributes to better accuracy, but allows that accuracy to be maintained during extended shooting. This is a real plus, and one any shooter must consider if restricting his shooting opportunities to a few heavy sessions per season.

Heavy barrels have another benefit. They hold on target better due to their added weight. This means less movement when shooting from a camouflaged position, and less difficulty returning to or relocating the target. The shooter doesn't become as tired of the actual shooting. Some may find this difficult to believe, but shooting is an exhausting activity, one requiring good concentration and coordination. This places unique demands on the body, unlike those of other sports or athletic endeavors. While these may seem unimportant benefits, their significance increases during long range shooting, particularly at small targets like ground squirrels or gophers.

In general, heavy-barrel rifles are capable of digesting a variety of ammunition. Combinations of closely related powder types, similar bullet weights, and various primer makes tend to shoot to the same point of impact. While this is not always true, heavy-barrel rifles are less load-specific than their lightweight cousins. Many shooters know that top performance in most rifles is only reached with one particular load, often after much experimentation and field testing. Heavy barrels tend not to be restricted in this way, and shoot extremely well with several different loads. Many times the same point of impact can be retained with widely varying bullet weights.

The benefits to this are real. In the field,

hollow point ammunition can be interchanged with spire point, or, depending on the shooting application, hard point ammo. There is freedom to assemble loads from a variety of components knowing there will be little change in end results. At times the same or familiar reloading components are not readily available, especially when travelling or having to reload in the field. The heavy-barrel rifle allows reloading flexibility unavailable with the lightweights.

There are good reasons for choosing a heavy-barrel gun over lightweight types or even sporting weight kinds. Where these advantages are needed, heavy-barrel rifles are the way to go. However, there is also a downside, and it is captured in one word—*heavy*. Heavy-barrel rifles *are* heavy.

All popular models in production today weigh in excess of nine pounds, and when outfitted with scope, mounts and sling will tip the scales at over ten pounds, with several going to 11 pounds when big variable scopes are part of the package. In a nutshell, where weight factors into the hunt scenario, the heavy-barrel rifle should be left at home.

Another issue is carrying the big rifle. Aside from sheer weight, heavy-barrel rifles are cumbersome to carry. The heavy barrel moves the balance point forward compared to a standard rifle. When slung over the shoulder the extra weight pulls the barrel back and pushes the stock forward, resulting in an awkward feeling carry. This is mitigated somewhat by slinging the firearm barrel down, but many hunters don't like this carrying method, simply because the longer barrel is easy to accidentally drive into the ground.

Military rifles avoided this by having front swivels well forward. Some hunters move the front swivel onto the barrel by using shotgun type swivels, but this is not recommended, as the tinkering will interfere with barrel performance. However, the move does change the balance point, allowing the hunter to carry in traditional fashion.

Much of the carrying problem is academic. Holding the barrel and placing the stock over your shoulder is a good carrying method, and no changes need be made to the rifle. Use the sling during shooting and not as a carrying device. Besides, in the hunting fields any rifle should be carried at quarter port, using both hands, keeping ready to bring the rifle into action.

There is one last complaint. It is alleged that heavy-barrel rifles are difficult to snap into shooting position, especially when shooting offhand. Stocks on these rifles have higher combs, wider forends and thicker butts, as well as being designed to favor prone or rest shooting rather than offhand use. The shooter must become familiar with these slightly different stock dimensions through dry fire practice. With practice, shouldering the heavy-barrel rifle is no more difficult than any sporter weight gun.

Using a rest ensures better accuracy, easy handling, and more long range hits with *any* rifle. With a rest the heavy-barrel rifle is capable of delivering its full potential as a specialized long range shooting tool. Small game shooters should always use a rest, and heavy-barrel shooters should consider the rifle rest mandatory

Here is one of the best ways to carry a heavy rifle. No sling, no problem.

equipment. Some shooters complain that the necessity to rest heavy-barrel rifles inhibits the shooting. That's doubtful, but it does focus the shooter on accuracy, and this extra attention will produce more and better downrange hits.

What about Barrel Length?

Once the decisions have been made about your shooting environment, action type, firearm weight, and the host of other factors outlined here, there is still the issue of barrel length. In the previous sections, we've discussed barrel length, but never really put the subject to rest. Shooters know that barrel length is given up with the lightweight rifles, and that carbines have traditionally sported shorter barrels.

Noise is a factor. Short barrels are well known for contributing to rifle report. Small game shooters know the difficulties any extra noise can lead to when hunting the urban fringe anywhere in North America today. No part of the modern world, even northern Canada, is free from this obstacle.

Carbines, as a rifle type, have been much maligned because of the noise produced by even so-called mild cartridges. As a teenager, my Model 94 Winchester took some getting used to, simply because every time I fired, the muzzle blast would shake my skinny face. Indeed, one reason mild cartridges like the 6.5x57 Mauser caught on with European hunters was the mild report they offered in carbine styled rifles when compared to the 8x57Smm. Also, many of the American carbines evolved during the closing days of the black powder cartridge. These cartridges generally produced less muzzle blast, and were easier on sensitive ears.

Short-barrel rifles are quick handling and easy to move through bush and tangles. On the other hand, long-barrel rifles give the shooter all the velocity the cartridge can produce and produce less muzzle blast. Either way, the shooter must make a trade off in picking one type against the other. Some cartridges are favored with longer barrels than others. The classic example is the .25-06. In most sporter weight versions, barrel lengths measure 22 inches. But for those models in .25-06, it's 24 inches.

The same holds true for the Model 700 Remington line. The Weatherby Mark V deluxe rifle, currently the longest barrel bolt action in production, comes in at 26 inches. Next in line is the Sako Custom Target rifle with a 25 1/2-inch barrel.

Many times in the past muzzle velocity loss accorded to short-barrel rifles has been overestimated. Using Wayne Blackwell's computer program ''Load From a Disk'', a comparison load for the .257 Roberts was developed. It showed that, in moving from 24-inch to 18-inch barrels, each inch of barrel length loss sacrificed about 20 fps of muzzle velocity when all other factors remained equal. The longest barrel produced 3050 fps and the shortest 2900, giving a muzzle velocity loss of 150 fps.

The question is, what importance does 150 fps velocity loss mean to the average shooter. In down range terms, using a .257 Roberts cartridge with an 87 grain bullet having a ballistic coefficient of .313, and fired from a rifle with a 24-inch barrel, remaining energy at 300 yards is 911 foot-pounds. Assuming like conditions, the same load in a rifle with an 18-inch barrel produces 812 foot-pounds of energy at 300 yards. The difference is 99 foot-pounds of energy. For the small game hunter, this difference is peanuts. Prairie dogs, rabbits, and ground squirrels taken at distant ranges require roughly 500 foot-pounds of energy to be humanely dispatched. There is plenty of energy left to do that, even at 400 yards.

The current tendency is for bush hunters to select short-barrel rifles and open plains shooters to go for longer barrels. As with the other decisions facing the shooter, accuracy and shooter comfort are important components in the equation. Personal preference is a real factor. I tend to favor short-barrel Mannlicher-styled stocks, while men like Townsend Whelan and

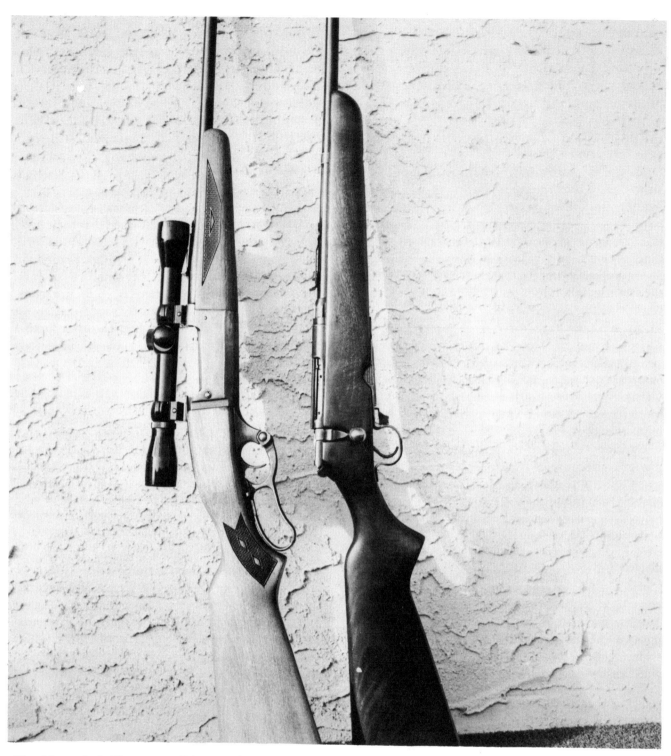

Short barreled rifles are well known for their handiness in the bush. Here the Model 99 and the Model 23, both very old models, offer quickness and light weight.

Jack O'Connor made heavy sporters famous. Having said that, much shooting is still done with traditionally configured rifles. There are a lot of us that like it that way, too.

Does Your Stock Fit?

In all the talk about choosing a rifle action and coming to terms with the technical aspects of modern day rifle shooting, nothing has been said about the stock or how it fits the shooter. Like any other aspect of the shooting sports, our rifle stock came from very humble beginnings. Originally, the stock was a mere stick bound to a crude barrel, serving to keep the shooter's face away from belching fire, burning powder, and acrid smoke. Later, stocks became works of beauty, serving as a medium for expressive carving and creative design.

In America the Kentucky style stock gained wide acceptance. For modern shooters these stocks carry too much drop, and the deeply curved butt plates are inappropriate for today's recoil levels. Some stocks were classic abominations, but this appears to have been necessary to advance our sport. The club-like appendage found on the British P-14 and American P-17 military rifles serves as a good reminder of the origin of our modern day sporting stocks.

Many cartridges failed to develop their potential, simply because the available rifles had stocks that helped produce a kick out of proportion to the cartridge's power. The Model 94 Winchester rifle in .25-35 was a good example. Developed in 1895 as a small game and varmint round, it was on its way to becoming the first dual purpose cartridge available to shooters. The future looked bright as gun writers of that era praised the cartridge as a valuable intermediate range rabbit and deer gun.

However, excessive drop and poor butt plate design on the Model 94 rifle gave shooters a whollop that made most think twice before taking another shot. As a result, the useful .25-35 hit the skids, and few rifles have been produced for this cartridge since World War II.

Shortly after this experience, the stocks on nearly all production lever guns were improved. This culminated with the stocks found on the Model 71 and Model 64 Winchester rifles. Bolt action stocks also underwent redesign. The stocks on both the early Remington Model 30 and Model 54 Winchester looked like thinned-down military versions. Writings by Townsend Whelan contributed to this awakening process.

Most shooters of average build will now find factory stocks, especially of the big three—Ruger, Remington, and Winchester-US Repeating Arms—are entirely satisfactory. This is especially true in the original sporter weight lines. However, the recent return to lightweight guns has caused some slightly different stock dimensions to creep back into our rifle lines.

The simplest test for sporting stock fit is if the shooter can naturally and quickly put the gun to his shoulder and have the sights line up, or very nearly line up, on target. No gun twisting or head realignment should be necessary for the rifle to sit naturally on target. Snapping the rifle to the shoulder six or seven times is the best way to complete this trial. Any rifle passing this test has good rifle-shooter fit, and average shooters will have no trouble sighting in or connecting in the field.

There are three critical stock dimensions that every small game shooter should know and understand. One, called length of pull, is defined as the distance from the center of the trigger to the center of the butt plate. Generally this came to be accepted as 13-3/8 inches. The hunter's physical build determines this length. Long necked, long armed shooters need longer than average pulls. Winter clothing greatly affects pull length, especially where thick clothing is necessary. Shooters who carry their heads erect need shorter stocks.

Two other stock concepts are *drop at heel* and *drop at comb*. Drop at the heel is the vertical distance between the line of sight and the top edge of the butt or heel. Drop at the comb is the

The best butt plate is the shotgun butt. Many early rifles featured crescent shaped butts that heightened the recoil of even moderately kicking rifles.

vertical distance between the line of sight and the forward end of the comb.

Drop is important because it influences felt recoil and helps align the eye, sight, and target. A well designed stock will have a comb high enough to allow the eye to look through the sights. High combs—rifles with little drop—are an important component of the sighting bridge. The entire bridge consists of a shoulder squarely on the butt, right hand on the grip, left hand on the forend, and cheek against the comb. Cor-

rectly designed drop lets the shooter take recoil at the center of the butt plate. This reduces apparent recoil because, with the right arm up in shooting position, shoulder muscles are spread over the entire butt plate. This arrangement of arms, muscles, and wood prevents the top of the comb from bashing the shooter's cheek, or the bottom of the butt—called the toe—from driving into the shooter's shoulder.

Pitch down is another stock measurement that is critical in establishing good fit. Pitch down is the angle formed by the intersection of the bore line and a right angle line connecting heel and toe of the butt. Essentially, too much pitch down from the muzzle allows the butt to slip upward. On the other hand, too little pitch down lets the rifle drop below the arm pit. In general, pitch down should range from three to five inches. The post-'64 Model 70 Winchester has 3 inches of pitch down. On the other hand, the Model 94 rifle in .25-35 has only one inch of pitch down. This alone accounts for the mule-sized kicks this little rifle delivers.

There are two stock refinements that developed over the years as scope sights came into prominence. First is the Monte Carlo comb. Once scope use became routine there was a clear need to reduce drop, thereby allowing the eye to better line up with the new scopes, some of which were two inches above the rifle's bore. For most shooters a Monte Carlo is a quick and easy way to get the eyes up to the correct height for scope use. In design, the Monte Carlo made the stock makers' job easier, as it was not necessary to critically decline the drop along the entire length of the stock. The Monte Carlo simply drops off very sharply toward the heel and slopes downward at the butt.

The second feature is the cheek piece. This helps in firmly holding the rifle and lining up the scope. Today, many of the so-called classic stocks don't carry the cheek piece. A good cheek piece should be thick, flat, and merge into the comb. The California school of stock design emphasized the rollover cheek piece. Many of these

Some early stocks, like this '86 Winchester, forced the shooter to stretch his neck forward to get down behind the sights properly.

Choosing the Rifle and Shotgun   155

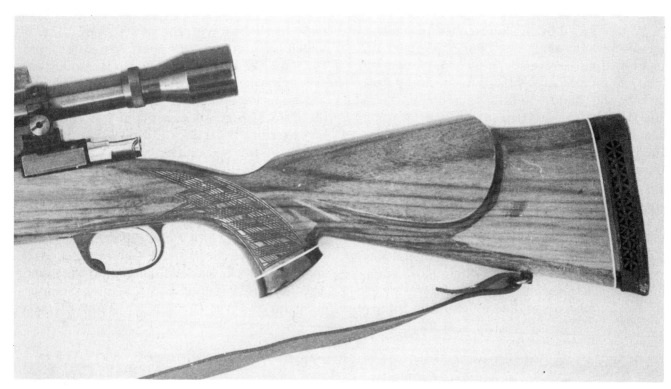

A cheek piece helps position the eye behind the scope.

The Model 70 stock represents a well designed Monte Carlo stock that lets shooters get their eyes lined up on the scope quicker.

The pistol grip is used to pull the rifle into the shoulder.

were large and gaudy. However, the cheek piece is a valuable tool that helps reduce shooting tension and aids in aiming.

Finally, forends merit discussion. Today, forends on most rifles are adequate, yet many quality sporters still feature fore stocks that are too heavy. Forends function very simply. For righthanded shooters this part of the stock is supported by the left hand. This hand holds the rifle true, but does not pull the rifle back into the shoulder in a tight death grip. The right hand, pulling through the pistol grip, draws the rifle tightly toward the shoulder.

Lightweight rifles have very thin forends, and much of the weight reduction in these rifles is accomplished by thinning down this portion of the stock. The forend need only be thick enough for the hand to grip firmly. Thin forends make the rifle quick to get on target and easy to follow through.

Pistol grip styles are changing. The latest Remington Mountain rifle features a lower pitched pistol grip. However, sporting rifles require a well curved grip so the hand is in a natural uncramped position and can exert back pulling pressure to hold the butt firmly against the shoulder. A full grip lets the shooter throw the rifle to his shoulder quicker and get on target sooner. It also feels more natural. Straight grips develop wrist tension and provide no guidance for the hand to line up with the eye.

In summary, the stock is critical, especially in an older rifle for small game hunting. While the modern numbers are well designed, good fit is still important and there is enough variation among manufacturers that new shooters are wise to shop around. Once you've given consideration to all criteria important to selection, pick the rifle that fits the best. The average shooter will have few problems, but a large framed hunter might have to consider a custom stock to get exactly what he wants. Also, watch that no quirks develop in your stance that may eventually force you to get a custom stock.

Shooting in the Cold

It is often said that cold weather is the shooter's friend—or is it? Cold winters and blustery days test your hunting interest; of that there is little doubt. It is true that bulky clothes, lumpy feet, and cold hands can sometimes characterize winter hunting. Yet these so-called miserable days produce game and keep less motivated hunters out of the field.

Aside from this, cold weather provides a vigorous trial of your equipment. Firearms are particularly sensitive to cold weather. They are subject to many performance variations because they are made of metal and utilize lubricants on springs and rails. Metal behaves differently (it contracts) during cold weather, and greases become more viscous. During extended periods of low temperatures these factors can create serious problems for shooters. Here's how to capitalize on the benefits and reduce the risks shooters face during inclement weather.

Firing pins are the source of the most common winter problem. When a trigger is pulled, the firing pin drives forward, propelled by the contracted energy of something called a main spring. These are surprisingly large coil springs that lie invisibly inside the rifle's bolt. They are also very well lubricated. Heavy grease is used to provide both lubrication and protection for this important element in the rifle mechanism.

During cold winters the spring is slightly harder to compress, since the metal has contracted and this renders an action slightly stiffer than on a warm summer day. The thick grease surrounding the firing pin becomes stiff, and instead of lubricating the pin's forward movement, the cold grease actually slows its forward travel. This can cause the firing pin to fail to strike the primer, or not hit with sufficient power to ignite the primer.

This problem can be easily cured for the winter hunter by disassembling the bolt and removing all grease from around the spring. Washing the spring in alcohol or gasoline will break down the heavy grease accumulations; next, the bolt, spring, and pin should be thoroughly rinsed. It's important to clean all grease away because even a small amount can cause problems at low temperatures. Allow the parts to completely air dry prior to reassembly.

Years ago, guns imported from Europe were heavily greased. This was done to protect them during shipment and storage. Military rifles are notorious for coming resplendent in gobs of grease. Firing pins in these rifles should always be cleaned, and even military actions that have been used for custom made rifles should be checked. The grease remains in place for years unless removed.

Trigger mechanisms are also susceptible to accumulations of oil and grease. Dust, dirt, unburned powder particles, bits of brass, and powder residues collect around triggers and bolts of shotguns and rifles, and become mixed with oil over the course of a warm summer.

The arrival of cold weather causes the mixture to stiffen and gums the action. This scenario can be avoided by regular cleaning and degreasing. Pre-winter preparation as preventive maintenance is a good idea.

Muzzle covers are another good idea. A piece of tape over the muzzle keeps out snow and mud. Any rifle carried in the barrel-down position is easy to clog with snow or mud. A more sophisticated approach is to make a sock-like muzzle cover that is kept in place by string or ties. These are very effective at keeping crud out of the rifle barrel and preventing a burst or bulged barrel.

Magazines and clips are real sources of difficulty. When cold weather hits, cartridges can easily become stuck in staggered column clips. This is avoided by having all magazines and clips scrupulously cleaned of grease and old oil. In particular, spare clips toted in pockets should receive special attention, as they often become clogged with lint and dirt. Basically, the follower spring becomes gummed by a combination of dirt and oil accumulated against the clip wall. This hampers upward cartridge movement and results in missed loadings at the most inopportune times.

Condensation, created by moving a rifle indoors from a cold outdoor environment, can be a problem. If you take a wet rifle back outside, the water will freeze. This is often what has happened to semi-auto rifle actions that freeze shut. Minute amounts of water vapor condense on the action, and condensed vapor—now water—drains from along the barrel onto the action. When the rifle is taken back into the cold,

Cold weather provides a vigorous test of firearms and hunter. Metal contracts in the cold, and this can lead to performance problems in the rifle.

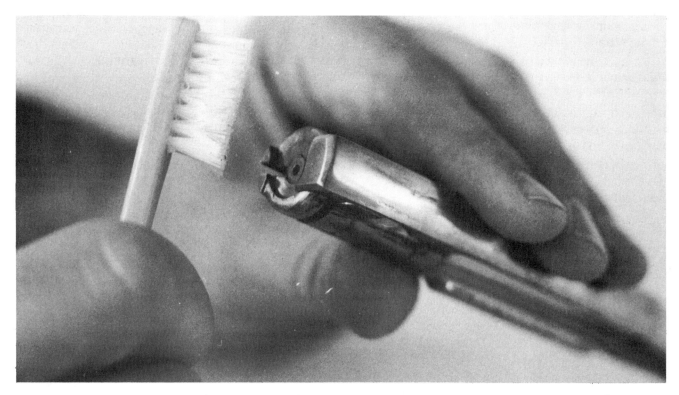

Scrupulous cleaning of all surfaces reduces the chances for old oils and grease to gum up performance.

water freezes the action shut.

Condensation problems can be avoided by proper firearm handling. The traditional advice has been to leave the gun out in the cold; don't bring it into the warm truck cab or cabin. It works well. Hunters living in rural areas will store their rifles in an unheated outbuilding, and this circumvents condensation problems. In camp, wise hunters store their rifle in a case and leave it outdoors.

Sometimes there is no choice, and a freezing firearm must be brought into a warm place. This occurs when the rifle must be carried in a warm vehicle long enough to allow condensation to occur. Under these circumstances, place the cold firearm in its case. Close the case completely. The rifle will warm very slowly and water vapor will be absorbed by the case rather than draining onto the gun. Camera buffs use this trick all the time when bringing their photo equipment from the

cold into the warmth. Rifle shooters will find that both scope and rifle benefit from this kind of treatment—and rust is prevented.

Ammunition also suffers during the cold. Primers become less sensitive, especially at extremely cold temperatures. Using Wayne Blackwell's Load From a Disk computer program, a typical .222 Remington load was developed. The program suggested that a starting load of 20.3 grains of any medium-fast burning powder pushing a 55 grain bullet with a sectional density of .157 would produce an estimated muzzle velocity of 2980 fps.

This information was then fed into the computer, but this time using Craig Chamberlin's Proware computer program to generate ballistic tables where only the temperature was altered. Two temperatures were chosen to represent the range in possible shooting conditions across North America. A quick check of the tables shows that when temperatures plummet to minus 40 degrees F from 75 degrees, muzzle velocity drops nearly 100 fps at 100 yards. At 200 yards the change is 173 fps, or about six percent. This may not seem significant, but by 300 yards this has grown to 237 fps, or more than ten percent. Similar changes occur in muzzle energy. The point of all this is to show how much cold temperatures affect cartridge performance.

Some hunters have always reloaded slightly hotter cartridges for use during the winter months. Others have moved to hotter and magnum quality primers with the hope of enhancing powder ignition. There are certain groups of cartridges, most notably older or semi-obsolete numbers, that have reputations for reduced performance during cold seasons. The age-old .38-55 was one such cartridge, and it was common for dedicated shooters to have a "summer" load and a "winter" load. The same can be done today with most modern high intensity reloads.

In general, it's safe to increase reloads by four to five percent during extremely cold winters. Experiment with different combinations before settling on one load. Some cartridges, like the .243 Winchester, don't appear to be affected by cold, and the summer load can be used during the winter with no noticeable performance loss.

The wood rifle stock suffers during cold weather, too. High quality stocks that are properly prepared—sanded, filled, and treated—can withstand considerable cold and moisture. Lacquer or varnish finishes seal best, but these glossy treatments are out of vogue with today's conservative minded shooter. Poor varnish finishes, the kind known as spar varnish, check and crack with age. Extended cold promotes cracking. A trick that military shooters used was to routinely polish their rifle stocks with shoe polish. This became unnecessary during the heyday of lacquer stocks, but with today's trend to dull finishes, stock waxing is a good habit to develop. It also leaves the stock looking better, and fills in many of the day-to-day scratches and nicks.

There are many other equipment considerations the cold weather hunter has to keep in mind. While paramount among these is rifle performance, safety is an important factor. Many times it's necessary to shoot while wearing gloves or mitts. Sometimes gloves cannot be removed fast enough to let the hunter get a shot away, and the rifle must be capable of being fired with a gloved hand. Trigger guards must be large enough to allow access with gloves. If yours is not, get a pair of thin shooting gloves, or build a new, more open, trigger guard. Also, the safety must be easily activated with thick gloves.

Heavy winter clothes mean changes for the hunter. The length of pull increases when thick mackinaws or parkas are worn. Also, elbow and shoulder room is sometimes cramped with certain styles of winter clothing, and this slows the hunter's ability to shoulder the rifle and sight quickly. In general, most rifles won't fit as well with heavy clothing in place, but extra practice and familiarity will cure these difficulties.

Head gear can also affect shooting styles. Broad brimmed hats are notorious for getting in the way of scopes, but toques, soft balaclavas, and watch caps are better. Don't allow your toque to work down over your forehead, as this can interfere with putting the scope to your eye. In really cold weather peaked caps with ear flaps tend to get pulled down tightly onto the head. Invariably, the peak bumps the scope as the rifle is quickly thrown to the shoulder. A balaclava gives full face protection and never interferes with sighting equipment. Watch caps are compact and well out of the way.

Scarves tend to go in and out of hunting fashion. Now they are making a comeback. For the active hunter concerned about utility, a scarf is a poor choice. They bind at the neck, and, when left hanging out of the clothing, are sure to catch in the sling or rifle action. Bandanas are good replacements for scarves, and serve the same purpose. They provide excellent wind protection for the neck area.

Wind plays a double role in creating problems

Follower springs can become gummed with old oil and grease, causing cartridges to become stuck on their upward travel.

for shooters. Not only does it affect where a bullet might go, it also influences the ambient air temperature. Even mildly cold days are made much more dangerous by winds that produce wind chill effect. For example, a day with an air temperature of only minus 10 degrees F combined with a 20 mph wind produces the chilling equivalent of minus 53 degrees. That's cold. Under these conditions frost bite to exposed skin can quickly occur. A bare hand touching a cold gun barrel could stick to the metal, causing a painful injury.

Heavy guns, cold weather, and bundles of clothing seem to go hand in hand. Movement in insulated clothing is difficult enough, but when deep snow and a heavy rifle are part of the package, the hunter had better be in good physical shape. Carrying a rifle can be bothersome under these conditions. A stout sling is needed, and the rifle should be toted in the barrel-upright military position to prevent snow from filling it. Frequently it's necessary to carry the rifle across the back rather than over the shoulder. This is because thick winter clothing rounds your shoulder area, leaving no room for the sling. The result is that the rifle slips off the shoulder with every step. By the way, be sure to alternate sides

on which the rifle is carried. The weight of the rifle, along with the sling pulling down into the clothing, reduces the insulating qualities at this point and causes a cold spot to develop along the back.

There was a time when scopes would always fog during cold weather. Often the hunter didn't notice anything was wrong until he threw the rifle to his shoulder and looked through the scope. Fog and ice crystals greeted the hunter's eye, and the scope was useless. Today scopes are fog proof; only those that have been damaged will fog.

Fogging occurs when warm moist air slips in between the lens and the scope tube. Upon exposure to cold, moist air inside the scope condenses into water droplets. This creates fog inside the scope, and when weather gets really cold ice forms on the inside of the lens. In the early years this gave scopes a bad name and some older hunters, like my father, distrust scopes to this day. As long as you hunted where it was warm there was no problem, but mountain or winter hunting would lead to foggy problems. This was overcome by employing better machine tolerance at the shoulder where the lens and the scope body meet. Scopes were slightly pressurized with nitrogen, an inert gas that left no room for water droplets.

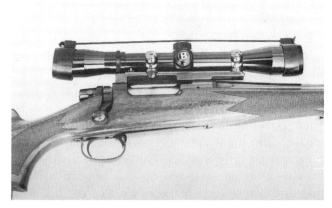

Scope covers are a must. Choose a good pair and always use them when hunting under snowy conditions.

Heavy winter clothing means changes in a shooter's style. Winter clothing tends to cramp elbow and shoulder movement. This changes the feel of the rifle and how it fits.

Finally, scope covers are an invaluable aid to winter shooting. During winter hunting snow falls from overhanging tree branches onto the scope body. It can cover the eyepiece, and even small amounts can melt, leaving a watery layer that makes viewing hazy, or turns to ice. Purchase good after-market scope covers, and read the instructions so you can benefit from the many advantages these products offer. Scope covers are good winter time hunting insurance.

What the Hunter Should Know About Shotguns

Most hunters think of rifles as the primary tool for hunting small game, while shotguns are considered applicable to several kinds of bird hunting. It's true most small game will be the purview of the rifle. However, it's fair to say that smoothbore shooters have a degree of flexibility not available to riflemen. The gun can be used on ducks, geese, upland birds, and even deer. The shotgun has a valuable place in rabbit and squirrel hunting. Indeed, many eastern hunters are familiar with no other tool for taking cedar swamp bush rabbits at close range.

Shotguns, of course, have limitations. Paramount among these is their limited effective range compared to the rifle. Any target beyond 70 yards is safe from standard loads. Precision accuracy, at least in terms of rifle shooting, is not available to shotgun shooters. The ammunition is bulky and heavy to carry compared with most rifle kinds, and generally the arms are larger and much heavier. Even avid shotgunners will tell you most shotguns are clumsy to handle and difficult to carry.

However, these limitations don't keep shotgun shooters from having fun; trap and skeet shooting are far more popular than any kind of rifle shooting.

Like rifles, shotguns come variously configured, but selecting the all-around choice is an easier decision than with a rifle. A few years ago some thought might have been given to choosing the proper gauge. Today that's not necessary as the 12 gauge is king, and all others—10, 16, 20, 28 and 410—have either withered on the vine or are considered highly specialized rigs with little practical field utility. Few guns are made in 10 gauge and the 16 is becoming increasingly rare. Shot and load choices in these are restricted. Unfortunately, while many other gauges—in particular the 16 to which I am sentimentally attached—are more pleasant to shoot, shotgun shooters are not supporting these older products. The handwriting is on the wall. For small game hunted across North America today, the 12 gauge shotgun in good hands will do just fine.

Shotguns are available in six action types. The oldest and simplest is the single-shot. Strange, in this modern day and age, there is still demand for these, and far more models are manufactured that in similar rifles. Many farm boys fondly recall their first shotgun as an inexpensive, break-action single-shot. These guns have changed little over the past five decades, and still offer the shooter safety and ease of handling.

Single-shots operate by using a lever to open the action. Most feature an external hammer that must be cocked prior to firing. These features are what makes the gun safe for beginners. Each step is a complete process, and one logically, as well rhythmically, leads to the next. Single-shots

are available in 12 gauge with a wide range of barrel lengths. On the negative side, single-shotguns tend to be light, generally weighing just over six pounds, and this produces a felt recoil that is more than younger shooters might like. Finally, remember that single-shots are just that—one shot at a fleeing bunny and it's time to reload. The rythmic motions learned in breaking the action allow many shooters to develop remarkable speed at ejecting and reloading. Only a couple of seconds are lost in getting a second shot off from the shoulder. In most small game situations there is enough time for reloading, so the single-shot action does not unduly restrict the skilled shooter.

The next obvious choice is the double barrel action. If the word traditional ever had meaning to shooters, it's here, where the double represents the essence of shooting conventionalism. From the moors of Scotland, to the open cornfields of South Dakota, the double shotgun is carried proudly and considered the ultimate in fowling equipment. For the small game shooter the double means an instant choice of two quick shots with different degrees of choke.

Double guns take two distinct formats. The traditional side-by-side, and the more modern over-and-under are today's choices. In general upland game bird shooters prefer the over-and-under, while waterfowl hunters choose the side-by-side as favorites. It really doesn't matter which the small game hunter picks; either style will effectively dispatch a bush bunny. Personal preferences usually dictate one over the other. Older double barrel shotguns tend to have wider sighting planes than stack barrel types. This makes over-and-unders easier to sight in the mind of most shooters.

Higher quality doubles feature automatic, selective ejectors which pop out the fired hulls when the action is broken. Unfired loads are raised slightly—enough for the shooter to grip the brass and remove the round. Less expensive models come with simple extractors that merely lift the hull from the chamber for removal by

The effective range of the shotgun is limited. However, within the limitations of the firearm some very interesting shooting can still occur.

hand.

Triggers have also evolved in double guns. The most expensive guns feature selective triggers—those giving the shooter the option to fire either barrel first and hence pick a choke for the particular distance at hand. Less expensive models have one trigger that fires first one barrel then the other. Older or reproduction doubles still have double triggers, one operating each barrel. The shooter makes his barrel choice and pulls the appropriate trigger. Selective triggers help the small game hunter deal with underbrush. At close range a more open pattern will spread shot, ensuring that some pellets make it through to the target.

Bolt action shotguns have declined in popularity. Back in the 1950s, inexpensive models were abundant, and many duck hunters preferred the length (over 55 inches) these guns offered. Most hunters felt these could be sighted like rifles, and shooters trained in military snap shooting methods were right at home with these long, almost exaggerated-looking, shotguns. They are exceptionally slow to use, but do allow for necessary follow up shots. Unfortunately, many are bulky and heavy, making carrying difficult for the small game hunter. For many years various hardware chains carried proprietary brand bolt actioned shotguns made by Iver Johnson or Stevens. All looked similar and were universally poorly finished, yet functioned very well, giving shooters much value for their money, especially compared to pump or single-shots. However, not much can be said about this action type today. They are a dying breed and serve little real purpose for today's small game hunter.

Having said this, I should add that my father still hunts ducks with a mint condition Stevens Model 58 bolt actioned shotgun in 12 gauge he bought in 1956. Large numbers of these can still be found in the hands of farmers, trappers, and general backwoods types throughout North America. They are considered duty guns, adequate for dispatching skunks from under out-buildings, rabbits that damage the garden, or potting at marauding mink that get too close to the chicken coop. Marlin makes one of the last quality copies available, and it has found a market niche among long range goose hunters rather than small game shooters.

Without doubt, pumps are the most popular shotgun action in North America today. Based on the action of a trombone, it was created by John Browning about 1880. The early Model 12 Winchester, Remington 31, and later the Model 870 proved that pumps perform. Herb Parsons, a Winchester shooter, toured the U.S. demonstrating pump action shooting. This publicity stunt established the pump forever. The action is reliable and time tested. Pump guns are quick, and unlike older automatics, consume all types of loads. What's more, these guns are typically less expensive than automatics. This combination of factors has put the pump out in front of all other action types.

Many pumps have magazine capacities of four or five rounds. There is now a bevy of pump guns on the market that come factory equipped for deer hunting. These have everything from good quality rear sights to slings. There is also a wide choice of barrel lengths and chokes. Small game hunters appreciate these features and can put them to good use in any serious rabbit or squirrel hunting situation.

Some critics claim pumps produce much felt or apparent recoil. Any 12 gauge shotgun of average weight yields about 24 foot-pounds of free recoil. This is more than any .22 centerfire, and ordinary shooters can't endure this pounding without some practice. Once the hunter is familiar with the gun, recoil becomes routine and goes unnoticed.

When fired with magnum loads, lightweight models such as the Remington 870 Special Field can produce uncomfortable recoil—especially for beginners. When young or inexperienced shooters encounter recoil problems, the best advice is to move down to a 20 gauge. The same Remington 870 Special Field weighing a mere six

Pump actions are the most popular shotgun type.

pounds, and firing 20 gauge field loads, produces less than 20 foot-pounds of recoil. This allows the shooter to get on with small game hunting, free from the worry about recoil and the bad shooting habits that can be developed in response to it.

The pump action is probably the easiest to adapt to small game hunting. Its advantages over other actions produce real results in the field. Unplugged, it offers good capacity and allows for quick follow-ups on running shots. It's inherently fast and easy to get on target. Short barrel models are easier to handle in close cover, and historically have proven particularly useful in cedar swamps or other brush-choked areas where rabbits hole up tight, and where oppor-

tunities for a target are limited.

Automatic, semi-automatic, autoloading, self-loaders,—the name game is similar to that covered in the rifle section—provide deadly fire on small game at short range. Today's high quality auto shotguns allow hunters to place three to four shots on fast moving prairie jacks or dodging bush bunnies in the blink of an eye. Early self loaders were unreliable, frequently given to jamming and misfiring. These guns were unforgiving of dirt and powder residue build up, and unless correctly cleaned would quit operating. Most were persnickety about the quality of ammunition used.

Part of the early problem was the great variation in loaded shot shells and the paper hulls used at that time. Today this has all changed and the automatic is as reliable as engineering technology can allow.

The first successful automatic was the Browning long recoil shotgun. It relied on the force of recoil, using a direct application of Newton's third law of motion, namely that for every action there is an equal and opposite reaction. It worked well, but resulted in a bulky, heavy gun. Even today, with modern lightweight alloys used in the action, the Browning short recoil auto tips the scales at eight pounds. It remains a bulky gun. In an attempt to reduce action size, gas operated designs were offered to shooters beginning about 1959.

Gas designs are common today. These function by tapping off some gas produced during ignition and piping it back to work the bolt. Briefly, gas-operated self loaders are activated by a short stroke piston that is moved back by the pressure generated from the cartridge. The used gas is then ported outside the piston area. In turn, the piston activates a rod that drives a reciprocating breech bolt rearward. In moving back, the heavy bolt compresses a return spring, cocks the action, pulls the fired hull from the chamber, and bumps the hull against an ejector plate. The return spring then propels the bolt forward once more to strip a hull from the magazine and carry it forward into the chamber. The shotgun is fully rearmed and ready to fire.

Self loading automatics provide shooters with a unique advantage. Recoil sensation is damped with gas operated shotguns because there is a millisecond delay before all recoil force travels back to the shooter's shoulder. The result is a feeling of gentle pushing rather than an abrupt kick. This single factor has made automatics extremely popular with trap and skeet shooters. It is also a very real advantage for small game shooters, where several quick shots can be fired in sequence.

There are two final concerns that must be covered in order to leave the small game shooter with a clear understanding of the auto shotgun. First, safety is critical with these guns. They answer only to the physics of their design, and correct handling is a must. When fired, self loaders recycle quickly, and it must be understood that a fully loaded firearm is presented with each pull of the trigger. This means close attention must be paid to muzzle control. The muzzle must be pointed in a safe direction at all times, and any lapse of concentration can produce fatal results. For old hands this is a natural, almost instinctive habit, but for younger or less experienced shooters an extra degree of concentration is required. Train for this extra element of safety.

Finally, auto shotguns still require attention to cleaning and maintenance. While engineering advances have been wonderful and responsible for moving the auto from the trap field to the hunting field, dust and dirt remain real enemies of this action type. Traditional advice has always been to keep the chamber and gas ports clean. Chambers can be cleaned with fine steel wool wrapped around a stick or cleaning brush. Gas ports should be kept free of unburned powder and residues.

Extra care is required when windy, sandy, or dusty conditions prevail. Exposure to rapid changes in moisture, dusty travel conditions, or even uncased travel—across the seat of a vehicle,

Most upland game bird hunters prefer the over-and-under style shotgun. These are also excellent for close range rabbit hunting.

for example—all influence the amount of crud a shotgun acquires. Learn how to clean your auto shotgun and do it whenever necessary.

Selection of a shotgun action type hasn't received the same degree of attention found with rifles. Indeed, it's easy to argue that shotguns and rifles are at opposite ends of the scale. Bolt actions are the growing choice with rifle shooters, while they are all but dead for shotgunners. The reverse is true with sporting automatics— lots of choice in shotguns, virtually none with rifles. There is no doubt that rifle shooters are demanding lighter weight firearms, reduced barrel lengths, trimmer stock designs, and less overall bulk. However, shotgunners have directed much attention to shot sizes, load performance, and power. While these are the trends, following any one may not work best for you. Choose the action type that suits your style of hunting and pocketbook.

Choke: What Does it Mean to Hunters?

Understanding choke is fundamental to good shotgun shooting. Waterfowl and upland game bird hunters are interested in choke performance, but it's important for small game hunters, too. Choke is defined simply as the amount of constriction designed into the end of the muzzle. It functions by pinching down on the shot charge just as it leaves the barrel.

Patterns are greatly influenced by the degree of choke. An open choked shotgun—one featuring only a small amount of muzzle constriction—is supposed to deliver wide or "open" patterns for easy hitting at close range. The opposite holds true for a tightly choked barrel. Shot charges are expected to hold together in a tight pattern, allowing better hits at long range.

A simple example will take the mystery out of chokes and choke performance. There are 280 pellets in a 12 gauge 1-1/4 ounce load of No. 6 shot. When fired through a shotgun carrying a cylinder bore choke, 98 pellets (35 percent of 280) should land within the 30-inch circle at 40 yards. With a similar load the other choke sizes would deliver the following—skeet, 98 to 126; improved cylinder, 126 to 154; modified, 154 to 182; improved modified, 182 to 196. Full choke should deliver 196-plus into the 30-inch diameter circle.

Variable chokes produce results within the ranges shown for standard choke patterns. However, shooters should not take this for granted. Many of these mechanical devices will throw tighter or more open patterns, depending on the load being used. There are really two types of variable chokes on the market today. These are the collet—represented by Poly Choke—and the interchangeable tube, exemplified by the Cutts.

Both make a shotgun more useful as a small game gun, especially for squirrels and rabbits.

The ten-percent variability from minimum to maximum pattern delivery shown in the table merely indicates the degree to which loads can vary between ammunition lots. The standard number of pellets in a load can vary by as much as a dozen in the smaller shot sizes, thus greatly influencing choke performance. Reloaders know several ways, through smart use of loading techniques, to open or tighten choke patterns. Random chance also enters into the equation. Nature follows certain physical laws that are always expressed in characteristic ways, but the chance of one event being repeated exactly the same each time is rare. Nature is playing the odds, and this is reflected by departures from the norm. Shooters can count on performance variation between ammunition manufacturers.

There is also much variability in how chokes perform in individual shotguns. Even consecutively manufactured shotguns of the same model with the same choke will display some differences, with one shooting tighter than the other. There is no particular scientific reason for this other than random chance, and hunters have to understand the kind of variability characteristic of their firearm.

Given the many sources of variation, the potential for having a full choked bore performing like a modified is real. For this reason even casual shotgunners should know how to pattern their gun. It's very easy and adds fun to the sport, as well as making the shooter more familiar with his gun and how it shoots.

The steps in patterning are very easy. First, find a safe place to shoot, and then erect a patterning sheet. By the way, nearly all gun clubs have patterning boards. Those shotgunners building their own need a sheet of plywood about four feet by four feet mounted on stakes about two feet off the ground. A sheet of paper big enough to trace a 30-inch diameter circle on is needed. Usually a piece about four feet by four feet, the same size as the target board, is best.

Two hunters check out the countryside for jackrabbits. Under these conditions choke size is important for small game hunters. Good patterns are necessary to connect on fast moving rabbits.

This sheet is stapled, tacked, or nailed to the plywood board.

Count off 40 yards, snap the shotgun to your shoulder, and shoot for the center of the paper. Don't aim as you would with a rifle, simply bring the gun up to your shoulder and fire. This tests whether the shotgun is centering its pattern.

Now the measuring process begins. Most shooters insist on taking five separate shots at clean sheets and then doing the calculations. Five does give a good average. Draw a 30-inch diameter circle around the greatest concentration of shot on each sheet.

This can be done by using a short pencil attached to a 15-inch string and scribing around the area showing most hits. Count each pellet hole within the circle, marking off each hole with the pencil to prevent any from being counted

twice. Determine your pattern percentage by dividing the total number in the circle by the total number of pellets in the charge and multiply by 100. Calculate the number of pellets in the charge by actually breaking apart a loaded shot shell and counting the pellets present. Do this with three shells to arrive at an average.

Just as an aside to the patterning process, try to avoid too much testing. Beginners or those not familiar with shotgun shooting may find recoil from the 12 gauge excessive. This can translate into flinching, especially when full powered loads are used. During actual hunting, recoil often goes unnoticed, or at least is not objectionable. However, during testing it is more noticeable, and it is best to have an experienced shooter do most of the shooting.

It's important to remember that shot shell

loads vary greatly in the way they respond to choke taper. The hunter who understands that pattern is the result of shot charge response to choke constriction is well on his way to a sophisticated approach to shotgun performance. The shooter can take this knowledge and apply it to all kinds of hunting.

Just what does all this mean to the small game hunter?. It means that by using this information with specific knowledge of game it's possible to pick load and choke combinations that will ensure success at small game hunting ranges.

Sir Charles Burrard, author of *The Modern Shotgun*, published in London during the 1930s, developed a mathematical method to compute the target area of game birds. Burrard's rule was simply that 88% of a bird's weight in ounces equaled the area, in square inches, of the bird. The same rule can be applied to most small game mammals hunted throughout North America.

Burrard further reported that it generally took two to five pellets of any size shot to yield a clean kill on a small game animal. This is a broad range, and can be influenced by many factors, including the toughness of a particular animal and the shooter's ability. However, from this spread it's safe to take a rough average and say that to obtain clean kills on game like rabbits and squirrels three pellets are necessary. Five would be better.

Before applying Burrards's rules, note that a 12 gauge, 1-1/4 ounce load of No. 8's contains 731 pellets, No. 7-1/2 holds 437, No. 6's carry 280, No. 5's 212 and No. 4's 168. At this point it's a good idea to use an actual animal to fully develop the example. While practical shotgun shooters may hunt any of several game species, the common bush rabbit is familiar to most shotgun shooters. Using Burrard's formula, a four pound jack rabbit would offer a target of 56 square inches (.88 X 64 ounces).

Now, using Burrard's formula as a basis, it's easy to pick the best shot and choke combination for our game hunting. If you're using an improved cylinder, the type most common on the right-hand barrel of doubles, 45% of the above loads would be 328 for the No 8's, 196 for the No 71/2's, 126 for the No 6's, 95 for the No 5's and 75 for the No 4's.

This would be the number reaching a 30-inch circle at 40 yards. Our bush rabbit was 56 square inches, while a 30-inch circle is some 700 square inches. This gives a relationship of roughly 12.5:1. Now divide 12.5 into the number of pellets reaching 40 yards, and it is clear that 26 No. 8's will arrive there, 16 No. 7's, 10 No. 6's, 8 No. 5's, and 6 No. 4's. Now recall that roughly three pellets much reach the boiler room of most small game animals to achieve a kill. Again, recall that five pellets would be better. This exercise shows that at short ranges of about 120 feet an improved cylinder, shooting any of the above shot sizes, would be adequate for small rabbits.

The full choke, most common on the left of a double gun, would produce 511, 305, 196, 148 and 117 respectively for the same shot sizes. Therefore, to continue the mathematics used above, 41 No. 8's, 24 No. 7 1/2's, 16 No. 6's, 12 No. 5's, and 9 No. 4's would arrive at our bush bunny target. It's now clear that a full choke using any of the above shot sizes is better than an improved cylinder bored shotgun, at least for small game hunting.

Figuring Lead

One of the most difficult shotgunning skills, for novice and old hand alike, is to understand correct lead. Lead is, of course, highly individualized, and therefore difficult to convey from one shooter to another. For many it seems automatic, while others struggle with its basics. Traditionally it has been considered important in duck and goose hunting, but successful small game shooters also require a basic appreciation of lead and follow through.

Three methods of figuring shotgun lead are in wide use throughout North America today: the spot and snap shooting method, where the shooter aims at a specific point ahead of the game; the sustained lead, where the hunter allows the gun to travel a measured distance ahead of the game, and then fires when the sight picture looks right; and the catch-up and follow through method, which is done by quickly mounting the shotgun, moving the barrel past the target, and squeezing the trigger in one fluid motion.

All three lead methods have specific applications in small game hunting. Rabbit hunting with a shotgun, in bush or open prairie, requires the hunter to get his shot off fast. Jackrabbits, taking advantage of minute cover, will usually present a fast moving target that hugs the ground. Under these conditions it's often necessary to shoot at a spot 12 to 15 inches in front of the rabbit. Actually, there are times where cover can be so limiting it's difficult to lead and follow through, leaving the hunter with no choice but to point and shoot.

When rabbits give the hunter more time—for example early in the season or under dense cover where the animals hold until the last possible second—greater lead precision can be attempted. At these times, the sustained lead method delivers good results. The gunner moves the muzzle of the shotgun ahead of the target for sufficient time to enable him to tell that his gun is travelling as fast as the rabbit. The gun is fired during the swing and continues to move after the shot to produce a correct follow through.

The catch-up and swing-through system can be applied in rabbit and squirrel situations, especially where animals are moving directly away from the shooter. The animal's position in relation to the shooter influence how the leading technique is used. Squirrels racing up a tree can be brought down by applying this technique, but with quartering shots it's necessary to use half the normal lead. Animals moving directly toward the shooter are very difficult to judge, and the sight picture, with correct lead, looks as if the shot will go into the ground.

A secondary factor, often forgotten in the haste to shoot, is that small game vital areas lie well into the forward half of the animal's body.

This is that classic heart-lung zone referred to as the "boiler room" by euphemism-seeking gun writers. Hits must be scored in this area. It's true that game can be taken when massive blood loss occurs to the back half of the animal. However, many times such hits will not immediately down the animal. The game escapes and can't be retrieved, only to suffer a lingering death. For this reason alone correct lead is a necessary skill for shotgun shooters.

Some of the older shotgun shooting literature reports that Remington Arms did a study during the late 1950s which indicated that 90 percent of all misses on game were attributable to insufficient lead. The failure to deliver a killing pattern on target was caused by poor judgement in either determining proper lead, or shooters not knowing the correct lead techniques. It's best to overestimate the required lead, and obtain a clear miss, than to hit too far back.

Imperative, too, is learning the methods outlined here and practicing these whenever afield. No one can really tell another hunter how far to lead an individual animal. No two shooters see the same sight picture. Nearly all shooters subconsciously apply the various lead methods, or some combination of them, without realizing it. Also, no two shooters possess the same speed of reflexes or muscle condition. Small game does not cooperate either. Few present good targets, and shots must always be rushed or taken at fast moving animals partly obscured by cover. The angles, speeds, and size of the animal all influence correct lead. Weather conditions are also important—the amount of light, fog or rain can change things. Cover is critical as well. However, the shooter should practice and always be conscious of the need for lead. Keeping close tally of the hits and misses will help any beginner better understand the results of his efforts. When in the field, keep in mind that what has worked once will work again. Look for a pattern. One will always emerge. Follow your pattern and success will confirm what is working for you.

The ability to determine lead brought this mixed pair of rabbits to bag. Figuring lead is important in shotgun hunting because of the distance at which targets are often taken.

Chapter 5

Reloading Basics for Small Game Shooters

An old Lyman handloader's manual, written in 1946, extols hunters and shooters of the day to consider reloading from a cost-saving point of view. The manual claimed that a box of twenty .30-06's could be reloaded for as little as 28 cents. If economy was needed back then, it is needed even more today. A box of reloaded cartridges saves between one-half and two-thirds the price of a box of commercial ammunition. There is little doubt that homemade loads are economical.

Economy is only part of the story. The wide assortment of components available today allows the shooter to tailor ammunition to a particular rifle or hunting situation. A variety of loads gives greater versatility to the rifle, pistol, or shotgun. Loads can range from light for short range plinking to high intensity loads for long range or big game shooting.

Reloading produces ammunition that equals factory ammo. Today's components, especially in the bullet line, make reloads as accurate as any offered by the companies. The rigid quality control on components such as primers and powder is unequaled in modern manufacturing.

This all makes reloading safe, as well as providing accurate ammunition.

Small game hunters benefit greatly by rolling their own ammunition. Most small game hunting demands a good supply of loaded cartridges. It's easy to fire off 200 cartridges in an afternoon shoot, whether 'chucks or prairie dogs are the targets. Rabbit hunting can consume a lot of cartridges. Ground and tree squirrel hunting usually provides fast action, so many cartridges get burned up there, too.

For long range shooters, reloading will improve the cartridge choice and provide an opportunity for the shooter to develop the perfect cartridge for a particular rifle. The options are many. For example, bullets can be seated further out of the case, allowing the bullet to nearly touch the rifle lands. This provides the best accuracy possible, and makes additional room for more powder. Different bullets, even custom made kinds, can be used, and a wide range of muzzle velocities created. Lead loads can be employed like rimfire cartridges for plinking and short range shooting.

There is also the option of developing high

Small game hunters benefit from reloading their own cartridges.

intensity loads. These require much care and experience in reloading, but commercial cartridge velocity levels can be significantly exceeded when the correct reloading components are assembled and fired in the right rifle. Many small game hunters become load developers in their own right, and an offshoot of riflery is often an interest in ammunition.

The most expensive part of the cartridge is the brass case. In many situations this is thrown away, but for the reloader the expended cartridge is only the beginning of a hobby that is both helpful to the shooter and economical as well. Cartridge cases can be used several times, with the actual number of reuses dependent on the case design and the kind of load being fired.

Reloading starts with an inspection of the case. Start by cleaning the cases, and then checking for cracks in the brass. Pay close attention to the neck area, and to the lower part of the case—the head of the cartridge. Cases with cracks should be discarded. Likewise, any case that shows a ring or bulge should be set aside. These can develop head separation—very dangerous to the shooter. Small game shooters have a tendency to reuse their brass several times. Reloaded and reworked brass cases can crack at the neck or develop head separation. Careful inspection reduces the chances for a bad case to pass through the reloading cycle.

Reloading rifle cartridge involves five basic steps:

1. *Depriming*—removing of the spent primer
2. *Resizing*—returning the fired case to its original size
3. *Repriming*—inserting a new primer
4. *Charging* the case with powder
5. *Seating* a new bullet

These steps can be accomplished using tools available from a number of manufacturers. Some of the best known are RCBS Inc., Lyman, and Poiness-Warren. Aside from the actual reloading tool, the beginning reloader will need a set of reloading dies for the given caliber, a shell holder, a powder scale, and one of the many reloading manuals.

A reloading manual is a must. They outline the steps in the reloading process and provide information on common reloading problems. They also include a table listing the many manufacturers of shell holders and the interchangeability of different makes. The manual presents the loads possible for a particular cartridge and breaks this down into beginning and maximum recommended loads.

This is a good time to strongly recommend that the maximum load never be exceeded, and that any experimental loading be carried out by working up the load a grain or two at a time. From time to time new editions of these manuals come out. It's wise for the interested reloader to avail himself of the most recent printing of these as they will contain new load information and point out new powders and bullets. Reloading manuals contain a lot of good information, and provide interesting reading for the amateur as well as a good review for the long-time enthusiast. These manuals are invaluable books and a source of information for all levels of shooters.

Buy one.

Step one of the above list is usually combined with step two. Cases must be lubricated prior to running them through the full length sizing die. Resizing restores the brass case to near-factory dimensions.

Depriming, full length resizing, and expanding of the case mouth to correct size are all functions that take place with a single stroke of the modern reloading press. On old Lyman dies, these functions were separate and a die was needed for each step.

The decapping is accomplished by a shaft that runs through the center of the die and pushes out the fired primer using an attached pin. Screwed onto the shaft, or incorporated with it, is an expander ball or button that passes through the neck of the cartridge. As it passes it leaves the neck with the correct diameter for bullets of the chosen caliber. The inside of the cartridge neck should be lubricated to help in this step.

Some reloaders are not particularly thrilled with the idea of having lubricant placed on the inside of the case. Powdered graphite eliminates much of the problem, as there should not be enough lubricant to damage the powder charge.

Sometimes, when home cast lead bullets are used, the expander button will not sufficiently expand the neck, and it will be necessary either to use a larger expander or expand the neck with a pair of needle nose pliers. In this step the important point is not to overexpand the case mouth.

Much has been written arguing the merits of full length sizing versus neck sizing. There was a time when neck sizing—that is, resizing only the neck area of the case to an extent that it would hold a bullet firmly—worked well. However, as case shapes changed toward the bottle neck style and away from the straight walled case, and chamber pressures increased, neck sizing was found inadequate. While reloading purists will continue to argue as to which is better, it is clear that neck sizing will work if the cases are used in the same gun. In many auto-

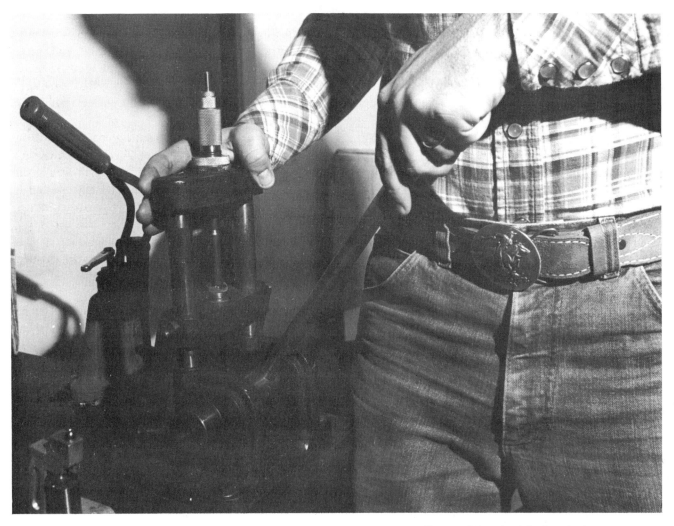

Full length resizing is one of the first steps in reloading. It is usually combined with depriming.

matics, lever guns, and pumps, full length sizing is necessary for the action to close properly. Full length sizing is always recommended.

Neck sizing has many advocates among advanced gunners and long range shooters. These types segregate their brass by rifle and load. Only brass fired from one rifle is used again in that rifle. The initial firing forms the case to the unique chamber shape and only the case mouth is ever resized. Resizing is only done to hold the bullet firmly during recoil and manipulation through the magazine.

However, the most ardent of neck sizers will admit that at some point all brass will have to be full length resized following repeated firings. The case just becomes too big for the chamber. Fire formed cartridges have the correct headspace for a given rifle and neck sizing preserves this fit. The argument favoring neck sizing says that the brass is worked more when full length sized. It's a tough debate. I have .243 cases that have been neck sized 50 times, and another batch full length sized a like amount. Neither batch has given out yet. It seems possible to get 60 reloadings out of most cases without worrying whether one is neck or full length sized.

Head space is defined as the distance from the face of the closed bolt to the point in the chamber where the cartridge is stopped from going any further. Basically, rimmed cases are prevented from going forward by the rim, and rimless cases are stopped by the shoulder resting against the chamber wall. Knowing what head-space means and how it relates to different cartridges is vital to successful reloading. For this reason, the sizing die must be set in the loading tool according to the instructions. Incorrect placement of the sizing die can result in incorrect head space.

Priming the resized case is the next step. This is a simple operation, but some precautions are necessary. The primer must be placed, anvil side up, on the priming punch or priming arm. Most reloading presses are designed so that priming can be accomplished when the case is extracted from the sizing die.

Care is needed in handling the primer. Oil or lubricant contacting the primer can break down the priming compound, rendering it inert, or severely weakening the mixture. So that the primer can be neatly placed within the priming pocket of the case, be sure any old priming mixture is scraped away with a deburring tool.

Primers are set in place with a gentle, steady

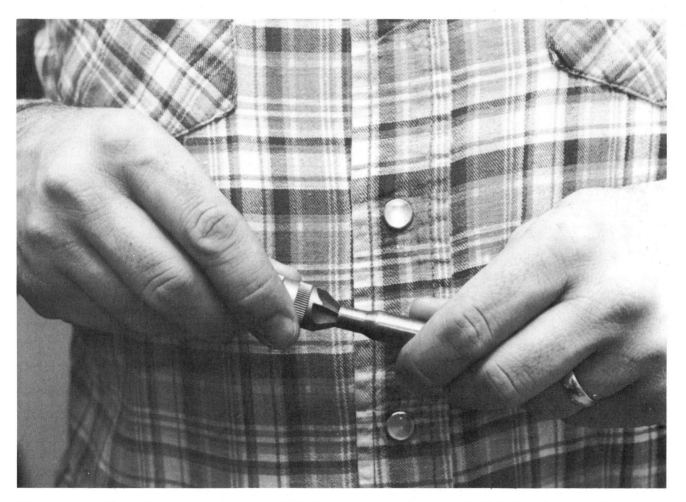

The case mouth is cleaned and deburred. This is necessary where lead bullets have been used or case mouths have become damaged.

Powder measures that throw accurate quantities are necessary for small game cartridges.

Primers must be handled carefully. Oil or lubricant collecting on any primer may weaken the priming mixture.

push on the press handle. The primer must be seated firmly against the bottom of the pocket. Failure to do this could result in a hang fire, since the force of the firing pin would be softened by the forward movement of the improperly seated primer. (Incidentally, you should never seat a primer into a case that has been charged with powder.)

After priming, the case is ready to accept a powder charge. Selecting a powder charge that meets the hunter's needs is what reloading is all about. There are a variety of powders and it is wise to consult a good reloading manual. In no case should you exceed the maximum recommended load. Many manuals suggest a starting load, and this is a good place to begin.

The charge values for powders are expressed in grains. The grain is the standard unit of measure for powder and bullets. All reloading scales are marked in grains. There are 7000 grains in one pound, so clearly a pound of smokeless powder will load more cartridges than most hunters shoot in a year.

Since there are several brands and types of powder available, selecting one can be bewildering. The best advice is to read several manuals and learn which powders are recommended for your needs. Generally, those loading for small game hunting choose faster burning powders than other hunting requires. Experiment with loads and powder brands until the desired accuracy results.

Once a load has been chosen, weigh out the quantity on the reloading scale and set the powder measure. Some writers recommend that each charge be weighed; there are times, especially during load development for a new rifle, that this is a good practice. However, the excellent quality of powder measures makes weighing each charge unnecessary. The scale is necessary to set the powder measure. The most important element in using a powder measure is to be systematic and consistent. The success of powder measure operation depends on a careful and routine technique.

Some powders, such as ball powder, pass through the powder measure more readily than conventional powders. This will influence the accuracy of the charge thrown, and it's wise to check every fifth charge by weighing. A powder measure is a great asset in the reloading process. Most of the IMR powders have more difficulty passing through traditional powder measures. For this reason IMR 4320 became popular with medium cased cartridge reloaders almost a generation ago. It flows through the measure

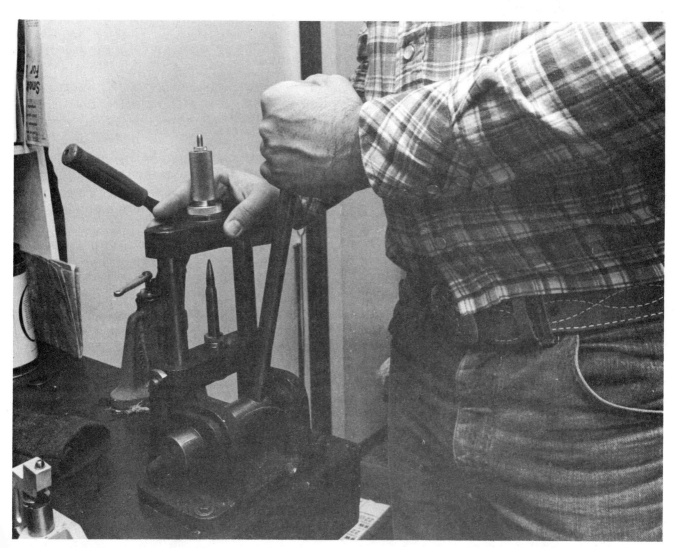

Bullet seating is the final task.

with ease and leaves behind accurate results.

The final step is the seating and crimping of the bullet. Again, set the die in accordance with the manufacturer's recommendations. A couple of factors determine the seating depth. In general, the rule of thumb for jacketed bullets is to seat the bullet to the bottom of the case neck. This rule will work for most bullets. Another factor is the total length of the case and bullet. In some clip model rifles, the cartridge will not work through the magazine if the bullet is seated out too far. Crimping is unnecessary unless lead bullets are being used or a tubular magazine is on the rifle. Bullets generally used in tubular magazines will come with a factory prepared crimping groove. Jacketed bullets generally grip the neck sufficiently so that no crimp is needed. The exception may be when particularly hot loads are used in the larger, heavy magnum cartridges.

Once seating is complete, the cartridge is ready for a final inspection. Wipe any grease or lubricant from the case and it is ready to go.

Loading shot shells follows the same general procedure. There are six basic steps:

1. *Deprime and size*
2. *Reprime*
3. *Place powder charge*
4. *Insert and wad on powder charge*
5. *Drop shot charge*
6. *Crimp*

The plastic one piece shot protector wads have greatly simplified shot shell reloading. In many cases powder charges have had to be reduced due to the superior sealing of these plastic components.

Loading tools for shotguns are usually designed for volume output. Many fine models now exist. The older tools that still abound are not usually effective in reloading modern plastic components, as they were designed for paper cases using wads of card and felt.

Shotshell reloading is much like rifle cartridge reloading. It is wise to choose a shell brand that is common in your area, and the same applies to your components. The combination of components is very important in shotshell reloading; use only those recommended for your particular load.

Reloading of rifle and shotgun cartridges is a fascinating hobby. Many shooters and hunters become serious reloaders when they learn the advantages of reloading. After all, the steps are basic and anyone with average intelligence can take up the hobby. And don't forget the economic advantage.

Choosing Correct Varmint Bullets

Bullet selection is a vital facet of small game hunting. Bullets do the job, and today's bullet must perform a number of things well in order to meet the requirements of our sport. Many hunters make demands on bullets that are contradictory. On one hand, we exhort manufacturers to produce accurate bullets, and on the other we expect varmint bullets to expand well at all ranges. There are many factors influencing bullet performance.

The major job of the varmint bullet is to expand violently and fragment on contact with a small game animal. It must kill quickly by transferring its energy to the tissue it strikes. In the case of a clear miss, the bullet must disintegrate upon striking the ground or surrounding vegetation. Penetration is not a factor, as the body and bone structure of most small game is soft and offers little resistance to bullet physics.

Factory cartridges are limited in bullet weights and styles available. In the .222 Remington the only expanding bullet is the 50 grain. The 55 grain bullet is found in the .223 Remington, .222 Remington Magnum, .225 Winchester, and the .22-250. The .243 calibers have only the 80 grain bullet and the .25 calibers have the 87 grain. These selections are too restricted and provide reason for the serious small game hunter to choose bullets from the many lines of commercial bullet manufacturers.

A bullet's job is complicated by many factors.

Bullet selection is important in small game hunting. Bullet types should be chosen with a specific application in mind.

Bullets must be matched to the velocity at which they will be pushed, the magazine length, and leed of the rifle, as well as the game hunted. How a bullet is constructed will influence how it behaves on animal tissue. The ranges at which animals are taken, and consequently the bullet's remaining velocity, also affect performance.

Accuracy is paramount in determining the proper bullet. Experimentation is the best method for deciding which bullets shoots best in your rifle. The process of elimination, based on a comparison of group size and muzzle velocity, is the best way to go. Serious varmint shooters will spend entire summers fooling with different loads, both on the range and in the field, in an effort to sort out the most accurate bullet for their particular rifle.

Sometimes shooters can go too far in choosing bullets based solely on accuracy. A bullet printing a three-quarter inch group is indeed more accurate than one producing consistent one inch groups. However, the bullet must also be an efficient taker of small game, and this means choosing a suitable accuracy level that also meets the requirements of field shooting. If a tight-grouping bullet fails to consistently kill wood-chucks at 200 yards, then group size has to be reconsidered in light of poor field performance. Perhaps slightly down-graded accuracy could be accepted from a different bullet that more consistently takes woodchucks.

Part of the testing process is becoming familiar with how the bullet performs under all conditions. There is no substitute for field experience. A bullet put to accuracy and field tests will reveal any weaknesses in design or misapplication of purpose. Small game hunting is the only sport where the hunter can actually take enough game over the course of a season to adequately test a single bullet's performance. A 150 grain bullet could not receive a similar test on deer, but enough 'chucks can be taken in a Saturday afternoon to get feedback on any 55 grain varmint bullet.

Range is critical because velocity is shed as the bullet travels. Shooting the .222 Remington with factory bullets beyond 200 yards leaves the bullet moving without sufficient velocity to expand rapidly. Some heavier bullets, like the 60 grain weights, lack enough velocity to expand the bullet at 150 yards. For long range practitioners this is an important consideration, because it suggests that hits at long ranges have reduced odds of anchoring varmints.

There are many commercially available bullets in the 50 to 55 grain range that open up well beyond the 200 yard mark. However, it's up to the hunter to find these by rigorous field testing on the game found in his home area. Bullet behavior on a small ground squirrel will be markedly different than on a rabbit or a badger. Pick the one that performs for your gun, for your game, and for your range.

Hollow point bullets have a great history of use in North America. This bullet style, sometimes called a dumb-dumb bullet, after Dum-Dum, the town in India where the British developed it, has an interesting past. In military

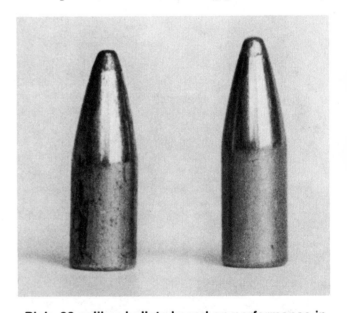

Pick .22 caliber bullets based on performance in the field. Accuracy and the ability to break apart at all ranges are critical factors. The 45 grain Speer and 55 grain Hornady spire point are typical of these bullets.

applications it expanded rapidly, creating large wounds, and was banned by treaty prior to World War I.

Under hunting conditions, hollow points are exceptional game takers, providing rapid expansion at nearly all ranges. However, there is a tendency for hollow points of all makes to perform erratically—one time penetrating deeply and expanding successfully, the next exploding on the surface of even rabbit-sized game. In .22 caliber the problem seems more widespread than in larger calibers like the .243 and .257. The jury is still out on this bullet design.

While gun writers might debate the hollow point's value, it has a large roll to play in active varmint hunting, and is a very valuable bullet design. No animal properly hit out to 200 yards will escape a .222 Remington using these bullets. The range extends an additional 50 yards using the .222 Remington Magnum or the .223 Remington.

Three excellent bullets for these applications are the Hornady 53 grain, hollow point match; 52 grain Hornady hollow point, boattail match; and the Speer 52 grain hollow point. The Speer bullet features a deep hollow point that assures expansion at intermediate level velocities. The Hornady 55 grain SX bullet will expand well at velocities as low as 1800 fps—reached at just over 300 yards with a .222 Remington. Don't let the discussion deter you from trying these excellent bullet styles.

Soft pointed bullets have traditionally given the best overall performance. Some of the better

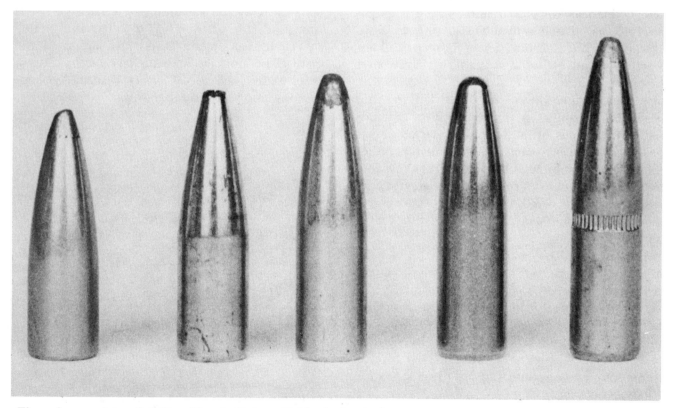

There is a variety of .243 caliber bullets suitable for both the .243 and 6mm Remington. Shown here: the 70 grain spire point by Hornady; 75 grain hollow point, also Hornady; 87 grain Hornady spire point; 90 grain Speer full metal jacket; and the 100 grain Hornady spire point.

choices available today include the Hornady SX 50 and 55 grain bullets, and the Sierra 50 and 55 grain Blitz. The Speer 50 and 55 grain spitzer are good choices in the .22 calibers. Recommendations for the .243 include the 70 grain Hornady and the 80 grain Speer spitzer. For the .25 calibers the best on the block include the 87 grain spire point and the Speer 87 grain Spitzer.

Commercial varmint bullets are constructed of light gilding metal jackets and pure, soft lead cores. Jacket walls are held to close tolerances and the entire bullet swaged—hit with a hammer into a die—to give uniformity. Bullets are probably better made today than at any other time in the history of bullet manufacture. Hunters benefit from assured performance and top grade accuracy.

There is a growing number of target bullets also labeled as varmint quality. These are also referred to as match or match quality. One classic example is the .22 caliber Speer 52 grain Golden Match—it's advertised as capable of target and varmint applications. Target quality bullets are, in theory, kept at closer tolerances than hunting kinds. For example, in Hornady bullets concentricity tolerances of hunting bullet jackets must be less than .0005 inches, while match bullet tolerances must be less than .00025 inches. The manufacturer achieves this by taking greater care with these bullets, and replacing the bullet swaging dies more frequently than on machines used with hunting kinds.

It really doesn't make much difference in hunting bullet performance, but strictly target types feel there is enough benefit to justify the higher price paid for bullets dropped from dies with tighter tolerances. Varmint hunters will find these bullets excellent for all small game, and it may well be worth the additional cost for extreme long range shooters to use these kinds for all shooting.

There is also much interest in solid jacketed bullets. Fur hunters find these bullets give better performance than soft points. In theory, hard point bullets leave behind a smaller exit hole and therefore less hide patching for the hunter. This may be fine for the fur taker, but these bullets have no place in small game hunting. Frequently they pass completely through an animal and don't transfer all energy to the animal. They are poor small game hunting bullets, and create an opportunity for wounded game to escape.

Bullet selection for varmint hunting is even more critical in the .243 and .257 calibers. Both calibers have a great selection of bullets available. The key is to select those designs and styles most suited for small game hunting, and that means picking varmint bullets out of lines designed for big game hunting—that is, choosing from bullets that give deep penetration and rapid expansion. These bullets need larger bodies to perform as designed. It leaves the small game hunter in a quandry, since eliminating big game bullet designs narrows the varminter's choice.

A good rule of thumb is to select only lightweight bullets. Again, these are designed for small game animals, with the two major criteria of providing an added safety margin by fragmenting upon striking the ground or vegetation,

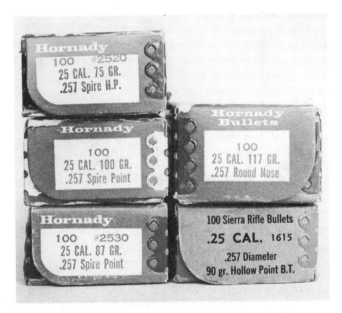

There is a .25 caliber bullet for every small game hunting situation.

and violent expansion against soft tissue. However, some selectivity among the different bullet companies is required. Lightweight can mean different things in different lines.

Nosler tends to produce bullets designed for deep penetration. For example, their 85 grain .243 Spitzer Partition will shoot through any prairie dog. However, their 70 grain .243 hollow point, boattail bullet is an excellent long range 'chuck and prairie dog bullet. The 85 grain Sierra .243 bullet is an excellent long range small game number, as is the Speer 80 grain Spitzer. In the .25 calibers, the Speer 87 grain bullet is frangible enough for small game. The Hornady 100 grain spire point is still suitable for varminting, while both the Nosler Partition and Speer in similar weight are too heavily constructed for routine varmint work.

There is a relationship between bullet performance and downloading that shooters must recognize. Care in downloading is required if performance levels are to be maintained. Shooters using .243 and .257 caliber cartridges must not drop velocities to levels where bullet performance becomes impaired. When velocities drop too quickly, expansion becomes unreliable and accuracy may suffer. Shooters who want reduced loads in the .25 calibers are lucky; they can select the Hornady 60 grain soft point bullet originally designed for the .25-20. This bullet can be driven as low as 1700 fps and still perform reliably at ranges under 125 yards. Shooters with .243 sized guns are not as fortunate, but can meet most shooting needs with the Hornady new 70 grain Super Explosive hollow point. It's designed to provide good expansion from ultra short barreled rifles, so it has real application in downloading. Downloading in the .22 centerfires is not difficult. Lightweight bullets, like the Hornady 45 grain Hornet and the .222 diameter 40 grain Jet, have been available for years and will accommodate shooters who want bullets that travel slower than 2000 fps.

In selecting bullets, keep in mind a cartridge's performance level. Truly long range shooting is

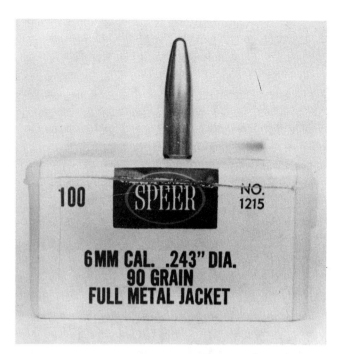

The full jacketed bullet has become popular for certain kinds of highly specialized varmint hunting, but small game not taken for fur should be dispatched using expanding bullets. The danger of ricochet is too great with full metal jacketed bullets.

best done with high intensity cartridges, capable of moving bullets with high sectional density to help buck wind with sufficient velocity to provide reliable expansion at 300 to 400 yards. Having said that, don't make the mistake of choosing the maximum load and thinking it will meet all your needs. Shots taken at 100 to 200 yards are the backbone of small game hunting, and cartridge-bullet combinations that meet those needs are all that's required.

Boattail bullets have become popular with varmint and target shooters over the last few years. Boattails, also called tapered heel bullets, offer greater stability over longer distances. The advantage is real, and extreme long range target shooters are convinced it tightens groups. For decades the military have used boattailed bullets for long range shooting in automatic weapons.

Slow moving, flat nosed bullet styles, like the aging .32-20, are particularly effective on varmints at short range. Pick your targets with bullet flight in mind.

Use them if you like. Chances are, the average shooter will never be able to hold his rifle in such a way as to fully benefit from these bullets. They are not necessary for good shooting, and can be expensive.

Safety has to be emphasized, especially for hunters doing their shooting near farm yards, small towns, or the urban fringes that seem to be everywhere. Big game bullets and so-called dual purpose bullets are out of the question. The potential for dangerous ricochet is too high. Care must be taken not to confuse the bullet types. Full metal jacket bullets are never used near habitation, as they will surely ricochet and travel for yards in errant directions, out of control.

Bullets fired from modern high powered rifles can travel over five miles from their point of origin. Varmint bullets, having reasonable sectional densities and light construction, can do damage even at the far end of their trajectory. The ability to expand rapidly and disintegrate means that some damage will result when they strike an unintended target. For this reason, the path beyond the target must be considered. Since many cartridges are fired during the course of one hunt, the need to understand where missed bullets travel is great. Pick your targets with bullet flight in mind. A solid backstop of dirt mounds or heavy trees will break up any varmint bullet with ease. An open expanse of soil, where a bullet strikes at an angle, will also induce fragmenting and provide a good safe catch area for your bullets.

At the risk of sounding like a nag, remember that before the trigger is pulled the shooter must have confidence in where the bullet is going to go, because he is ultimately responsible.

Chapter 6

Special Equipment

Optics: Binoculars

Binoculars help you see, plain and simple, but choosing a pair for your type of small game hunting is not always easy. The buyer is faced with a bewildering array of powers, sizes, shapes, and prices. Unfortunately, the advertising is geared more to sell than to inform. In selecting binoculars, careful consideration to a few basic points can mean the difference between having a useful outdoor tool of lifelong value or a nearly useless, bulky encumbrance.

Choosing a pair with coated lenses is a must. Older models may lack any coating, or it may be worn away, so you have to check secondhand binoculars closely. Hold the binoculars, whether new or second hand, at waist level, at a slight angle, to allow overhead light to be reflected in the lens. The lenses should appear as an even bluish-purple to amber color. These colors are caused by the coating of metallic salts that have been evaporated onto the lenses. Single coated lenses reflect a purple to violet color, while multiple coats produce a greenish purple color. A white reflection means at least one surface is uncoated. Don't buy binoculars without coated lenses.

When light hits a lens or prism, some reflects back, and the remainder passes through the glass. Coating the glass surface allows more light to pass through into the binocular. This improves binocular efficiency. The terms coated optics, fully coated optics, multicoated optics, and UVC coated optics have meaning for all binocular users. Coated optics have a magnesium fluoride cover on one side of the objective lens, one side of the ocular lens, and the long side of the prism.

Fully coated optics extend the coverage to both sides of the lens, and the long side of the prism. Multi-coated optics means that in addition to magnesium fluoride, zirconium dioxide and aluminum oxide are added. Finally, UVC stands for ultraviolet coating. This is done to fully coated optics by adding cerium dioxide to one side of the objective lens system. This produces the purple color seen on some lenses.

Good binoculars have two focus adjustments. One, located in the center, serves to focus the binoculars quickly; the second, found on one of the eyepieces or on one of the objective mounts, is called the dioptric ring, and serves to compensate for any difference in the strength of the eyes. Once the dioptric ring setting is determined for your eyes, memorize your setting to eliminate the need to adjust them later. The binoculars will then require focusing only with the center ring, resulting in quicker, sharper focusing.

Both focusing rings should work smoothly, yet hold their position when not turned. They should definitely not bind or have any hard spots

The selection in binoculars includes compact types, mid-sized porro prism kinds, and large, heavyweight, high power traditional binoculars.

when they are turned. Binding suggests misalignment of the binocular barrels, and means a reduction in the ability to produce clear, sharp focus. Compare several models in the various price ranges, and the differences will be very noticeable.

Binocular power is identified by a number on the top cover plate of the right-hand barrel. The second number, usually preceded with an ''X'', is the diameter of the objective lens in millimeters.

Powers range from six to 20, with seven power binoculars considered the standard. The power you choose depends on the use you will make of the binoculars. For general hunting or casual animal study, choose 7X magnification because higher powers are difficult to hold steady. Varmint hunters who can be deliberate in their targets can use the higher powered kinds. Ten power is tops for most hunters to hold freehand. Hunters who have to slog their way to their favorite varmint patch will not want higher

powers, because they are large and heavy. Purchase the lowest power that will suit your needs.

The whole area of power and suitability for hunting needs some additional discussion. Small glasses in big powers are here to stay. Some binoculars are no larger than a box of cartridges and about as heavy. Yet large, full sized, glasses are still produced and readily purchased by wise outdoorsmen. There is a reason for this.

Lightweight, high-powered binoculars are difficult to hold steady for long time periods, and require exact eye alignment behind each barrel. This is a very tiring process. Hunters should use lightweight binoculars when possible, but also have a pair of the heavier type for use when extended viewing is necessary. These are easier to hold and less fatiguing.

When most varmint hunting is done from or near a vehicle, a heavier pair of binoculars is fine. Where hunters have to hike into their preferred area, lightweight versions are the way to go. A good binocular kit would include one light-

Holding binoculars can be a problem. Here the thumb against the cheek method demonstrates one way of holding binoculars steady with one hand. This works well out on a prairie dog colony.

weight and a heavier, traditional style pair. This allows the hunter to select binoculars that fit the circumstances every time.

The size of the exit pupil is another major consideration in binocular selection. The exit pupil on binoculars can be seen as a distinct disk of light on the lens surface of the eyepiece. The bright circle is the amount of light reaching the eyes after passing through the binocular. To determine the size of exit pupil for a particular pair of binoculars, divide the magnification into the objective lens diameter. For example, a 7 X 35 millimeter binocular produces a five millimeter exit pupil.

The exit pupil must be sharp, clear, and absolutely round. If it appears ragged along the edge, or anything but round, the unit may have poor prisms or badly aligned optics.

To understand the significance of the exit pupil, you must consider how the human eye functions. The pupil of the eye will contract to about 2.5 millimeters in bright sunlight. In low light, however, the pupil dilates—gets bigger—to as large as seven millimeters.

When the exit pupil in a pair of binoculars is as large or larger than your own pupil, that pair will supply all the light your eyes require. If the exit pupil is smaller, the brightness of the image will be considerably reduced.

Exit pupil becomes important if you intend to use your binoculars in the dawn, dusk, or at night. For night work, an exit pupil of about 7 millimeters (which you'd get in a pair of 7 X 50's) is desirable, as this corresponds to the widest opening of the human eye.

One other consideration is the field of view. This number generally decreases as magnification increases. The average 7 X 35 binocular offers about 390 feet field of view at 1000 yards, whereas a large 20 X 50 produces a mere 157 feet at the same range. Field of view is the width in feet the hunter sees at 1000 yards. On some binoculars it is expressed in degrees. One degree translates to 52.5 feet at 1000 yards. In practical terms, the average varmint shooter will see about 80 feet across at 200 yards.

Wide-angle binoculars in the 7 X 35 magnification have fields of view in the 525-foot-plus range at 1000 yards. Wide-angle binoculars are useful for sporting events and for hunting in wide open areas. A minimum field of view has been established for wide angle binoculars. The 7 power must have 487.5 feet, while a 10 power must exceed 341 feet at 1000 yards. Any binocular with a field of view less than this cannot be called a true wide angle.

When purchasing binoculars, well-known brands are best. The better makers offer long-term guarantees on quality, performance, and workmanship. Many maintain service shops at the factory, as well as having selected dealers and repair centers across the country. Bushnell, a division of Bausch & Lomb, offers a lifetime warranty on their products. Their products are worth considering when field glasses will be used under harsh conditions.

There are several body configurations, the result of rearranging the internal elements. There are two prism arrangements: the porro-prism arrangement, consisting of offset prisms, and the roof-prism, the name being derived from the shape of the prismatic assembly. This changes the profile of the binocular into a more compact unit.

Professionals say that light transmission is somewhat better in the older, time-proven porro-prism type; however, many top-name binocular producers are marketing roof-prism models. A go-light hunter would logically select the more compact roof-prism model; on the other hand, the older porro-prism binoculars are often less expensive than the roof-prism models. Also, there is greater selection of power and objective lens diameters in the porro-type.

In binocular optics, the capacity of the instrument to retain sharpness of detail is defined as resolution. For the hunter, this is the ability to discern detail. The potential buyer can make a

Compacts can fit in the hand—very handy for serious shooters.

Wide-angle binocs provide the viewer with a broader view of the surrounding area.

simple test right in the store. Pick a particular set and observe some object, preferably at a minimum distance of 35 feet, then repeat this with a second pair. The difference in detail in the confines of a sporting goods store will give the shooter a good indication which is the better pair of binoculars. Pick those giving good resolution, as this is a prime indicator that lenses, prisms, and workmanship are correct.

This also is a good time to check for eyestrain. The human eyes will compensate for misaligned prisms by adjusting themselves to eliminate a double image. But the result is eyestrain or headaches if you use this kind of binoculars over a long period of time. This consideration becomes very important if you are doing intense nature study or scanning hunting areas for long periods. With good resolution there should be no risk of eyestrain during extended use.

Eyeglasses can influence the type of binoculars chosen by outdoorsmen. The eye must be within a certain distance of the ocular lens. In most magnifications, eyeglass wearers have no problem, but with higher power models the eyeglass does interfere with this minimum distance. If the eyeglasses are left on, the wearer experiences a decreased field of view. It's necessary to remove the eyeglasses to correctly focus the binoculars. This constant removing of eyeglasses can become a bother, but if they are left on, the reduced field of view is unsatisfactory.

To eliminate the problem, some manufacturers offer flat eye cups which are used by eyeglass wearers in place of the regular eye cup. The regular ones are merely unscrewed and the flat cup screwed into place. Another method used by manufacturers to solve this problem is to build binoculars with flat cups and include as part of the ocular an eye cup consisting of a rubber disk. The eyeglass wearer rolls the rubber cup back and has, essentially, a flat cup. The regular user would leave the rubber cup extended.

Rubber cups have one additional advantage. During winter's cold, rubber is far more comfortable to place against the cheek than plastic. While temperature is only a problem until the plastic warms from body heat, it can be bothersome and inconvenient during frequent repeated use. This advantage should be considered by winter rabbit hunters or anyone facing cold weather situations.

Rubber has made another important inroad into binocular design. Rubber-covered binoculars—all outer surfaces except the lenses—are now the rage. These are referred to as armored, and nearly every line has at least one style. The covering does protect, but not to the degree many think. Binoculars are still precision instruments, and any bad drop will misalign the prisms of rubber armored types as easily as uncovered kinds. The covering does protect from minor bumps, and reduces the noise in the field. Also, reflection from the body is eliminated. The rubber armor comes in camouflage or green, and is generally a good investment. One model, the Jason Perma Focus, is blue.

When it comes time to selecting your binoculars, ask yourself how you will use them. If you are a go-light hunter, perhaps the lightweight, compact pair or roof-prism binoculars of medium power is what you need. On the other hand, if you're interested in natural history and studying animal behavior while hunting, you may want the highest power and largest objective lens size available. This would necessarily mean bulkier, heavier framed binoculars. Perhaps you specialize in hunting colony-living animals, so wide-view binoculars are needed to give the desired view. Whatever your activities, trade-offs between binocular characteristics and the use to which the binoculars will be put must be made.

Remember, binoculars offer many advantages. The hunter can spot game that would otherwise go unnoticed, can bring small game closer to to the eye and check the route ahead. Binoculars are necessary to study wildlife and gain insight into the behavior of animals. The binocular gives the user the vision of most game animals, and therefore improves chances to detect and identify them. It makes it possible to observe or to hunt without moving, and reduces the risk of disturbing the game. This is most notably true for those hunting ground squirrels. Above all, a set of binoculars lets you cure your sense of curiosity. Consider the use, and take a clear look at any binocular you select.

Scopes

There is no room for debate. Scopes are a must for accurate small game hunting. Scopes have made today's small game hunting possible. No longer restricted by iron sights, shooters are free to take on more challenging shots previously impossible with the best iron sight. The modern scope is a rugged instrument, no longer fog prone and impossible to mount on the rifle. Most are reasonably priced and within the means of all hunters. Scopes make hunting what it is—accurate shot placement under a variety of conditions.

When hunters were restricted to iron sights, any woodchuck was safe at 200 yards. There was a brief period of time when receiver sights became popular, but their application was addressed more to big game hunting than varmints. In fact, it was scopes and scope mounts that markedly improved the sport of small game hunting.

Early scopes were delicate and cumbersome. Mostly made in Germany, where technicians struggled with lens manufacture for years, few practical models were available. While the use of scopes dates to the American Civil War, hunting uses were limited until the 1950s. Scopes were approached more in the way of a surveying instrument than a practical hunting tool.

Interest in varmint hunting—especially of woodchucks—grew throughout the period from 1930 to 1960. Along with this, the use of the scope grew. At first target scopes, like the early Fecker Combination Target/Spotting scopes, were used by woodchuck shooters. The scope went from the range to the field. Scope technology also grew, and it was Bill Weaver that provided the first commercially successful, American made scope featuring internally adjusted cross hairs. Other scopes remained target kinds, with external adjustments. Today, shooters can select from a broad array of scope models, designs, and configurations. For small game hunters, the choices in modern scopes have never been better.

Small game shooters have needs that any scope must meet. The scope must be matched to the rifle, the game, and the conditions likely to be encountered. In the West, black-tailed prairie dog hunting often means long range pot shots taken under windy conditions. In the East, woodchucks hunkered along the treed edge of some pasture demand a scope that can discern detail and separate the shadows. Optical considerations are important because of the great ranges at which small game can be taken and the

A rifle scope that mounts one and one-half inches above the center of the bore is highly desirable.

variability in ambient light conditions.

Scopes can be broken into fixed and variable powers. A fixed powered scope is one in which the magnification is set at the factory and cannot be changed. A variable powered scope can be adjusted up and down in magnification.

The power to choose is determined by many factors. It's critical to understand the field conditions under which the scope will be used and how this influences scope power. In open, long range shooting at distant targets, high powered scopes are generally recommended. These help define the target and make it appear larger. Low powered scopes are preferred for short range shooting under bush or low light conditions.

Range is critical. When all shots are taken at short range, and under good conditions, any scope performs well. Most small game hunters will find their shooting confined to under 300 yards. Beyond this, shooters generally have to use a rest of some type to hit consistently. Better and more specialized equipment is also needed. Even with long range prairie dog hunting, it's impossible to define targets beyond 300 yards. Vegetation, topography, or stones often obscure the target. Three hundred yards represents a typical top-end distance.

At very short ranges, like 50 to 75 yards, a scope's field of view becomes important. Without some practice, quick moving game, like a rabbit, is difficult to find in the scope. A wide field of view lets the hunter locate game more easily and line up on target quickly. Standard fields of view include 18 feet at 100 yards for the Leupold M8-6 power and for the Redfield Golden Five Star 6X. Specialized scopes, like the Redfield Widefield 6XLP offer wide fields for rabbit hunters and others who need the width. This scope gives 23 feet at 100 yards.

Fixed four and six power scopes work best under these conditions. Scopes like this can be used in many hunting applications from big to small game. These power levels have become associated with general hunting use, and over the years several manufacturers have developed ex-cellent examples. They are thought of as dual purpose scopes—used for small and large game. They offer the combination that works under field conditions for most game.

Scopes of the fixed four and six power variety offer several advantages. Shots at moving game are easily made, as human quavering is easily overcome at these power levels. Mirage and heat wave effect go nearly unnoticed. These scopes are generally compact and light. There is also a tremendous variety of reticle styles available.

Extremely long range shooting—distances over 300 yards—demands additional thinking. Scopes of ten-plus magnification will help the hunter discern targets, but field of view is sacrificed. Wobble and shake are also magnified, and mirage effect can limit use. With these factors in mind, high powered scopes do have a legitimate place for those who specialize in long range prairie dog or similar hunting. The word specialization is important here. The pluses of high magnification must be added to other advantages the rifle might offer—target weight barrel, special bedding, and fine tuned load. These, in combination with a high power scope, make a highly specialized package designed solely for long range shooting. High powered scopes are part of the package.

High powered scopes are not suited for general shooting. Wobble, mirage effect, restricted field of view, and size are too great. There are no advantages. These scopes are slower to get on target and more difficult to hold there. The shooter must be more deliberate, taking time to focus correctly and be sure the target is clear. It takes at least a few seconds longer than with a regular hunting scope to set, line, and place a high powered scope on target.

High powered scopes substantially add to the weight and profile of the overall shooting outfit. They are bulky, and their size produces minor problems in fitting gun cases and storing in gun racks. Any sporter or lightweight rifle outfitted with a large scope loses its inherent advantages of lightness and portability. These rifle traits took many years for the gun manufacturing fraternity to recognize as important to shooters, and they are lost when big, bulky, large diameter, variable powered scopes are clamped onto the receiver.

Variable powered scopes are one way to meet the needs of both varmint and other hunting in a single package. The 3X to 9X is now considered the industry standard. The low end powers provide suffcent field of view for close-in work, and the 9X is good for varmints at long range. The variable scope does, of course, offer versatility over fixed power models.

Variable powered scopes suffer from many of the same disadvantages as high powered kinds. There is, of course, the added expense—most variables average one third more than equal quality fixed power scopes. They are more delicate than the fixed power kinds, thus being more prone to breakage and high repair bills. Rough use is out of the question for these scopes—no matter what the makers might say.

Variable powered scopes are experiencing considerable popularity. The 3X to 9X offers a wide range of settings and neatly accommodates small and big game hunting with the turn of a wrist. The 2 to 7 power is also widely accepted. Both offer the shooter great versatility, and weight factors are not significant when they are teamed with sporter rifles. A Leupold Vari-X-II weighs 10.4 ounces, and when mounted on a Model 70 Featherweight produces a total package of 7 pounds ten ounces, including mounts. At this weight it remains light enough for mountain or woods use.

A point often forgotten in the discussion is that variable powered scopes can be turned down. When heat and mirage effects are extreme, dropping a scope to four or six power will let the shooter continue. In pre-dawn periods and toward the evening, or in dark woodlands, lower power settings will gather enough light to allow the shooter to spot targets. The added versatility of the variable can't be denied in these circumstances.

On rifles designed for a single use, choose a fixed power scope. Varminting rifles should carry a six power as a minimum, and as the shooter becomes more specialized in his shooting, power can be increased until about 24 is reached. Beyond this, power becomes a limiting factor. There are many times during the summer, out on the average prairie dog town, where heat waves and mirage will make shooting with the high power scope challenging. Heat waves and mirage will alter the point of aim significantly, and a clear miss is possible, even when doing things right.

High power scopes often require a sun shade. Leupold makes one for their line of scopes, and other after market designs are available. Bench rest shooters often design their own from rubber pipe or plastic hose. One fellow I know uses a toilet paper roll. Shooting toward the sun will obliterate the scope image, so a shade is a must. In the field it's sometimes necessary to improvise with cardboard, or even birch bark.

Reticle selection is pretty much a matter of personal choice. The four most popular designs are the cross hair, dot, plex type, and post. Everybody interested in shooting knows about the cross hair. It's the original design and offers the beginning shooter a good choice. It provides an aiming reference that is easy to use and understand. Big game hunters prefer fairly coarse cross hairs, while varmint shooters like the thinner kind. Under good light conditions the thin cross hair covers less of the target at long range.

Leupold makes something they call the CPC, which is really a cross hair with a steady taper down to the center intersection. Under poor light conditions this offers a faster reference to the target than the conventional cross hair. Other makers produce a fine cross hair specially for target and bench rest shooters. Varmint shooters find these useful, but light conditions must remain bright for these to be useful.

The dot reticle is a modified version of the cross hair. A dot is superimposed on a fine cross hair. It seems to float as the cross hairs disappear in bright light or against dark vegetation. The shooter need only place the dot on the target and shoot. Varmint hunters like this method. The dot covers just under two inches at 100 yards and provides a good reference for aiming.

The plex type reticle is currently the most popular and widely used by small game hunters. It consists of four posts that meet in the center like a typical cross hair except the outer portion of each hair is thicker. These point prominently at the intersection, making it easy to line up quickly on target. Small game hunters prefer these because of the speed at which game can be sighted. There is no time wasted in delivering an accurate shot.

The post is also a variation on the cross hair. It provides a thick black post rising up from the lens bottom with a fine wire running horizontally. The heavy post is easy to spot and line up on target. It's preferred by hunters working dimly lit bush country. Small game hunters don't usually use this reticle, as the heavy post will obscure game at long range.

In recent years illuminated cross hairs have become available. A switch is turned on to electrically light up the reticle. Batteries are used as a power source. In poor light the reticle appears red to orange. Rabbit hunters might find this an interesting option, especially for those hunting in deep cedar swamps and heavy bush or in northern areas where winter-shortened days create poor light, even in the middle of the afternoon. However, battery performance may drop during cold winters or after a rifle and scope have been left out in a cold truck.

There are many options available to the scope user. In 1977 Redfield began offering a range-estimating device on their 3X to 9X variable scopes as a special order feature called Accu-Trac. It works by rotating the power ring to fit the animal between two top wires. Range is read on a scale that appears in the lower right hand portion of the lens and is then dialed into the elevation turret. The hunter simply holds dead on, and the scope automatically corrects for the extended range.

Small game hunters can put this device to good use. The scope functions by comparing a known height to an unknown distance. The wires on the Accu-Trac are set for 18 inches—the same height as a standing woodchuck. As the power ring is turned, the animal is fitted between the wires, producing a good estimate of distance. The hunter has the option of using the hold-over compensator or judging bullet trajectory for himself.

There are many detractors of these systems. Some say they are too difficult to use under field conditions. The most common observations are that holding the rifle correctly is difficult, or that game doesn't wait around for a hunter to make a calculation. Others say not all game fits the 18-inch category. Gophers are, at best, nine inches high, meaning that some mental arithmetic is needed to arrive at the correct estimation. These are valid criticisms, but a number of situations do work out, especially in long range varmint hunting where the hunter has sufficient time and the animal cooperates by remaining in range. Good, solid, long range hits are nearly assured when the hunter does his part.

Another option that has proven very popular with practical field shooters is the compact scope style. First brought out by Leupold in the late 1970s, these scopes are lighter, smaller and less bulky than their larger cousins. They are at home on the current crop of lightweight rifles, providing a true weight conscious combo. Many lightweight rifles look odd when outfitted with large scopes, and the compacts fit well with downsized rifles. Compacts have a reduced field of view; Leupold's has 26.5 feet at 100 yards compared to the M8-4X with 30. Redfield now produces compact scopes with an extended field of view.

Some forms of varmint hunting, especially rabbit shooting, require that the hunter cover many miles. The lightweight packages are ideal under such conditions. My Leupold compact mounted on a Sako Hunter in 6mmPPC has proven to be a deadly rabbit and gopher outfit.

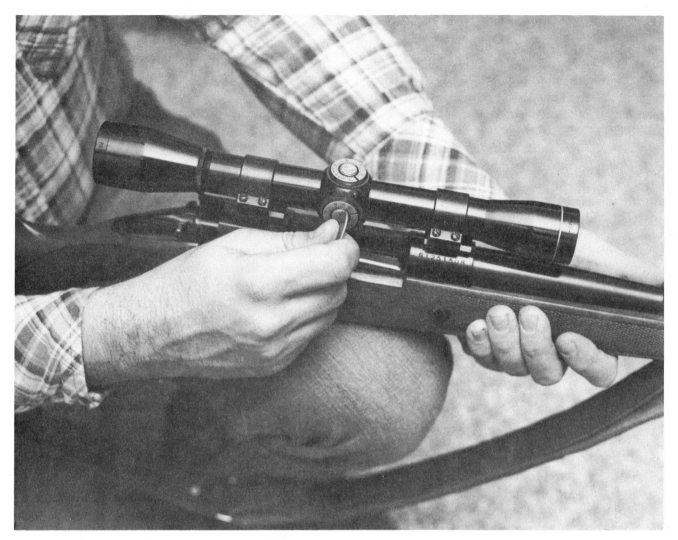

Some scopes are graduated to adjust the reticle in one-half inch increments, and others at one-quarter inch increments.

At less than seven pounds with sling and mounts, it goes anywhere and doesn't tire the hunter. It not only looks nice, but leaves the hunter more energy for hunting, as less is needed for carrying unnecessary steel, wood, and glass. Redfield has specialized in producing scopes with extra wide fields of view. These provide more field of view than regular scopes. For example, the Traditional Redfield 6X has 18 feet available at 100 yards, while the Widefield of the same power provides 23. Most varmint hunters never need the extra field. A case could be made where rapid breaking jackrabbits provide some additional challenge for the hunter, but in most other kinds of small game hunting there is little need for wider field. This is an option meant for bush country deer hunters.

A word about scope adjustment systems is necessary. Some are graduated to adjust the reticle in 1/2 inch increments, others at 1/4 inch, and still others at 1 inch increments. Be sure you know the scale your model is graduated in for adjustment purposes. Target models tend to feature fine adjustments, while older kinds are wider. Audible click adjustment settings are preferred over the noiseless variety. One click should equal one adjustment graduation on your scope. Remember, too, that adjustments are based on some fraction of a minute of angle, which is one inch at 100 yards. Thus, any scope with 1/2 minute adjustments would require two clicks to move the bullet one inch at 100 yards.

Scope parallax exists when the image being viewed through the scope doesn't fall squarely on the reticle. Older scopes produced parallax more than modern types. It can be detected by moving the eye up and down, left to right while looking through the scope. If the images appears to move, then parallax exists. This gave rise to the myth that "edge to edge sharpness" was a requirement of a good scope. On target and varmint scopes, parallax can cause a complete miss at long ranges. Most high quality varmint scopes now come from the factory with adjustable objective lenses to allow parallax to be removed. This adjustment allows the image to be focused correctly onto the reticle, and sighting error is eliminated.

What would the ideal scope selection look like? If a hunter had unlimited funds he could have whatever he wanted, but for most of us money becomes the central issue to having all the scopes or other equipment the heart desires. However, some basics are in easy reach of the dedicated hunter. Every hunter should have a rifle, outfitted with a six power scope, that can be used for all small game covered in this book. A varmint rifle, used solely for long range shooting of animals like woodchucks, rockchucks, and prairie dogs, should be topped with an eight or ten power scope. No more is necessary. Any lightweight rifle should have one of the compact models offered by Bushnell, Leupold, or Redfield. These make an excellent combination.

A high powered variable, something like the Leupold Vari-X-III in 3.5 to 10 power, should be fitted to one of the top end calibers for varmint hunting, like the .25-06. Basically, this means that three scopes will cover all the possible small game shooting situations any North American hunter will encounter.

Special features, like range estimation capability, bullet drop compensators, or illuminated reticles are nice, but not necessary. Go with a model that provides range estimation. It has broad application across the entire hunting spectrum. It will let the hunter concentrate on wind drift and mirage, but demands that the hunter understand bullet trajectory. Compact scopes are a must on lightweight rifles, and can't really be thought of as an option.

Spotting Scopes

The spotting scope is a highly specialized piece of equipment—and something beginning hunters might consider unnecessary. Equipped with a rifle scope and good quality binoculars, the hunter may see the spotting scope as redundant. Yet serious varmint hunters, especially those adept at long range shooting, cherish this extra equipment, and many won't go afield without it. All hunting can be made more successful through correct use of this valuable tool.

The selection in spotting scopes has really burgeoned over the last five years. In 1981, when I co-authored *The Hunter's Book of the Pronghorn Antelope*, there were scarcely a dozen models on the market. Pronghorn hunting and spotting scopes are made for one another. At that time, working as a wildlife biologist, I had ample opportunity to test nearly every available model, and found these scopes needed almost ideal conditions to be useful. Today that's all changed, and there are over 50 models offering the hunter a wide selection. Technology has improved the spotting scope, making it easier to use and a handier tool afield.

Perhaps there *are* some forms of small game hunting where a spotting scope is not necessary.

A spotting scope is a highly specialized piece of outdoor equipment. It is best used in combination with other optical gear like binoculars and scopes. This scope is fastened to the car window with a special window mount.

On the other hand, let your imagination work, and you will see many opportunities. A few years ago if someone had told me that a spotting scope would help rabbit hunters, I would have paid scant attention. Nevertheless, it's a fact that prairie jackrabbits can be easily observed with a good quality, high powered scope.

Varmint hunters need a spotting scope. It's used to find animals and to sort them out from their surroundings at distances where binoculars and rifle scopes can't help. It makes varmint hunting safer, simply because targets are positively identified. The landscape beyond can be studied and judged safe for shooting. A spotting scope is also a great way to confirm distant kills without disturbing the remainder of a colony.

There are two kinds of spotting scopes: the prismatic scope, and the catadioptric, or mirror optic type. Prismatic types are slightly bulkier and heavier. Catadioptric models predominate in the market.

Early spotting scopes were difficult to focus at long range. This was both a function of design and the great power of these tools. Many early models seemed to slip out of focus without being touched. These technological problems appear to have been overcome.

Spotting scopes are available in two basic configurations: fixed power and something annoyingly referred to as a zoom lens. Fixed power scopes, like binoculars, offer only a single power, while zoom kinds let the hunter choose his power preference with a turn of the wrist. On many fixed power models the eyepiece can be easily replaced with a broad selection of alternate powers. Most scope makers, especially in the Bushnell and Kowa lines, offer a wide selection of powers. Small game hunters are wise to choose a 20 power and a 40 power eyepiece. These will cover most hunting situations.

The choice between fixed power and zoom is strictly one of personal preference. Magnifications higher than 30X power are rarely used. Mirage effect, dust, and heat waves will distort viewing on most summer days, leaving top powers almost useless. However, for those who want it both ways, Redfield makes an excellent spotting scope that provides a choice of fixed 20 power and an interchangeable 18X to 40X zoom eyepiece. Simmons also produces a similar model. It's easy to pick one eyepiece and then change as shooting conditions alter.

Too much scope power can be a problem. Sixty power scopes are difficult to use on hot days. Heat waves distort the image so that it appears to move in and out of focus. Under these conditions selecting lower powered eyepieces is about the only way to go. Usually early morning is free of visual disturbance, but even during warm, fall afternoons distortion is possible.

Rubber armor is now common on spotting scopes. This is a great feature. Generally, spotting scopes are bulky items that are hard to transport. They rest on the truck dash, in a back pack or slung over a shoulder, all places where they are likely to receive rough treatment. Rubber armor will not save a scope from a fall from the dash onto the floor but it will help prevent damage suffered from light knocks and bumps. In today's downsized vehicles, gear left on a seat will invariably collide. Rubber armor helps in these situations.

Color is more important in spotting scopes than in binoculars. Used from a fixed position, a camo colored spotting scope is less likely to reflect light and warn distant animals. Since most spotting scopes are large when compared to binoculars, there is more surface area to reflect light. Dark colors, deep greens, camo, and brown prevent this. The traditional grey, pebbled surfaced metal of the better quality older scopes also reduces reflection, but as the surface wears over the years it becomes smoother and more reflective. Rubber armor will also wear, but a reflective surface never develops. When selecting a scope keep in mind the color and the light conditions under which it will be used.

Since spotting scopes carry much greater power than binoculars, they are more susceptible to body vibration and movement. Hand holding a spotting scope, especially when scanning for small game animals, is nearly impossible. A camera tripod, or a specially designed spotting scope tripod helps get around this problem.

Some hunters claim they need only rest their scope over some nearby vegetation and it's steady enough for most ground checking. One key advantage the spotting scope offers is the ability to discern detail. This is best accomplished with the scope rock steady at all times. A tripod helps do this well, and while resting the scope over a rock or tree is better than nothing, the tripod simply can't be beat for providing maximum advantage to the small game shooter.

Tripods help hunters in other ways. Once set, they remain lined up on target. This means less time is spent relocating the target, refocusing, and checking for hits or misses. A hunter shoot-

Some scope models feature a little iron sight that helps the hunter line up on target quickly.

ing prone, overlooking a woodchuck or prairie dog town, can easily move his head over to a set spotting scope and check for results. This leaves the hunter in nearly perfect shooting position for either a longer range shot or a follow up. It adds an interesting dimension to varmint hunting and helps the hunter become more familiar with distance, bullet trajectory, and downrange performance.

Spotting scope makers have now recognized these shooter-oriented advantages. Several models come factory equipped with quality tripods. Two recent examples are the Bushnell Zoom Spacemaster and the Redfield Regal series. Another feature for the shooter is dual rotation eyepieces. This means it's now possible to turn the eyepiece a full 360 degrees for more convenient line up of eye and eyepiece. Some models also come with their own carrying case.

Sighting-in at the range becomes easy with a spotting scope, and this is often a major justification for purchasing one. Since it is no longer necessary to chase each bullet downrange, a rifle can be quickly checked and reset. Even .22 caliber holes are easily seen at 100 yards under high power, and, with a target divided into one minute squares, scope setting becomes quick and efficient.

There are three kinds of ocular designs now used in spotting scopes. The rotational eyepiece has already been mentioned. Although available on few models, it's a boon to the hunter wanting a spotting scope for several kinds of shooting—it's good for target work, varminting and simple spotting. In short, it's versatile. The straight-through eyepiece type is the most common and easiest to use. Locating objects is simply a matter of lining up the scope and placing the eye to the ocular. Some scope models have a little iron sight to help aim and locate the target. The third type is the 45-degree ocular favored by target shooters. This kind is more difficult to use, but once on target is very good. Speed in lining up should not be critical with these scopes.

One accessory very useful for the long range shooter is the car window mount. The mount, tightened against a partly rolled down vehicle window, provides a steady base almost equal to a tripod. From inside the comfort of the car or truck, it's possible to scan the countryside with ease. It's an expensive accessory, but one every varmint hunter should own. In strong winds the vehicle might rock somewhat and interfere with focusing, or someone moving inside the cab might do the same thing, but these are small inconveniences when measured against the ease of spotting. It's particularly handy when checking new country from backroads for woodchuck, ground squirrel, and prairie dog mounds. It's a compact accessory that can be quickly removed from the scope, exchanged for a tripod, and tossed into the kit bag. The mount is a truly useful piece of hunting equipment which no varminter should be without.

Another trick used by many hunters is to mount the spotting scope on a cast-off rifle stock. The stock is held the same as a rifle and provides a steady hold. It lines up about the same as a rifle scope and eye relief set, and can be rested against a tree or over a rock. The scope must be a straight see-through model to mount properly on the stock. By the way, the spotting scope is heavy and must be mounted correctly;

Another favorite idea is to mount the scope on a cast-off rifle stock. It is a handy trick for heavy spotting scope use.

most hunters use heavy rubber bands and heater hose clamps to firmly join the stock and the scope. It's not a difficult project. It does seem strange that none of the scope companies have marketed the idea.

In small game hunting, especially varminting, a spotting scope is necessary. With other forms of hunting, like deer, it's not required. For the spotting scope to be a really successful adjunct to the hunt, it must be used in conjunction with binoculars, the rifle scope, and the rifle. Each optic has its special function, and enhances the others. Together, they make the shooter a more successful hunter.

Range Finders

These tools are a useful option for long range shooting. They are particularly helpful in small game hunting because there is often sufficient time and enough targets to dope out the distance. For years, the major criticism of the range finder was the amount of time needed for the device to go into action and produce an answer. This delay favored the game animal every time. However, not all hunting is the same, and varminters often have plenty of time to sort out distances. A partially hidden hunter can successfully use his rangefinder on several different animals. He can first determine distances and then begin shooting.

There are two models of range finder available to shooters. Both types work well under the right conditions. One model, the Sportview Compact Rangefinder, works by comparing animal body size to a series of vertical lines and reading, spreadsheet fashion, the appropriate distance. This is the same principle used by range finding rifle scopes.

The other kind, represented by various Ranging models, operates by bringing together split images of a different color, and using triangulation to determine distance. A double image appears in the viewfinder. Turning the distance dial merges the images into one. Once the images coincide and produce a sharp, clear object, the precise range is read off the distance dial.

A good range finder will provide an accurate estimate of the distance over which you must shoot. However, the device must be correctly calibrated. The model I used over the last eight years required frequent correction, and a calibration ritual became part of my regular trip to the shooting range. Calibration must be done against a known distance—the more exact the better. I found it easy to check settings against the 200-yard target stands. Any long range shooter regularly relying on range devices should develop the habit of checking the tool's accuracy.

Many shooters think optical distance finders can only be used on live game. This is not entirely true. One of the best applications of distance finders is range estimation out to various objects where game will be commonly seen. A good example would be determining range to active prairie dog mounds or woodchuck holes. Record these distances, especially at the 350 to 375 yard mark, and some astounding shots can be made. With the distances predetermined, there is no guesswork when an animal appears, for instance, at a den mouth.

This technique can be applied in another way. Determining distances from your position to various landmarks at the 200 and 300 yard mark gives the hunter a real advantage when game does appear. It's easy to read game as closer to 200 or nearer to the 300 yard marks and aim accordingly. Getting the range quickly and accurately is all part of this kind of hunting.

There are some technical advantages to estimating range with an optical range finder rather than the wire of rifle scopes. One is accuracy. The Ranging device is accurate to within one percent at 100 yards and five percent at 500 yards. Optical finders are not restricted to the precise 18 inch top-to-bottom measurement guideline. Also, not all of an animal must be visible for the range finder to function. It's common in small game shooting to have only a head and perhaps part of the shoulders visible. An optical range finder can work with any size target.

The Ranging product I have, an old Range-matic Mk 5, reads distances between 50 and 1000 yards. It uses a 6X18 lens. Today's models, like the Spectrum 500, estimate to only 500 yards, and that's good enough. I have yet to make a shot at 500 yards—on any game animal. Most prairie dog shooting is done around the 300 yard mark. Ground squirrels are commonly taken at a maximum of 250 yards, and woodchucks are large enough to be good targets at 400 yards under the right conditions. I never used a range device for direct crow hunting, although I have estimated ranges to various roost sites from hidden points in surrounding wind breaks when no crows were present. There is no doubt that an optical ranging device is necessary before hits beyond 450 yards could be made on most small game.

The range finders made today are a vast improvement over those only five of six years old. The optics are sharper and the adjustments more precise. Some are more compact and rugged. Others are even designed for short range bow hunting.

The benefit to all small game hunters, and varmint hunters in particular, is simply the accuracy with which distance can be judged. Mili-

Optical range finders are accurate but slow to use. They are useful for hunters determining extended ranges—say, 450 yards.

tary tests show that most people cannot estimate distance well, even on flat ground. When the terrain is more rugged, the ability to estimate accurately declines further. When all other factors are equal, range or distance is the most critical element in the small game equation. The better our range knowledge, the better we should shoot. Overcoming the limitations of our equipment across some distance is a real challenge in varmint hunting.

There is one final point about optical range finders. It won't matter if the hunter has doped out the range accurately unless he also combines this with knowledge of where the bullet will strike at that distance. Long range rifle shooting requires two things—accurate judgment of range and an understanding of bullet trajectory. A .222 Remington sighted in for 200 yards drops just over ten inches at 300 yards and a whopping 33 inches at 400. Where would you hold for a 225 yard shot on a 'chuck standing beside its mound? The answer is dead on—the bullet would drop marginally in the intervening 25 yards.

Chapter 7

Dressing the Part

Outfitting for small game hunting is important—perhaps more important than in other types of hunting, because of the wide variety of conditions and circumstances under which most small game is taken. For North American hunters, outfitting has come to mean how we dress and prepare for the hunt. It can take years to become adequately equipped and to discover what works right in one area.

Small game hunting takes place over a great variety of circumstances and weather conditions. Open prairie dog towns on hot, windswept plains, or winter rabbits closeted in deep, snow-choked forests, make unique and separate demands on hunt clothing. Walking conditions can vary from easy, to sticky or slippery mud, to deep, powdery, or crusty snow. The weather can vary from day to day and also within a day. It may be cool in the morning, warm and sunny in the afternoon, only to have high winds and low temperatures toward evening. In the North these variations can all be encountered in a short time span. Much is demanded of outdoor clothing.

Travel conditions can turn into emergency conditions. Those picking remote back country to do their hunting can be faced with impassable roads. Road conditions can change quickly, and even the most careful hunter can find himself stuck in mud and snow, where digging and winching become part of the hunting activity. Rain in the spring, dust in the summer, and blizzards in the winter are potential hazards for the hunter any time he leaves the comfort of his living room couch. It's easy for a hunting trip to develop into a full blown survival epic if the climate is not recognized as a major influence and possible danger.

Hikes away from parked vehicles are part of hunting strategy. Yet hunters forget that they will be out of easy reach of this comfort. Wise choices in clothing and good use of gear can greatly influence the success of the simplest hunt. Weather changes, like rain, can catch the unprepared hunter and his expensive equipment away from the shelter of the vehicle. Without proper clothing both the hunt and equipment can be ruined.

Those using all-terrain vehicles or snowmobiles have special clothing needs in order to be comfortable and practically dressed. The key to outdoor dressing is to have the right garb at the right time. Summer shooters face a far easier task

Hikes away from parked vehicles are part of most hunting trips. Clothing choice is important, and the quality of gear will influence the success of even the simplest hunt.

than hunters going after winter game, as the needs are simpler. Winter rabbit hunters face many decisions. The hunter should consider the winter months most challenging, and prepare with attention to detail.

Proper dressing for hunting starts at the top with well chosen head gear. Scientists specializing in hypothermia tell us that nearly 65 percent of the heat loss from the human body occurs in the head and neck region. Therefore, the easiest way to retain heat is to wear a hat.

There is a grand selection of seasonal head gear from which the hunter can choose. The cowboy or western style hat is good for warm weather use, but is out of place in cold weather small game hunting. Many shooters complain that western style hats catch on vegetation, bump the scope, and telegraph movement for yards in any direction. However, this form of head gear remains an item of fashion and is commonly seen in the field, being used for all types of hunting.

A light cap is best during warm seasons. Caps with long peaks are good if the hunter wears glasses. The peak shades the glasses and there is less opportunity for reflected facial light to betray your position. In colder parts of the range, a quilt lined hunting cap can be used. Those with storm flaps are best, and can be crushed to fit into a pocket or used with an improvised rifle rest. Mostly made of some kind of processed wool, these hats are excellent hunting gear.

The best piece of head gear for the small game hunter is a watch cap. These can be found in most army surplus stores, and the outfitter Eddie Bauer still sells them. They are excellent under a camouflage head net or cover during cold weather. Camouflage hoods that can be drawn up tight around the neck are also made more snug with a watch cap worn underneath. It's compact and easily stored in a pocket when not needed.

A watch cap offers shooters real advantages. It doesn't obscure vision. The lack of any peak means it will never interfere with bringing the scope to the eye. The best way to wear it is with the ears exposed, to pick up the telltale sounds of snapping twigs, crushing leaves, or breaking snow as an animal moves or breaks from cover. When winds build it can be tightly pulled over the ears. Wool is the best material for one of these; the one I have used for years is an old military type. It is about worn out but still performs well enough to get me through some of Canada's toughest winters. A watch cap is a highly recommended piece of equipment.

Heavy, well insulated caps are not popular with the fashion conscious. However, for hunters going out into extreme cold, a wool cap with folding ear flaps is an excellent investment. Some rabbit hunters actually prefer this type of hat. It is characterized by a pommel, smack dab on the

Wool caps and toques are some of the best outdoor gear ever designed.

top of the hat. In ranch country these are commonly worn during the winter months and are jokingly referred to as "cattle feeding caps". A hunter will never be out of style wearing one these in rural America.

Somewhat similar to watch caps is the balaclava, a knit cap that pulls down over the face and onto the shoulders, leaving only the eyes, nose and mouth exposed. Some models are incorporated into full body sweaters. They are good if using a snowmobile or staying out on very cold winter days.

A particularly well designed winter hat is the kind once common to police and military types. It lacked any kind of visor and was usually made of fur. During the fifties and sixties these became popular, or at least respectable, Sunday-go-to-meeting wear. The ear flaps, folded up along the outside, were tied at the top with a ribbon. In really cold conditions this ribbon was used to fix the flaps tightly to the ears by tying it under the chin. The one I use was given to me by a postman friend. My father uses one he got in the 1940s. They are excellent hunting hats in cold, windy country, and with no visor never get in the way of the rifle scope or obscure vision. If you can find one today, it's a worthwhile rabbit hunting hat.

An article of dress uncommon to most hunting literature but with good value for small game hunters is the bandana. A traditional piece of attire in the West, it was worn by cowboys and teamsters. It had pretty well died out until revived by sporty rodeo cowboys seeking ties to the past, and the more recent wave of urban cowboy mania. A bandana gives protection to the neck area. It can produce the warmth of a scarf, but does not slip, twist, or become caught in equipment and vegetation the way a scarf can. It is my own observation that a hunter can wear one less layer of clothing if he wears a bandana. This saves weight on long walks. Although traditionally made of silk, most today are made from various combinations of polyester, cotton, and nylon. Some also contain wool.

Bandanas have recently taken on new importance for small game hunters. Now available in camouflage colors, this traditional piece of gear helps modern crow and varmint hunters hide the neck. It reduces the need to slop camo face paint over the neck and chin. Serving two purposes—extra warmth and camouflage—this improvement has made the bandana doubly useful to the hunter. Winter rabbit hunters suited in white or snow camouflage can wear a white bandana to achieve the same goal. Both tricks work well.

Gloves are also helpful and can be used by both warm and cold weather hunters. Hunting literature fails to mention one significant fact: gloves used to handle or dress freshly taken game should never touch the metal portion of a rifle. Blood and other fluids soaked into glove material are very destructive to gun blues and some stock finishes. This is due to the acids that form and react with the metal or finish. Wise hunters use two different pairs, one for handling animals, another to keep the hands warm and to carry the rifle.

Use white gloves in the winter and the appropriate camouflage pairs in other seasons. Gloves vary from light, protective covers useful in the heat to those that protect from extreme cold. In truth, gloves and mitts are not the hunter's friend. They interfere with the feel needed to squeeze the trigger, and bulky gloves make gripping the rifle's forend difficult.

Gloves and triggers have been age-old enemies. Trigger guards on the old Colt Double Action Army were enlarged to allow a cavalry man to fire his revolver with gloves on. For years the military used mitts designed with special finger slits allowing an exposed finger to contact the trigger. These are now available for hunters and shooters. Most hunters leave their trigger hand bare and keep it warm by frequently placing it in a pocket or folds of the winter clothing. However, the fact remains that during extended winter hunting sessions the trigger hand can become very cold. It's a source of discomfort, but can be avoided by using correct equipment.

In conditions of extreme cold a pair of mitts are mandatory. Outfitting stores are now routinely featuring large, insulated, gauntlet type mitts made of cotton and Cordura nylon. The design is copied from the many armies of the world that must function in winter or northern climates. These mitts are especially good where hunters use a snow machine to get around, though their size makes them difficult to remove when quick shots must be taken. For this reason the best cold weather hunting advice is to leave the large gauntlet types behind and use a good pair of wrist length mitts. This will serve the needs of most hunters.

Wrist length mitts are best attached to the winter coat by a string running across the shoulders and down the sleeves of the heavy coat. My kids call these "idiot strings"; this is the method used to keep children from losing their mitts. When removed quickly to shoot or use binoculars, the mitt drops away leaving the trigger hand free to shoot. It will not, however, become lost or filled with snow. By the way, any mitt can be quickly pulled off the trigger hand by using an old Eskimo trick. Simply bite into the mitt and pull back, letting it fall at the same time the rifle is brought to the shoulder.

When temperatures are particularly cold a pair of thin cotton gloves can be worn inside large mitts. These gloves can be used for shooting with little loss of trigger feel or interference with shouldering the rifle.

One final note about gloves and hunting. I mentioned that gloves used for cleaning and skinning be kept separate from the those used for carrying the rifle. It is also important that hunting gloves or mitts not be used for other odd jobs. Filling the gas tank or greasing the front end of the vehicle will leave strong odors permeating the glove material, odors that can be picked up by resting animals at amazing distances. Having several sets of gloves or mitts, including those for hunting, a pair for cleaning, a pair for general use, and maybe even an old pair for changing a tire or pouring gas from a

leaking jerry can is the best advice. Keep dirty pairs away from your other clothing to avoid transferring odors.

Into the Breeches

The selection of pants available to a hunter is not as good as it could be. In years gone by hunters wore their old army clothes or used surplus versions. Wool riding breeches were considered top hunting fashion for years. Now blue jeans or cotton pants are the hunting rage. But for small game hunting in fall or winter conditions, especially where wind can come up suddenly, wool pants are hard to beat.

The selection of pants available to the outdoorsman is varied. Blue jeans or cotton pants are now the rage.

Finding a pair is usually the problem. Those made by Woolrich are excellent for this type of hunting. Also, Eddie Bauer supplies good hunting weight pants. The pair I use are called Penbucks.

The use of suspenders seems to be back in vogue, which is fortunate—they are excellent for holding up heavy wool pants. It also lets the hunter use a separate belt to carry a knife, handgun, ammo pouch, or compass. Suspenders let the hunter move without the binding at the hips common to a belt, and this is appreciated when changing shooting positions or squirming for cover. Suspenders are recommended gear.

The best shirts are heavyweight cotton. Traditionally, hunting shirts have sported bright colors and broad checks, but have now been updated with more modern colors and camouflage patterns. Western shirts, identified by the cut of the yolk and bright colors, are favored by many hunters, but they are usually tapered and not roomy enough when an undershirt is also needed. They give a bloated look. Thick cotton hunting shirts are roomy, do not bind at the wrist, and offer some padding to protect the shoulders from a rucksack or rifle.

Common in my father's era, heavy wool shirts are still very good hunting attire. They do not seem as popular now and can be hard to find. However, a long sleeved cotton undershirt, now often called a beer shirt, or long underwear uppers worn under wool give a hunter incredible protection from the cold—enough that one less clothing layer is required. These old shirts are usually outfitted with two large breast pockets excellent for storing a game call or a couple of extra cartridges.

The late Townsend-Whelan, an avid hunter and firearms writer, once said that wool socks are compulsory footwear for the serious hunter. He favored lightweight, medium weave wool socks that went almost to the knee. With hunting boots or boots with rubber bottoms and leather tops, wool socks are the only way to go. Medium-weight wool socks are hard to find, but a hunter's need can be met by using those wool socks favored by the cross country skiing clan. These are heavier than traditional wool socks, but go almost to the knee. A thin cotton pair of socks can be worn under the woolen types when rubber boots are used. Wool socks are mandatory for snowshoeing and hunting winter rabbits.

Since socks of 100 percent wool don't wear well, most manufacturers include nylon or other material to increase durability. Wool percentages as low as 60 percent are still good for hunting. With repeated washing and wearing, though, the amount of wool is reduced, producing a corresponding decline in comfort and insulating value. Because this happens quite rapidly, a hunter should outfit himself with three or four pairs at the beginning of every hunting season. Worn out socks have little use except for cleaning windshields.

The boot insole is closely allied with socks and boots, and is bargain priced warmth. An insole is, essentially, a foot-shaped liner placed inside a boot along the sole, offering super protection against the cold and extra comfort while walking. Rubber boots should always have insoles, as should rubber bottomed, leather topped boots. A wise hunter working in wet or snowy conditions should always carry a spare pair, either in the rucksack or in the vehicle. Most insoles are made of felt. They are inexpensive and add greatly to the warmth of boots, as well as absorbing moisture from sweaty feet or wet boots. In these conditions they should be dried out each night.

When temperatures drop and the wind rises, serious outdoorsmen wear long underwear. Many wonder about the old trap door, one-piece underwear made famous in countless western movies. The old hunting texts all recommend light weight wool "long johns" as the ultimate in cold weather safeguards. This advice is still valid. The rabbit hunter working fencelines or small bushes will really appreciate the one piece feature of the old "long john". The advantage to this old piece of gear is that there is no separation of the top and bottom pieces when

A good example of the type of footwear needed for cold winter hunting. Note the felt inner liner that keeps the foot toasty warm under all conditions.

sitting or bending, and thus no cold spot develops along the back.

Today long underwear need not be wool, and its use not confined to outdoorsmen. Two-layered suits with cotton on the inside and polyester on the outside make excellent light-weight outfits. Heavy cotton work-quality underwear will also prove useful. The choice of materials and colors is better than ever. Small game hunters might want to check the types used by skiers.

This author has a pair of 80 percent wool underwear, which are still best for extreme cold. Even under blue jeans, cold can be kept at bay for hours with moderate body activity. Some complain that pure wool is too itchy when worn next to the skin. This is cured by wearing a cotton layer below the wool. This makes an effective combination for all kinds of outdoor use. Breathability, heat retention when the hunter is inactive, and the ability to retain its warmth when slightly wet are points which still argue strongly in favor of wool underwear.

A Boot to Shoot With

Perhaps the single most controversial article of equipment is the hunter's boots. Boot making was once an art, but now it's a competitive manufacturing process. Unfortunately, many times this does not produce a boot that suits the hunter's needs. This is especially true in the northern states and Canada. Here hunting seasons can range from soaking wet to bone dry, and comfortably mild to bitter cold; snow conditions can vary from mere skiffs to drifted, dense snow packs that change the character of the landscape for the remainder of the season. Given the variety of conditions, it's clear no one footwear type or design can be adequate in all cases.

The hunter deals with this by outfitting with several kinds of boots to cover a variety of conditions. Any well shod small game hunter will want three or four types of footwear. Rubber boots are especially useful during the spring when searching for sign, or in wet autumns when fields become soft and muddy. The kit should also include a good pair of heavy leather summer hunting boots. These are the kind the outdoor magazines talk about and advertise. Most of the year these provide adequate foot coverage, but they are impractical in extreme conditions of wet or cold.

The third pair would be Foresters or Lumberman's leather topped, rubber bottomed boots. In the area I hunt, these are the closest thing to an all-around small game hunter's boot. With a wardrobe of footwear, conditions from warm to very cold are covered.

When temperatures drop and winds whistle, the so-called snowmobile boot, "skidoo boot", or snow pac is perfect. While there are dozens of variations on the market, the best have inner felt liners that can be removed for drying. Felt, a reprocessed wool product, is preferable, as other materials lose their insulating value when wet. Liners on some boot designs are permanently fixed to the inside of the boot. Avoid these at all costs. The material wears along the interior and they are more difficult to keep dry.

All boots, no matter what the manufacturer says, will leak at the stitching. This is especially so where threads have broken from harsh use. It is also true of the Forester type boot where the rubber portion joins the upper leather part. Any hunter working under wet or muddy conditions must keep boots well conditioned and guarded with waterproofing. Frayed or broken stitching should be redone. Also, it's wise to regularly apply waterproofing compound along seams.

With wear, the lining of boots compresses and the boot often becomes loose. A boot that fit well when new is now too big. Most outdoorsmen choose lined boots using the criteria for non-lined kinds. A size-eight boot and liner will adequately fit a size-nine person, once the liner has flattened with use. Excess foot room within a lined boot lets the foot slop around, and this quickly wears a hole in the liner or socks, and insulating value is lost.

Another tip is to tighten the laces no more than necessary to comfortably hold the boot in place. Over tightening reduces the insulating value of the boot. Some hunters cut the lace in half and tie the lower half of the boot separately from the upper half. For the best insulation the bottom half is laced loosely but firmly in place. The upper portion is then laced snuggly to the leg. This allows good circulation around the toes and heels of the foot—the two areas that become cold first—yet holds the boots tight to the feet.

Moccasins or mukluks are effective footwear in conditions of extreme cold where there is little chance of encountering wet snow or puddled water. These soft kinds of footwear don't provide much comfort, and most modern feet are used to arch support and ankle protection. While there are great numbers of hunters who believe that moccasins are good for sneaking noiselessly around the countryside, they offer little protection to the feet and are easily poked by sticks, stones, and roots. Also, moving from outside to a warm vehicle will cause the snow accumulated on the outside to melt. This

Some hunters prefer heavy, one-piece suits for their winter rabbit hunting. However, these suits can become too warm for the walking hunter.

soaks the leather in minutes, rendering them ineffective in the cold and leaving the hunter's socks wet.

These days gym shoes of all types are pervading the market place. Some of these have been designed specially for mountain climbing and hunting. Made from heavy nylon called cordura, and in some cases bits of leather and canvas, these boots should not be totally disregarded by hunters. They are light in weight, have good insulating qualities and are reasonably durable. They are, however, a very poor choice in damp conditions; melting snow quickly wets these boots.

A comment must be made on cowboy or western boots. These boots are made strictly for horseback riding, for which they are excellent. However, even those with the so-called walking heel are poor for walking. While providing leg protection and comfortable in their role, these sturdy boots are not for hunters.

Finally, what about jackets? A hunter, outfitting along the lines given here, will find that heavy overcoats are necessary only in extreme cold. Wool, especially in layers, will keep the hunter warm and dry under a variety of circumstances. Dressing in layers reduces the need for thick bulky overcoats.

In the North the popularity of the heavy parka grew from the desire to wear just one coat rather than several layers. In by-gone days those working outdoors in the coldest part of the winter would peel off layers of clothing as their bodies warmed. When they slowed, or the weather became colder, they would replace layers. Today there is less continuous outdoor work, even in pursuits like logging or farming. Thus the principle of layered dressing has fallen by the wayside and become replaced with the one thick parka or mackinaw.

Outfitted in woolen ''long johns'', heavy cotton or wool shirt, wool pants, good quality socks and footwear, a hunter need add only a top grade jacket insulated with goose down or newer Thinsulate. Dressed this way, it's easy to hunt in temperatures below zero.

Winter jackets should be finger-tip length and have a wide collar or hood attached. Many designs have a nylon lining with down quilted pockets. Unfortunately, many also have nylon outer shells. While this does provide light weight and sturdy construction, nylon is very noisy. It easy for a rabbit to key in on the swishing noise of a passing hunter. Luckily, down filled jackets with cotton shells are available.

Some hunters prefer heavy one-piece suits for their winter use. These evolved from the wind- and cold-proof clothing needed for snowmobiling. The combined chilling effect of the air and wind is much greater than that of still air. High speed snowmobiling is capable of producing very high wind chill factors. The snowmobile suit acts a lot like the old trap door underwear described earlier, except it's worn outside all other clothing. It contains all body heat in one outfit and leaves few places for cold air to penetrate. The air next to the body is trapped within the garment. It works extremely well for most outdoor uses. However, at times the suit can become too warm. Perspiration results and dissipating the heat can be a real problem since opening the zipper exposes the chest area to the cold air. Legs, back, and thighs are still wrapped in the warm suit, and the body does not cool down correctly.

Dressing for any hunting requires the right clothes, and going after small game is no different. Clothing should be comfortable and suitable to varying weather conditions. Weather specific clothing makes the hunter safer and in a position to better deal with emergencies. A vehicle breakdown, even close to safety, can present serious problems to the improperly dressed hunter. Match your clothing to the weather conditions common in your area.

Clothing needs for small game hunting vary according to area, season, and weather conditions. Proper clothing can ensure a pleasant hunting experience, while improper attire can make it an activity you won't want to repeat.

Chapter 8

Using Old Cartridge Guns and Muzzleloaders

It was late in the fall and most ground squirrels had gone underground for the winter. The weather was crisp, and although no snow had fallen the sky was overcast and dull. The trees were nearly bare and the fallen leaves produced a dense vari-colored carpet. There were gophers still active and they were fat from feeding on the grains lost during harvest.

The small gopher colony was before me. I knelt down on the edge of some scrub poplar. Knee deep in snowberry brush, I felt camouflaged enough to try my luck. Easing back the hammer, I quietly raised the 1886 Winchester to my shoulder. I held into the wind and a bit high and toward the rear of a fat ground squirrel standing straight up on the opposite side of the colony. The 260 grain bullet would drop onto the head-neck region of the pest rodent, I thought. A mild report, and I was on my way, pacing the distance to the still gopher. When I reached the fallen animal I could see that the old .40-82 Winchester cartridge had done its job well.

As I stepped toward the gopher I bent down and picked up my expended cartridge. I examined it closely. Finding it in good condition,

I placed the hull in my pocket and continued to the colony. This was my tenth year of gopher hunting using an old rifle and cartridge combination. Each year there have been successes, and the old equipment has never disappointed. Hunting any small game with obsolete equipment is a tremendous experience, and really challenges the hunter's shooting skills.

Black powder hunting has increased in popularity to astounding proportions. However, most of the hunting is done with cap and ball, or flintlock type rifles, with hunters showing little interest in old cartridge weapons. The result is that few have experienced the fun of small game hunting with old or semi-obsolete cartridge rifles, or are familiar with the rigors and demands of using old-style cartridges and rifles.

Any hunter undertaking a hunt using old gun and cartridge combinations is looking at a year-around effort. Many aspects have to be considered in the off-season: the gun to be used, the cartridge employed, the most suitable load, and getting in some concentrated practice. The search for an old gun in good, safe, working order, and the location of sufficient brass, can become major off-season activities.

Hunting small game with an old cartridge shooting rifle challenges all the hunter's skills.

Many hunters feel that the older cartridges are not suitable for small game or any other type of hunting. They feel these cartridges are underpowered and ballistically inferior. This is not correct. While some cartridges can be considered insufficient for deer, almost all are potent when used against ground squirrels, prairie dogs, rabbits, and badgers. In reality, many old cartridges develop good velocity and killing power.

Some of the better cartridges are the .45-70, .45-90, .38-56, .40-82, and .50-110 in the Winchester line. Others include the .40-50 Sharps (straight), the .40-70 straight, and the .40-90 straight Sharps. The Ballards .40-80, .40-70, and the .38-50 as found in various Marlin lever guns also are good.

This list of cartridges represents those still considered effective and capable of delivering good killing power. They all feature well designed brass configurations, all are Boxer primed, and use large rifle primers.

There are several advantages to using an older

style cartridge. Aside from the nostalgia, the older cartridge, because of its generally higher trajectory, requires that the shooter become a better judge of range distance. The hunter who gets a little practice with his old rifle and cartridge combination becomes a better marksman. These advantages extend to all the hunter's shooting efforts, and result in more enjoyment with shooting and hunting overall. A hunter making a good kill using his increased hunting skills and the obsolete cartridge derives a feeling of achievement.

Good, safe killing velocities are available from these old-time cartridges. The .45-70, which is probably experiencing the greatest comeback ever made by an obsolete cartridge, moves out of the barrel at 1350 fps. The old Winchester .45-60 with a factory lead bullet travels at 1320 fps, while the .45-90 with the same bullet weight

The Marlin in .45-70 is a good candidate for reloading with lead bullets weighing 200 to 400 grains. At reduced velocities, these old bullets are very capable small game performers.

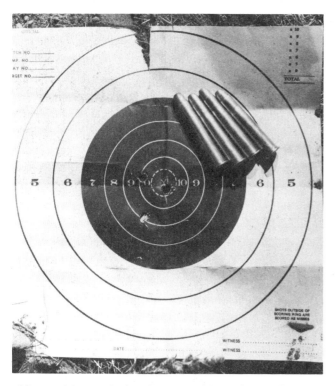

Many old, semi-obsolete cartridges have plenty of power and are accurate for most short to intermediate range shooting.

leaves the barrel at 1900 fps.

For comparison to smaller calibers, the .40-82 Winchester carrying a 260 grain bullet travels at 1500 fps and the .40-70 with a 330 grain pill flies at 1340 fps. These velocities are actually adequate for any North American big game at moderate ranges, and serve particularly well on small game taken at intermediate ranges. Since most small game is taken around 200 yards, these velocities will provide sufficient killing power.

One other advantage is the noise level created by these cartridges. All are classed as low noise producers and are very mild on the ears, although it must be said that the blast from a .50-110 equals that with any modern belted magnum. Generally, though, the muzzle blast is considerably less, and this is a definite advantage in heavily populated areas or when shooting near farm yards or the urban fringes.

Many of these older cartridges produce less recoil, or at least a more gentle recoil, than many modern calibers. This is a real advantage and allows the hunter to practice more without the fear of pounding his shoulder to hamburger. Recoil is often the source for a case of flinching, and reducing the physical punishment will help keep hunters from developing this habit.

Now that we have discussed the advantages of the old cartridge in comparison with the modern, one other problem remains. That is finding a suitable gun. There are actually thousands of old rifles around, but few of them are in condi-

tion to be used for hunting. A functional shooting piece is what you must look for, rather than a collector's item of no hunting value.

The overall appearance of a gun is often a good indicator of the internal condition of the piece. The first thing to check is the condition of the bore. If it is shiny and free of marks, with the rifling still sharp and clear, it is probably in good condition. However, the old corrosive primers in combination with black powder have often eroded the rifling of older guns. Obviously, one in this condition would not shoot accurately and have little value for the small game shooter.

Checking the chamber is a wise decision. Sometimes, while the rifling may appear in good

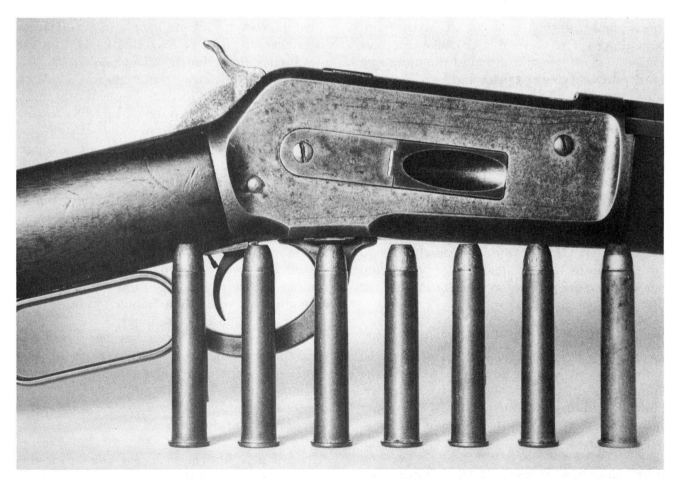

An older style cartridge demands new skills of the shooter. Better range estimation, more practice, and greater control of the shooting situation make the hunter a better marksman.

Using Old Cartridge Guns and Muzzleloaders 221

condition, the chamber will be somewhat worn. A sloppy chamber can lead to case extraction problems, or worse, blown and cracked brass. Also, case re-sizing can later become more difficult, and the number of times cases can be loaded is reduced.

In general, check the action of any older gun, seeking one that is tight and free of binding by any parts. Later, clean the rifle thoroughly to free it from accumulated grease and dirt. Pay particular attention to the action so as to remove any rust, and closely examine the parts for wear, pitting, rust, or damage.

Having considered what to check, the next problem is obtaining a rifle that is in the category of old or obsolete. Many fine Sharps or Winchester Low and High walls make excellent single shot hunting guns. Both Marlin and Winchester offered several large caliber repeater models. Then there are several of the more rare rifles which, because of price and lack of availability, are not really practical as hunting guns.

I think the best rifle model suitable for hunting is a repeater. Two of the best models ever made were the Winchester 1886 and the Marlin 1895. Both were made in a variety of calibers and large quantities of each were produced. Since such a large number were marketed, it's easy to locate a rifle in good, safe, working order. The Winchester 1886 had a production of 160,000 rifles, and the Marlin 1895 had nearly 40,000 produced in its lifetime. These large production figures mean good odds for locating a particular rifle in a desired caliber.

I have hunted with both the 86 Winchester and the older Marlin 1895. Both perform well, are well made, and reflect a workmanship that is unavailable in modern guns. This is one of the things the old gun user will immediately notice. The wood-to-metal fit, the quality of the wood, and the close tolerances on many of the parts would impress the most avid of modern gun users.

The availability of cartridges for the older calibers is often thought of as a problem. However, with the .45 RCBS basic brass, nearly all the large, old-time cases can be reproduced. This brass is a boon to the old cartridge user, as some 25 different cases can be formed in various stages from this three-inch hull.

A good source of cartridge cases are the gun shows held throughout the country. Watch out for cases still loaded with black powder and corrosive primed. The best cartridges are the later smokeless kinds. Many old cartridges made the transfer from black powder to smokeless, and a surprising number are still around. These, while often primed with corrosive mixtures, can be broken down and the corrosive primer replaced. A good, clean brass case is the result. This case can be safely reloaded and used several times with moderate loads.

Another supply of old loads can be obtained from custom cartridge reloading firms. Companies such as Beals Bullets in Landsdown, Pa., are willing to provide custom ammunition. Much of the ammo is hand loaded. Most of the brass forming operations are done with RCBS dies, or, in some cases, dies made by other custom die makers. The ammunition from custom cartridge reloaders is usually of excellent quality, although somewhat expensive.

The major reason for ordering custom ammo is to obtain a supply of correctly sized brass. Once this is fire formed to your rifle you can continue to reload the fired cases. Purchasing 20 or so from a custom loading outfit, and maybe finding another 20 at gun shows, will provide enough hulls to keep a hunter shooting and reloading for the entire summer.

Once a supply of brass has been secured, reloading becomes the most economical and suitable means of feeding an old cartridge rifle. As most modern handloading manuals don't cover a broad range of obsolete cartridges, where does the shooter find reliable load information?

Fortunately, the most recent edition of the Lyman reloading handbook does have a section describing loads for a few old-time favorites.

The aging Marlin Model 95 in .38-55 and the recent Winchester .375 BB show that lever gun lines are essentially unchanged.

Actually, any older reloading manual will cover some old cartridges. The older the manual, the greater the variety of old cartridge loads, since many old cartridges shared the same history.

Obtaining an old manual may be difficult, so it's important to know the book *Cartridges of the World*, by Barnes, which describes most obsolete American cartridges. Not only does this book give correct dimensions for the cases, but it also provides loads using modern gun powders. Many are good starting points for developing and working up a new load. The ballistic information also gives the reader some idea of cartridge performance. Another good source of information is *Handloader* magazine, as it usually carries an article outlining the history and suitability of a particular cartridge. Old *American Rifleman* magazines are also a good source of load information, and the earlier *Shooting Times* magazines often carried information on older cartridges.

Cast bullets are the backbone of reloading old cartridges. Some feel that good velocities can not be obtained behind these lead bullets. But with careful handloading, good velocities can be obtained. The use of paper wads behind flat base bullets allows some increase in velocity. Often the most common material used is blotting paper or hard waxed paper. Some shooters place a wax wad between the base of the bullet and the paper wad. This serves to absorb some heat, and reduces gas cutting past the length of the bullet, as well as allowing increased muzzle velocity.

Another method of improving the velocity in lead bullets is using a hollow base bullet. The skirt on the bullet expands to fill the bore, preventing gas from escaping. Also, paper patching will enhance velocity on cast bullets. Paper patching should be done on bullets that do not have their grease grooves filled. The paper should be long enough to lap the bullet about three times, and have the edges cut on a suitable angle so that they neatly meet when the bullet is patched. It's not necessary to use glue of any kind, and the paper need only be wet enough to

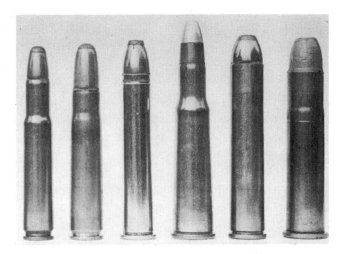

Older and bush type cartridges that can be reloaded for small game hunting include the .32 Remington, .35 Remington, .375 Winchester, .348 Winchester, .444 Marlin, and the .45-70.

adhere to the bullet. In this way, when the patch is folded, the center of the base of the bullet will be uncovered.

Gas checking provides the best method of increasing lead bullet velocity. However, this feature is no longer available on molds for .40 caliber size bullets. The entire selection of .40 caliber molds currently available is very small, and this is indeed unfortunate. Gas check style bullets are still available in .375 caliber, and there is one style available in .45 calibers. Gas check bullets should be cast as hard as practical, and the gas check then set on the base.

Jacketed bullets can be driven with high velocities and often will allow reloading beyond the original factory offering. Speer makes a .458 caliber bullet and this, loaded with 3031 or IMR 4064, provides a potent load. However, it should be stressed that to digest loads of this nature requires a rifle in excellent condition. The Marlin 1895 or the better 1886 Winchesters are the only rifles that should be used with these loads. Arms such as the .45-70 trapdoor Springfield should not be used.

Some mention should be made of cast, hollow

point bullets. Hollow point bullets are very good for small game hunting, but their effective expansion varies with the hardness of the bullet alloy and the velocity at which they are pushed. These two characteristics conflict, since the bullet will not expand if lead is too hard, while a bullet cast too soft can't be driven at sufficient velocity to expand. Another factor affecting expansion is the depth and diameter of the hollow point. If a hollow point is too deep, a rapid expansion or tipping occurs and poor penetration results. When hunting small game, a shallow hollow point in a soft cast bullet will allow good velocity and adequate performance on small game tissue. Don't expect the dramatic, explosive expansion from lead bullets commonly seen with modern, jacketed hunting bullets.

A good bullet mold is essential to reloading the old cartridges. Early Winchester molds cast their bullets the correct bore size. Today, if such a mold in good condition can be located, it is worth acquiring. The bullet weight is usually correct for the particular caliber, and if the bore of the rifle is in good condition a good group can be expected.

Lyman also made tools that had very good quality molds attached. Locating these is not very difficult, and the bullets left by these molds are just as good. Modern Lyman molds cast bullets oversized by a couple of thousandths of an inch. This excess can easily be sized down and should be sized if the rifle bore is still good.

A good bullet mold should leave bullets with sharp edges and clear grease rings. The mold halves should line up true and the top of the mold should not be pitted or damaged. The sprue

A receiver sight greatly improves accuracy. This Lyman, about 50 years old, will enable old guns to shoot as accurately as modern kinds at intermediate ranges.

cutter should not be bent. Checking a mold to ensure these qualities can mean that several may have to be passed over until a good one turns up. However, the result is well worth the wait.

The biggest concern in reloading obsolete cartridges is greasing the bullet. Beeswax has always been the traditional bullet lubricant. It is fairly soft and manageable, and at one time was very abundant. I still use beeswax in a mixture with Vaseline. The petroleum jelly acts to soften the harder beeswax, and makes the concoction last longer. Beeswax can still be obtained from apiaries or purchased from sporting goods stores. Get to know a local beekeeper, and you will ensure yourself a longterm supply of this valuable lubricant.

If beeswax cannot be found, paraffin wax mixed with petroleum jelly will make a good lubricant. Melt the wax and slowly add the jelly until you have about a 60 percent paraffin wax mixture. Let the mixture cool and set until required.

Getting the grease onto the bullet can also be a problem. The use of a Lyman or RCBS greaser-sizer is very valuable at this point, but not always necessary. Grease can be melted into a tinfoil pie plate and the bullets set in this and then left until the grease hardens. The bullets are then cut out of the grease, leaving the grooves full of lubricant.

It's not necessary to fill the grooves completely with the wax. As long as some wax is in the grooves, the bullet will receive sufficient lubrication as it follows the rifling. The problem is to be as consistent as possible, so that relatively the same amount of lubricant is placed on each bullet. Wide variation in greasing technique will show up in scattered shots and wide groups.

The final items to consider are the sights. Good sights are imperative to shooting an old rifle and cartridge combination. The sights on most rifles are adequate for short range shots or shots that must be taken quickly. However, the receiver type sight is superior to the buckhorn or similar sight. Superior accuracy and longer range shots are possible with the receiver sight.

Any model of receiver sight works well as long as it has a hunting type disc in the sight. For really serious shooting buffs, the old Lyman and Winchester peep sights make excellent sights and are surprisingly accurate. There are none better made or easier to adjust for height. These sights were calibrated for the various calibers, and the adjusting post is interchangeable. Be careful to check that the sight you use is correct for the caliber of bullet being fired.

The shooter is the most important factor in the old rifle and cartridge combination. The saying that practice makes perfect applies very much to shooting the old gun. The hunter has to practice until he is familiar with the trajectory, the sighting and the handling of the old combination. Plinking under field conditions helps a lot, and concentrated target practice develops a feel for how the gun and cartridge shoot. Practice not only makes perfect, but it burns up the ammunition. This gets the shooter reloading his old cartridges more often. This helps develop good reloading technique, important in this type of shooting. The more shooting that is done, the more discriminating the hunter becomes, the more reliable his shooting becomes, and the greater his confidence.

When I reached my gopher, I looked down at my heavy 1886 Winchester. I thought about the previous owners of that particular gun. Who were they, and how many times had that old combination been fired? I was sure that no old hunter would have used his .40-82 for shooting ground squirrels. Times change, and new life was being breathed into an old gun. It was useful again, and it was fun. Hunting with an ancient cartridge and old rifle has added a new dimension to my small game hunting, a dimension that other hunters may want to try.

Rabbits and Muzzleloaders

Can you pick the single species that's tailor made for hunting with a black powder shooting, muzzleloading rifle? Any rabbit at all, you say? How about one of my favorites, the cottontail. No other rabbit offers the shooter the opportunity to test his shooting skills at close ranges in rugged country. Cottontails are easy to find.

Let me qualify that last statement. Cottontails of several kinds exist throughout the U.S.A. and Canada. Essentially a broad, paint-brush-wide swatch across the map of North America covers their range from north to south.

For the muzzleloading hunter, this is a virtually untapped opportunity to partake in rabbit hunting at its best. The cottontail is a challenging target that demands the hunter stalk close for effective shooting at black powder ranges. He is also a skilled escape artist, or can hold tight, letting the unsuspecting hunter walk on past. All things considered, it is a combination that is hard to beat.

The cottontail offers something many black powder shooters like. The animal is as good for eating as any whitetail, and when properly field dressed yields a meat that is succulent and unique in taste. And since it's possible to stalk these animals right in their own back yard, the chance of finding one that has been pumped with adrenalin, and chased by dozens of other hunters, is greatly reduced. In short, it is an animal

The muzzleloading rifle is one of the more unusual ways to go after small game.

worthy of our tables and an experience for the palate.

The transition from modern scope outfitted rifles with the trajectory and high intensity offered by modern cartridges to muzzleloading can be difficult for some. This is especially so when hunting out on the open prairie, where distances can be deceiving, and wind and mirage are always present. In dense bush, handling characteristics between the two kinds of rifles are different, too. It's difficult for unpracticed shooters to become comfortable with the longer barrels and seemingly odd balance common to black powder rifles. Just going back to iron sights is a problem for most of today's modern hunters. Cottontails, because of their natural ability to blend into the environment, make careful sighting more crucial than when hunting with a scope.

A black powder shooter going after any game must practice intensively before heading into the field. The practice required is greater than with a cartridge rifle because there are additional skills to learn and routines to follow. Get to know your rifle, how it feels when you throw it to your shoulder, and what the sight picture looks like at different ranges and under varying light conditions. Practice, practice, and more practice are the three keys to success.

Most small game is just that—small. Problems about penetration and animal weight are unimportant in this kind of hunting. Yet good accuracy is critical due to the distances and conditions under which shots are taken. For this reason, many black powder shooters prefer heavy caliber muzzle guns as opposed to smaller caliber versions. They also give shooters some versatility, allowing adequate power for big game during the right season, and letting them move back into small game hunting to keep up shooting skills. This means there's a tendency for black powder shooters to select the bigger caliber rifles needed to deliver the downrange energy necessary to dispatch deer as well as rabbits.

Although muzzleloaders come in .36, .45, .50,

.54, and .58, along with countless custom sizes in between and beyond, your best bet is with something over 50 caliber. These larger calibers develop proper knock-down power and the range necessary for successful hits on all small and large game.

It is important for the hunter to use loads that are powerful and provide the kind of down range ballistics that make the rifle a sure performer. In my favorite .58 caliber, I routinely use 110 grains of FFg with a 285 grain ball, which would produce somewhere around 1500 fps and a muzzle energy of 1425 foot-pounds. This delivers about the same striking energy as the modern .30-30 or .32 Special cartridge and is sufficient for deer. In terms of outright load versatility, it's here the muzzle loading rifle shines. Loads can be easily altered. For cottontail hunting at intermediate ranges I would download a full one-third, to around 72 grains. For squirrels, a light load of 50 grains of the same powder has proven adequate for close range shooting. In all loads sufficient power and accuracy over the required ranges is maintained. By the way, for prairie dogs and badgers, I duplicate the deer load.

Iron sights are a problem for some hunters not used to them or just coming over from scope use. The best sighting tip is to learn the six o'clock hold, where the top of the front sight is placed at the bottom of the chest on the animal. This leaves the entire body of the animal in full view of the hunter, and makes it easier to concentrate on the front sight while squeezing the trigger.

Sighting can also be greatly improved, as can accuracy, by using a peep sight. Over the last few years the peep or receiver sight has become more popular with black powder shooters, and for good reason. The sight is easily used by even a novice hunter. By looking through the aperture and placing the front sight on the animal, good shooting is almost assured at reasonable ranges. The aperture disk is allowed to appear blurred, while the hunter's eye fixes on placing the post-shaped front sight on the exact spot he wants the bullet to go. This sighting technique is

The transition from scope-outfitted rifles with modern cartridges to muzzleloading types can be difficult for some.

particularly useful to rabbit hunters as most of this hunting activity is done under good light conditions. The average muzzleloading hunter can wring out an additional 50 to 75 yards of performance by simply using a hunting sized aperture sight.

Trigger pull is also very fundamental to good shooting, and correct pull pays good dividends for small game hunters. Most mass-produced muzzleloaders come with factory set trigger pulls around the eight-to 12-pound mark. Some judicious gunsmithing can reduce the trigger weight to about four pounds.

The dividend comes when shooting. It's possible to get a shot off quickly as the rabbit springs from its morning bed or courses along a back trail or path. Light trigger pull also means less flinching and more controlled shooting. In most types of shooting a light trigger will often produce tighter groups, but in overall small game hunting it often means more hits on moving animals and better success at ranges greater than 125 yards.

Although many factors influence muzzleloader accuracy, consistent reloading practices are most influential in determining group size. Uniformity throughout the loading procedure is necessary to achieve good shooting. Equal charges of the same type of powder must be used from shot to shot, and a measuring device helps ensure that this happens correctly. Seating the patch and ball has been singled out by professional black powder shooters as the most critical factor to repeat accuracy when all other considerations have been eliminated. The ball must be seated on top of the patch and into the barrel in the exact same fashion for each shot.

Start the ball the same way each time, that is with the sprue mark in the same position, up or down. It doesn't matter which, as long as it's the same from one time to the next. A ball starter is used to seat the ball into the bore, followed by a short starter that pushes the ball a short way into the bore. Modern black powder shooters use a tool called a two-legged ball starter to do this. The ramrod is then used to firmly seat the ball against the powder charge so that the powder grains are not crushed.

Small game hunters should follow some additional advice that black powder shooters going after big game can ignore. Number one is to wipe the bore with a damp patch followed with a dry patch after each shot. This softens the fouling and preserves accuracy. This advice is particularly valid where smaller bore rifles are used and several dozen shots are taken over the day. Small game shooters should be careful not to load down too greatly. Enough powder should be used so that the rifle delivers a sharp, crack-like sound. Underloaded shots, or shots where the ball is not sufficiently seated, create a hollow, boom-like sound. Weak loads create a thud-like sound.

Although many shooters don't practice this, it's sound advice to wear safety glasses when firing percussion or flintlock guns. This is more a case of do as I say, not as I do, but fragments from caps and burning powder embers can get in the eye. Remember too, the material coming off the pan or cap is burning, so it does double damage—striking with force and causing burns. Indeed, this is one reason experienced muzzle shooters wear broad brimmed hats. A wide hat lets the shooter peek out from under the rim and deflects any flying particles generated at the time of firing.

A properly functioning muzzleloader, with correct load and in the hands of an average shooter, should group into two inches at 50 yards. If it doesn't, it means load components must be varied. Experienced field shooters begin by altering powder charges by a few grains or changing the patch. The patch lubricant can also affect group size. Sometimes a simple trick like doubling the patch will increase accuracy significantly.

One thing frequently overlooked by beginning muzzle shooters is the effect of wind on the round ball in flight. It all boils down to sectional density; round balls have less sectional density than bullets of similar weight. The round ball presents more surface area in relation to weight than does an elongated bullet. As a result, the round ball is more susceptible to the wind than a similar weight bullet. Practically speaking, this limits long range shooting, and means that species like prairie dogs and woodchucks can be taken only with well-planned shots.

Cottontail hunters might want to try using a muzzleloading shotgun. These are fun—one of the real workhorse guns of yesteryear. At short range, cottontails can be easily taken with one of these, and provide a source of fun gunning unavailable anywhere else. They are surprisingly economical to shoot.

Unknown to many, black powder shotguns will produce the same kinds of patterns as modern smokeless arms. Dedicated shooters can do a round of trap with a black powder shotgun and perform as well as anyone using a modern pump

Large caliber muzzleloaders are preferred because they have adequate power for both small and large game.

shotgun. In short, the hunter is not limited by these arms, and surprising results are possible.

These guns require only equal measures of shot and black powder. The grade of powder poured down the barrel seems unimportant. Any kind will deliver good results, but FFg is preferred. Sometimes Fg is used in the ten gauge. Finer granulations are not recommended. Any shot can be used, but size does influence pattern, so some experimenting may be necessary.

Loading one of these is simple. The correct amount of powder is poured down the barrel. The stock is slapped to set the powder, and two card wads are placed over the powder and tamped. This is followed with the appropriate amount of shot. Wads are necessary and can be cut from pasteboard. Milk carton cardboard works well. Commercially available felt and older overshot wads work well, too. The wad is placed over the shot and pressed lightly with the ramrod.

Under hunting conditions, which usually means overcast skies, excessive wind, thick fog, rain, snow storms, and animals obscured by vegetation, the difficulty associated with cottontails being a small target is made plain. It is for

these reasons that the hunter has to practice long before going afield. Add to this the difficulty of estimating range, and it is clear that the hunter must be intimately familiar with his rifle's performance and fit.

Cottontails demand that a hunter shoot speedily. In the bush country that's home to most cottontails, the animal wastes no time putting distance and cover between himself and the hunter. This means any animal carelessly disturbed by your approach will not wait around attempting to sort out the danger. The animals simply move out. In the late fall and early winter, when most of this hunting occurs, the cottontail lives a solitary life, in a relatively fixed home range, occupying five or six acres. They don't move unless pushed and then do so quickly. A shooter must be ready to shoot just as quickly.

Some hunters feel the flash of a muzzleloading rifle puts game into flight. This may be partly true with some big game. However, it seems neither the flash or the large amount of smoke generated at firing disturbs the cottontail. Rifle report is more likely to provoke animals into moving than anything else.

Getting close to your quarry is the bottom line in this hunting. Even a crack shot who has practiced all season is hopelessly lost if he cannot stalk properly and get himself within the taking range of his muzzleloader. Some hunters who are very dedicated to the hunt and truly skillful outdoorsmen, will attempt too close an approach. A hunter has to be cautioned against this. Any stalk to within 50 to 100 yards is sufficient for the average hunter. Trying to reduce the range under 50 yards brings with it increased risk of spooking the rabbit just as the rifle is moved to the shoulder. Remember, all members of the rabbit family have large, well developed eyes that are alert for movements in the surrounding countryside, and respond to any shadow that looks like an approaching predator. The key is to get close, but not so close as to cause a frustrating runoff or an overly hurried shot at a moving animal.

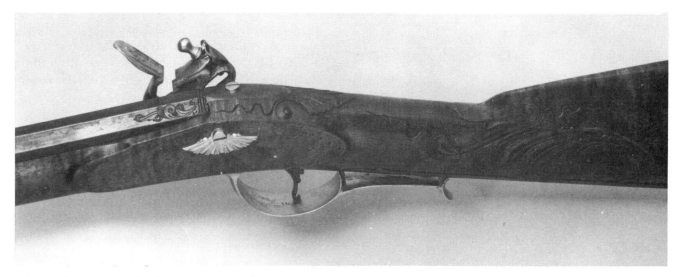

Some hunters prefer flintlock rifles. Cap types are the other option.

Soft lead balls travelling at moderate velocities will not damage a lot of game meat. On a rabbit, lung shots are always best for the two traditional reasons—quick kills and little damaged meat. However, both can be assured by using soft cast balls of pure lead, as these will deform on contact and provide some of the mushrooming effect common to modern bullets. In deforming, soft lead transfers its energy to the animal's tissue, creating shock and hemorrhaging in its path. Essentially, this is how any bullet kills, but the round ball does this job at a much slower rate than the modern hollow point with a thin jacket. The result is less damage to edible parts of the animal.

Rabbits react differently to being taken with a muzzleloader than a centerfire rifle. Many rabbits will show little reaction to being hit with a muzzle gun. Some, especially those running, will not miss a step and quickly move out of sight or into deeper cover. It's then important to find tracks and check for sign.

Remember, too, that any muzzleloading rifle has to be prepared for winter and late fall use. Heavy grease and oil that protect the lock during the summer will create problems in the winter. On flintlocks, stiff grease can reduce the strike needed to ignite the pan. Hammers on cap and ball guns can likewise freeze. Triggers become stiff, and some commercial muzzle guns come from the factory with such rough triggers—the result of poor polishing—that this is aggravated. Trigger pulls become creepy and uneven. Removing oil and grease from around the lock spring, and additional polishing of the trigger parts, help reduce these problems.

Muzzleloading hunters are not limiting themselves when they go after cottontails. Rather, they are using a completely new or different set of skills and abilities to bring game meat to the table. For the average blackpowder hunter, cottontails are an excellent beginning on the way to taking big game with a muzzle gun. In no other kind of hunting are the challenges exactly the same and as varied. The cottontail is tops in terms of matching the gun and shooting skills to the game. It requires good effort on the part of the hunter, demands black powder skills, good rifle handling, and accurate shooting with all this put to the test in a bush-like environment.

Chapter 9

Shooting Skills and Tips

Game at a Distance

Game at a distance—long range shooting, is the major challenge of varmint and small game hunting. It demands most from the hunter. Here, it's all on the line. Skillful use of firearms, knowledge about animal behavior, use of terrain, stalking, and marksmanship all come together. No two shots are the same, conditions change quickly, and action is fast. Any hunter with red blood coursing through his veins will be challenged and thrilled.

Excitement isn't enough. Good technique is needed, but what does good technique really mean? How do I know when I've got it? Some hunters may hit from time to time, while others only take close in "easy " or "sissy" shots. Good technique means hitting game consistently, every time, or almost every time, you shoot. It means being in full control of the shooting situation, finding, selecting, and turning down shots as required. It means reading the environment and methodically putting your shot together—marshaling skills you've learned. Prairie dogs, open field jackrabbits, the various ground squirrels and woodchucks are tempting targets, but re-

quire that the hunter does his part before this kind of shooting becomes anything more than long distance frustration. Routine success is the measure of a good long-range shooter. The ultimate test of good technique is repeatability. Can I repeat that 250 yard shot every time out?

Fundamental to consistent shooting is the ability to judge range accurately and reliably. There is nothing complicated or magical about determining distance out to game. It's done by practice and familiarity with the countryside. Over the years, techniques have evolved that, when applied carefully, provide good estimates of distance. All are easily learned and can be combined together to help the shooter sort out how far is too far.

The *football field* method has been foisted onto hunters for years as the quickest way to become a good judge of distance. Based on the dubious premise that everybody knows how long a football field is, it takes the familiar and attempts to transpose this to the unfamiliar. It's not my favorite, but it works where hunters are able to relate clear images of football field lengths to the outdoors. Most never develop this ability to a high enough degree for the technique

Successful shooters develop mental pictures of the distances over which they shoot.

to be reliable. Unless you're an avid fan going to every game, (television doesn't count), and paying strict attention to the distance the ball is moved with each down, retaining a strong a mental image of this distance, the dissimilarity between a football field and the back forty will defeat your best efforts. Yet for some it works well, and there are hunters who brag about their ability to compare distance to football fields.

There are other problems with this method. One is the hunter's inability to reliably judge successive increments of range.The first 100 yards is no problem for even casual hunters, but inaccuracies creep in when attempting estimates for the following 100 yard increments. These incremental guesses are each subject to some error, and the combined result produces misjudgement. For some reason, the human eye tells the brain to compare each succeeding unit of 100 yards with the previous. In our mind we try to

make each 100 yard unit look equal to the first, producing a gross overestimation of actual distance.

However, these eye and gray matter problems can be gotten around by discarding the incremental approach and developing mental pictures of certain fixed ranges or distance examples. For example, my mental image of 250 yards out on my favorite prairie dog town can be transposed to another prairie dog town where conditions are similar. It works well, especially where new countryside resembles my mind's photograph. Comparing an unknown distance to a known range, in similar country, is one of the best methods of range estimation available to the hunter.

Measuring to successful long range hits is a good way to build up a catalog of known distances in your mind. Measuring can be accomplished by using a tape, chain, or rope of known length, but for most hunters this is too much hassle. Range finders can be helpful. Cyclometers, the kind used by joggers, will help give accurate distances. However, good old pacing is the easiest and most familiar technique for hunters. Simply practice pacing on level ground. Measure about 20 of your paces and record the average length somewhere in your loading records or field book. Every time you make a successful shot, pace off the distance to the carcass and record the figure. Whenever possible, do the same with clear misses as these will often be more instructional than solid hits.

The advantage of recorded information is never lost. Back in high school my shooting buddy, Doug Blakely, and I routinely measured the distance to our gopher kills. We had a mutual friend, Wayne Yerhoff, a guy who by today's standards would be considered a math nerd, who took our recorded distances and compiled some enlightening statistics. He was also a reasonable shot, so he understood the kind of arithmetic interesting to shooters. He told us our average range for hits, average range of misses, the range most commonly used, and had separate columns for average short and long range hits. Wayne even supplied confidence levels.

These figures, gleaned by mere high school boys in the early 1960s, are as revealing today as they were interesting then. Our average long range hit with a .222 Remington was 125 yards, average for the short range was 75 yards. Longest shot, taken in 1963, was 234 yards on a lone gopher, along a fence line, at the edge of the pasture. Looking at these notes today, I know exactly what 234 yards looks like out on Clarence Weinberger's farm. The gopher patch still exists, and I could stand today in as near the same spot as my mental picture would let me, and repeat that shot. I might use a different rifle, I am much older, I wear glasses now, and I weigh a hell of a lot more, but that distance is 234 yards, and that hasn't changed. There would be no question on the distance.

Hunters can also judge distance by *perspective*. This is done by comparing the relative size of the animal to its surroundings. For this technique to work, hunters must be familiar with the silhouette shapes of various small game animals, especially those routinely taken at long distance. Woodchucks and prairie dogs fit this category.

Perspective means keen judgement based on lots of field experience. Aside from human error or lack of familiarity, light and atmospheric conditions can complicate this method of long range estimation. Dust in the air is always a problem. Back country is full of winding, dusty roads and any vehicular travel puts up lots of dust. Hot days can produce shimmering heat waves that move and bounce across the countryside, making judgement at ranges as short as 200 yards difficult to accurately ascertain. Shadows too, usually created by clouds, coulee walls, hillsides, and valley slopes will throw off this kind of estimation. The color of the countryside will also introduce error. Yet judgment by perspective is the method most hunters unconsciously apply. Looking through a rifle scope and relating to past hits, hunters develop an instinctive feel for distance. Many are unable to translate this feeling into yards or meters, but all can tell when the target looks right.

Going hand in hand with good range estimation is the ability to call shots at all ranges. Every long range sight picture is unique, and hunters doing much shooting will soon learn to associate distance with picture. Experienced shooters rely on how the sight picture looked just as they squeezed the trigger, to tell them how the bullet travelled. Good target shooters can reliably tell where their bullet struck the target. Many are able to say, with certainty, whether the bullet cut a nine, ten, or six. Calling shots accurately means the shooter is using correct trigger control and doing things right The aiming eye is open and the crosshairs fixed on target at the moment the bullet leaves the muzzle.

The phrase *calling the shots* means just that— the bullet will strike a particular area, either high, low, to the left or right or some combination of

Chuck Cadieux and friend Orvill Sandal take on prairie dogs. One watches while the other shoots—a good way to test the ability to call shots accurately.

these, and the shooter is able to state, with reasonable confidence, where that shot will touch. Attention can be focused on other factors like wind, weather, mirage and distance. For practical varmint shooters, the ability to call shots well means all shooting skills are being applied properly for a particular range.

Calling shots helps long range shooters in another way. Shots not going where called implicates other factors affecting results. Shots missing distant woodchucks, and kicking up dust to one side, suggest that winds at the target may be different than those near the shooter. A quick follow up shot, compensating for wind, should give the desired result. Knowing how to call shots helps correct errors and provides a method for evaluating down range field conditions.

On Using a Rest

Admonishing shooters to use a rest any time long range shots are taken may seem like overstressing an obvious point. However, not everybody knows that a solid rest is fundamental to successful long range shooting. Small game targets are tiny, often hidden, and capable of fast movement. This makes general shooting hard and precise shooting more difficult. A properly supported rifle helps overcome these difficulties by delivering shots more accurately and consistently than one fired offhand by an upright shooter waving in the wind. Accurate shooting at small targets is a lot easier when any kind of rest is used.

There are obvious kinds of rests that shooters

have been familiar with for years. Things like nearby rocks, fallen trees, upright vegetation, old ant hills, rotting tree stumps, sturdy fence posts, solid rails, leaking water troughs, abandoned windmills, unused corrals, unfrequented wells, and active prairie dog mounds are old stand-bys. Shooters who hunker behind these natural features shoot with greater precision. Natural rests are where you find them, and some creative thinking will come up with several more. Sometimes old abandoned farm machinery, junk piles, power poles, and snow fences will prove worthwhile. Take advantage of anything available to help steady your rifle.

Many hunters drive to their shooting sites, especially those looking for prairie dogs and woodchucks. Any vehicle is a good source of shooter rests. Cars offer good spots along the hood and roof, but an open box half-ton truck works best. Where permitted by law, shooting from the box and resting the rifle along either the cab or box wall provides shooters with a perfect opportunity to score on distant vermin. Standing in the truck box gives a better view of the surrounding countryside. Car doors work well, too. A shooter seated comfortably in the car can easily rest his rifle through the open window of the driver's side door and make exact hits at incredible ranges. Shooting across the hood gives almost bench-like results.

Improvised rests must be padded from the recoil waves generated at the instant of shooting.

Improvised rests must be padded from the recoil generated at the moment of shooting.

Sometimes a fence post makes a perfect rest.

Some recoil energy is always transferred to the rest, and since the rest does not move, the energy is passed back to the rifle. This causes the gun to jump and consequently shoot high. The rifle simply can't be laid across some hard object and expected to yield consistent long range hits.

For years the best advice has been to place a jacket or some other soft material, like a rug or sandbag, between the rifle and the rest. This is still mandatory. A rolled up jacket, vest, or coat works best. A back pack works well, too. Place your pack directly on the ground or on top of some rocks. Push the rifle down into the pack, cradling it into a fold, and shoot. A rucksack is probably one of the best improvised rifle rests a shooter can have.

Where the rest is a tree or some similar natural object, use one hand, arm or elbow to keep the rifle from directly touching the object. The key is having something soft to absorb energy developed during recoil, thus preventing the shot from being thrown high.

The many advantages offered shooters through natural rests led to the development of commercial shooting rests. Why not bring your own rest, and ensure having one available for that "once in a lifetime" long shot? Rests support

the rifle in some way, usually at the forend, and are adjustable for height. These newly manufactured rests are all after-market purchases, and sometimes it's difficult to understand why varmint rifle makers don't include one of the models with every rifle they sell. It would sure make sense.

Shooters dedicated to long range varminting often take portable shooting benches with them into the fields. These must be properly set up. There are several commercial models, and countless home made kinds, that work extremely well. Getting the bench level and stable is usually the problem. Rough ground or rocks have to be dealt with.

It's necessary to have the bench hidden—at least partially—and to perform the set up with little disturbance to woodchuck or prairie dog colonies. Either species will disappear the moment they see an intrusion into their environment, or when too much commotion is created. Perform the set up function quietly, with minimum movement, and without silhouetting your position. Once in place, an incredible afternoon of shooting awaits.

One useful product is the Micro Rest Shooting

Some hunters fashion a pair of shooting sticks into a long bipod. The technique works very well.

Portable shooting benches can be taken into the field. It's important to properly set up the bench, making sure all legs are level and there is no wobble.

Stand, available from Cravener's Gun Shop. It's of all steel construction, and gives shooters an extremely rigid tripod capable of holding the heaviest varmint grade rifle. There is an adjustment wheel and three chains that move leg positions, allowing the shooter to use the tool either sitting or prone. It's a fine product, and one that will really help the extremely long range shooters.

MTM also markets a quality rest, called the "walking stick", useful for varminting under field conditions. Although favored more by long range pistol practitioners, riflemen can use the tool, too. The rest moves up and down the stick, allowing shooters to choose prone, sitting, or kneeling positions. The stick is pushed into the

ground to a suitable depth to give it stability.

While these rests are useful, they do represent another piece of gear that must be carried into the field. When the shooting is intense, and little movement from place to place occurs, there really isn't much problem. But, when hunters have to move, especially over tough terrain, more gear becomes a headache. Few of these products are adaptable to quick moves, and where the hunter must do a lot of walking rests become cumbersome. In practice, shooting tables are usually left at the initial shooting spot. Other rests are carried and eventually left behind, usually with some other equipment, to be picked up later.

Perhaps the single most popular shooting aid

Rock piles are also good rests. The author has placed a folded hat between the rock and the rifle forend.

today is the famous Harris Bipod. It's a boon to varminters and intermediate range shooters. Predator hunters are also fond of this rig. It's simply a bipod that ingeniously fastens to the front sling swivel stud of any rifle. A swivel stud mounted on the bipod allows the sling to be re-attached. This means a rifle outfitted with the bipod can be carried in the normal manner, leaving the hands free.

The legs fold forward to the front of the barrel, thus out of the way when the rifle is slung over the shoulder. When it's time to shoot, the legs are folded down and held in place by spring tension. Legs are individually and fully adjustable, meaning that shooting from sitting, or prone, or on uneven ground can be easily accom-

The Harris bipod.

modated. There are two models. The larger bipod has legs 12-1/2 inches long, capable of telescoping to 23 inches, and the smaller has eight inch legs telescoping to 13 inches. Most long range varmint shooting is done from the sitting position. It gives the hunter a better view and room for movement from close-in shots to those farther out. The larger bipod is more useful in this type of shooting.

Everybody likes the Harris Bipod, and more hunters are showing up in the fields with these every year. Even deer hunters can see the value of this product. However, there are a couple of minor disadvantages. On older rifles, like my Model 70 .225 Winchester, it's necessary to replace the old fashioned screw-in swivel with the newer post and swivel type. It's necessary to remove the bipod prior to placing the gun in a case. As yet no rifle case has been designed to take a rifle outfitted with bipod. Personally, my biggest beef with the bipod is the clumsy way it makes the rifle look. In my ultra-conservative gun mind, adding a bipod destroys the clean lines of the rifle. It makes my Model 70 look like a World War II Bren gun. Now that's picky.

Some shooters cart their bench rest stands into

There is probably no such thing as the perfect rest. The key is to use whatever is available to help steady the rifle. Improved accuracy at all ranges will result.

the field for varmint shooting. It works, although it's mighty inconvenient. In the field, stands work particularly well when combined with portable shooting benches. Folding or compact portable shooting tables are also commercially available. One model, called the Earth Anchor, has adjustable legs for overall heights between 14 and 21 inches. The table features a turnbuckle that attaches to an anchor stake, allowing the user to fully stabilize the bench by pulling the bench to the ground. It measures about 36 by 16 inches. This makes it ideal for shooting from the sitting position, and any bench rest stand placed on the table top is easily used to good advantage.

There are many home-made rests that work equally well. My old friend Rick Schumway designed a long bipod or cross sticks on a pattern he alleged was used by early buffalo hunters. He made it from two dowels, each about 45 inches long and two inches in diameter. They were covered at the top with leather thonging or babiche strapping, to protect the rifle, and joined together, about four to six inches from the top, with a large wing nut screw.

The bottom ends of the dowel were sharpened. The screw acts as a pivot point, and a surprising variation in height can be achieved using this set up. The sharpened dowel ends are pushed into the ground at a chosen height, and positions from prone to sitting can be easily accommodated. The rifle, placed in the crotch created by the sticks, rests directly on the soft leather lashing, or a small sand bag can be placed in the V. The shooting begins. Most hunters will find this an inexpensive, eminently practical, and easy-to-use bipod.

Another favorite homemade shooter's rest is constructed from easily obtainable boards about four to six inches wide. Two boards are required. The first should be about 14 inches long and the second about seven or eight. An inexpensive set of hardware-grade one-inch hinges is then used to join the two pieces together producing a hinged board arrangement that is now about 21 inches long. A V shaped notch can be cut where the two boards hinge, but this is not mandatory for this rest to work. The long board faces the shooter acting as the back part of the rest, and the shorter board, working on the hinge, determines overall rest height. Prone shooting is best done with this tool. Some shooters modify the design offered here by driving short nails into the board's bottom edges to prevent the rest from slipping during shooting. This is not necessary, but can be a nice touch, especially if your shooting is done on very hard ground. Others cut a V on the bottom end of each board to form legs.

I have taped a piece of index card to the long board, and between shots scribbled distances directly onto the card. A jacket or small sandbag can be laid over the rest to make a perfect combination for prone shooting at distant targets. By the way, be sure to paint the board some suitable color to help camouflage it.

No discussion of rests can conclude without something on sandbags. Those with some military background hate sandbags of every description—a reaction that comes from having filled and emptied one too many. For long range shooters, though, the sandbag is an incredibly useful tool that provides any rifle with correct support. Easily repositioned during use and simple to transport, it is not affected by recoil and remains stable throughout the shooting session. The sandbag might be old hat, but it is one of the surest tools in the shooter's bag of tricks. Today, there are many specially designed sandbags, made mostly for the bench rest crowd. Familiar names include Koplin, who offers contoured canvas bags, and Hoppe's leather and vinyl bags the shooter fills himself. These are all good, and when properly filled—which means not overly full—with soft sand or lead shot, will enhance long range shooting every time.

Home made sandbags also work well. A small sandbag—no bigger than a pant leg, is really all a shooter needs. Long ago I learned to carry two empty bags that I fill on site, when required. The lower leg portion, from the knee down, of an old pair of blue jeans has provided an excellent sack for years.

My wife has sewn the bottom closed. In the field, clean sand, from the edge of the road or from one of many gravel pits that dot my area, fills the sack. These sacks work best when about three quarters full and then closed off with a piece of twine. In farm country, soft dirt from the edge of a freshly summer fallowed field adequately fills the sack, too. Any shooter should feel free to use whatever material is available in his area. For example, sand from along a beach, river bank or open sand dune is excellent. Sometimes the sacks remain full for most of a season, other times they are emptied after the shooting session. On calm days one sack placed over the vehicle hood makes a perfect rest for shots up to 300 yards.

There is probably no such thing as the perfect rest. And in reality it doesn't matter what type the shooter uses. The key is to use a rest any time precision shooting is attempted. Rests are not restricted to long range shots either, short range offhand shooting, say at ranges like 80 yards, can be markedly improved with an improvised rest. The hunter must train himself to think of using a rest, even if it's a fallen tree or a stock watering tank. It's simply another good shooting habit that can be developed with some thought and practice. Commercially made rests are great assets. However, where hunters move from site to site the extra equipment can be burdensome. Sandbags are a traditional shooting accessory and something no shooter should be without. Home-made rests are good, too, and some simple designs are available that require no special tools or equipment to build. Like much of the other equipment available to shooters, there is no perfect answer. However, we know shooting over any rest helps.

Sighting In

Jack Bonnell was a sheep herder. When he came home recovering from wounds at the close of World War II, he found work in his home hill country. Sheep ranching had become highly profitable during the war years. Wool was a critical war material, and so was the mutton needed to feed hungry European and Russian mouths. Now, sheep was a big industry—the biggest it had ever been and ever would be again. It was easy for a ranch raised soldier to find work on a large place. Besides, there he could rebuild his strength, living and working in the open hill country not 20 miles from where he was born.

All through the decades of the 50s, 60s and into the 1970s, Jack carried a Model 94 Winchester in .25-35. With it he shot everything. Marauding coyotes were his favorite, but deer and antelope routinely fell for the fall stew pot to feed his growing family. Sick dogs, horses out of luck, and foundered cattle were dispatched with that gun. It was carried on foot, bounced around in a war surplus jeep, and saw more than its share of time in a saddle scabbard. It was also carried on a crude, homemade motor bike where it probably received its roughest treatment. Commercial ammo was used exclusively, and if Jack had 50 cartridges, 48 would kill something.

Shots were never wasted on vermin—gophers, prairie dogs, or squirrels. Rabbits would be taken, but only when the opportunity was right. An easy head shot at close range would mean no edible meat was damaged. Besides, cleaning for the stew pot was quicker and less messy if a good shot was made. With seven mouths to feed on a sheep herder's wage, every morsel of meat was not only important but a pleasant change from a diet of lamb and mutton. The .25-35 performed well at these tasks.

When I first met this man I was impressed with his back-country knowledge. His understanding of livestock and natural history, and his breadth of practical experience were inspiring. For someone who, other than during the war, had never been more than 40 miles from home, his understanding and perspective of world events was better than most academics. On more than a couple of occasions during the long hot August evenings that characterize the open west, his marksmanship was also impressive. Coyotes, usually inexperienced spring born young, would sneak, sniff, and snake their way toward the corraled sheep Jack was overseeing. The .25-35 would crack and the small coyote would fold up for keeps.

By this time in my life I considered myself a not too bad shot and a fairly sophisticated rifleman. On one hot evening, while drinking tea on the steps of his trailer, I ventured to ask Jack if he ever sighted-in that .25-35. Did he know where that gun shot? The answer was simply no. Jack didn't really think sighting-in was necessary. He'd done it in the army but that was the last time.

In his mind only army rifles required sighting-in, and everybody that was anybody knew those Winchesters came from the factory with the sights set, so there was no need to check where a gun shot. It also saved ammunition. Besides, the army had lots of money to waste on such things, while Jack had to get on with the business of herding sheep.

Few shooters today have the luxury afforded Jack. Deeply familiar with one gun, the country he worked, and life in the outdoors, his gun probably never needed sighting-in. His Model 94, a rifle version with a 24-inch barrel and sights 21 inches apart, worked well for him. It probably would have taken a psychologist to analyze the sight picture Jack saw every time he threw that rifle to his shoulder but there were no delicate optics on his rifle. Open, iron sights served all his needs.

Nevertheless, few hunters would go afield without scope mounted rifles. Black powder enthusiasts will attempt it, but most often even they use receiver sights. Many small game shooters use the same rifle for big game hunting and can benefit from the practice and familiarity gained through small game hunting. Today's scope is a rugged shooting tool that enhances all hunting.

Good pre-sighting is, for most of us, a must in small game hunting. It's necessary to sight-in with ammunition that will be used for the actual hunting. The performance characteristics of all ammunition will change with lot number, primer type and bullet weight, thereby delivering different groups at various ranges.

Remember, too, that distances are greater, targets smaller and conditions constantly changing. It is folly to go into the field with a rifle not sighted for the prevailing shooting conditions.

There are three basic considerations fundamental to good sighting-in for small game hunting. First is *point blank* range. While this varies somewhat with game sought, small game hunters are best served with a point blank range of 250 yards when using the .22 centerfires or 300 yards with the .24's and .25's.

The second consideration is the *quality of the equipment*. Rifle and scope must be capable of producing group sizes within one and one-half inches at 100 yards.

Third, *mid-range trajectories* should not exceed three inches in this kind of hunting. It is common practice to sight-in big game rifles to print three inches high at 100 yards. For the typical .30-06 with a 150 grain bullet, this means the highest trajectory will be 3.2 inches at about 140 yards. Trajectories this high can produce a clean miss on small game where the hunter misjudges range. These are called mid-range misses, and are often perplexing to beginning shooters. However, shooters insisting on using hunting rifles sighted for big game can still be successful by using a deep six o'clock hold on all small game. That means holding slightly low on shots under the 150-yard mark and dead on for anything beyond. For most varmints, a mid-range trajectory of no more than two inches is best.

Hunters wanting to shoot at targets over 300 yards distant require a different set of rules. Any rifle zeroed for 300 yards will assuredly produce a miss on small game at 100 to 150 yards. Those with a special interest in super-long range shooting must train themselves to pass up shots under their chosen distance, or learn to correct for

Sighting-in at short range (25 yards) and then rechecking at 100 yards makes good sense for the small game hunter.

mid-range miss by holding low on closer shots. Range estimation skills must be honed. Most shooters will find it easier to learn how to hold high at long range than to hold low at mid to short range. Strict long range shooters must discipline themselves and take time to closely dope out their shots to prevent mid-range misses.

Point blank range is defined as the distance at which the shooter can hold dead on his target and still be assured a hit within the animal's vital zone. A standing prairie dog offers a target about ten inches high, a badger gives much more, about 18, any of the gophers or picket pins about six to eight, while the woodchuck gives about a 12

inch target. In all cases, the vital zones are considerably less than the height of the standing animal. Clearly, the shooter has to pick a point blank range suitable for the particular species he is going after. Indeed, one major reason woodchucks and prairie dogs became popular targets over the years is that their height allowed shooters to use rifles sighted-in for big game hunting.

As noted, a standing prairie dog is about ten inches high. However, the animal's vital area—head, heart, lungs, and liver—covers about four inches of this total height. Thus any bullet striking within the four inch vertical plane will dispatch the animal.

Any rifle held dead on the center of this vital area can place a bullet either two inches high or two inches low and still ensure a clean kill. The maximum distance at which the bullet will still drop into the vital zone is called the point blank range. Thus a .243 sighted-in to place a 75 grain hollow point bullet two inches high at 100 yards would have a practical point blank range on prairie dogs of 320 yards. At this range the bullet would strike the bottom of the vital area. However, what would happen on one of the shorter animals like any of the gophers? The same cartridge would have a point blank range of around 270 yards. This is because the smaller vital area on these animals is only about three inches.

Equipment must be satisfactory for the job at at hand. Quality scopes must be mounted correctly. Parallax, eye relief and focus must fall within manufacturers' specifications. Scopes must be mounted securely and all mounting screws must be tight. Lenses must, of course, be clean.

With these basics out of the way, sighting-in can be easily accomplished in a simple three-step process. Begin with a good job of bore sighting, followed by a short range shooting check at 25 yards, and end by completing a final, down range sight-in for zero. Many rifles, especially those continually used under constant climatic conditions, rarely change their point of impact without very good reason. Change in ammunition lots, reloading components, and commercial brands frequently accounts for subtle shifts in point of impact. However, damage to the rifle or scope, usually caused by a bad bump, is the most common reason for radical shifts. Rifles moved across extremes of climate—for example, very dry to very moist—will also experience change. Those subjected to much vibration, usually during transport, will need resighting.

Bore sighting is the first step. With a bolt action rifle, this is easily accomplished by removing the bolt and lining up the bore with a target bull placed some 25 yards distant. Hold the rifle firmly, and adjust the scope's crosshairs to coin-

cide with the bullseye, and the preliminaries are over. Autoloader, lever actions, and pump actioned rifles are more difficult to sight-in this way. A good bore scope can be used, but it might be difficult. The quickest solution is to use a collimator. This is a sighting device that fits on an arbor that slides into the rifle's muzzle. There are many inexpensive models on the market, and no serious shooter should be without one. Many hunters still take their rifle to a local gunsmith for bore sighting.

Collimators are easy to use, and a varmint hunter should have one as part of his shooting kit. Essentially, the device contains a printed grid which acts as the target. The bore sighter is aligned with the bore, using the accompanying arbors. Arbors are made in different calibers to allow use with different rifles. While looking through the scope, the reticle is aligned by moving the horizontal and vertical scope wires to match with the grid. This gives a bore sighted rifle.

Many shooters have bad opinions of collimators and how they work. They claim these devices are inaccurate and therefore a waste of time. These observations are not true, but a collimator can be incorrectly used. Their value comes, though, in giving a shooter the freedom to move one scope onto several rifles, and make adjustments quickly, many times right in the field. These devices are not meant to replace actual shooting for group.

Once bore sighting is complete, the next step is to try a *group at 25 yards*. Knowledgable shooters choose this distance for preliminary sighting because the bullet, in most calibers, first crosses the line of sight at this point. Until later in the trajectory—at zero range—the bullet travels above the line of sight. Bore sighting reduces the need to experiment with other distances. At 25 yards all information will be relevant to the 100 yard mark.

Test groups are best fired from a solid bench and proper rifle rest. Most gun ranges are now equipped with good facilities for this kind of

Change in ammunition, reloading components, and commercial brands will cause the point of impact to shift slightly.

shooting, but when no other options exist a rolled up jacket or back pack can replace a rest. If you're doing this under field conditions, use the sitting position and a natural rest like a fallen tree or stump. Also, be sure to pad the rest with a jacket or pack. Steadiness is critical at this time.

When shooting for group, always apply your best shooting skills. Control breathing, concentrate on the sight picture, squeeze the trigger correctly, and ensure a proper fit of rifle to shoulder. Aim for the center of the bull. Fire the initial shot and set the rifle down to allow the barrel to cool. Take a few breaths, blink your eyes to remoisten the eyeball, and rest for a few moments before resuming the shooting.

It's important to let the barrel cool, as this reduces the chance of the point of impact shifting. It duplicates the hunting situation where only one or two shots may be fired. Always sight-in with a cool barrel. Under intense varmint hunting, where several shots are fired in quick succession, any gun barrel will heat up quickly and minor shifts in impact will occur.

Fire two additional shots to give a three-shot group. There was a time when any red blooded shooter would have insisted on taking ten shots to produce a group. Later, five shots were considered the minimum for reliable information. Now, three are considered adequate, and will give the shooter everything needed to make intelligent decisions about where and how the gun is shooting. There is also a school of thought that says if properly done, one shot is really all that's necessary. Stick with three.

The three shots should have produced a tight group somewhere in the paper. Don't feel bad if the group is too high or low from the bullseye. This will happen, even with collimater sighted rifles. The key now is to move the group toward the bull by working the crosshairs. Modern scope adjustments are graduated into minutes of angle, with some graduated into one-quarter minute, or four clicks per inch change at 100 yards, while some others employ one-half minute or two clicks equaling one inch. Many sighting-in targets are now measured into one inch squares, and it is easy to count the inches high or low, left or right from the center of the group. Once done, the rifle should be shooting well enough to try at the next range.

For the final check, sighting is best done at *100 yards*. This distance is used by all modern shooters and gives an easy way of comparing performance among many different guns, scopes, ammunition types, and components. Again, a three shot group is sufficient. This group should confirm your initial group, and height above the bull should be very close to what is required for your particular small game species.

Groups at 100 yards give shooters a lot of information. For example, a group that shows bullet holes one above the other, several inches apart, suggests there is a bedding problem. Wide open groups indicate either a poor reload or poor shooting technique. Overly warm barrels will cause shots to string vertically. The ultimate group is clover leaf shaped and contained within one square inch or minute-of-angle, or less. Groups left or right of their location on the 25 yard target suggest wind may be a factor.

This procedure works because the 25 yard sight-in ties closely to the ballistic performance of most small game cartridges. The rifle barrel is never perfectly horizontal, but rather at some angle upward. This elevation imparts trajectory

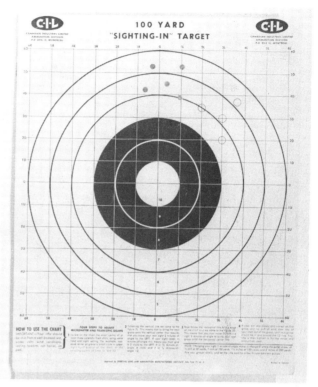

Shot landing on the target should produce a tight group. Next, adjust the scope, following manufacturer's instructions, to move the group into the correct location on the target.

to the bullet, and some degree of trajectory is needed to overcome gravitational pull. The bullet's path is not straight as many hunters think, but forms a curve. The bullet intersects the line of sight at 25 yards and travels upward until gravity pulls the bullet earthward, intersecting the line of sight again at the zero range.

Let's look at an example. A factory loaded 80 grain bullet striking the black at 25 yards will hit two inches high at 100 yards, one and three-quarters inches high at 200, land dead on at about 245 yards, and strike 5.4 inches low at 300 yards. Combine this with point blank range information and it's easy to see how prairie dogs, woodchucks, badgers and standing jackrabbits can be taken at nearly 300 yards. Good sighting-in is critical. Jack Bonnell never had to sight-in,

Frequent checking keeps the rifle shooting where the hunter wants.

but he only shot at what he knew he would hit, and then only at distances he was already familiar with.

Varmint hunters have to go further than performing the simple sighting procedure covered here. How a particular rifle shoots at all ranges should be part of regular checking. Wherever possible, groups fired from rest at 200, 250, 300, and 350 yards should be attempted. These groups will be much more open, but until the hunter knows how his rifle and cartridge shoot at these distances, long range shooting will be only a guess.

The question arises as to how often grouping and sight-in should be checked. When a rifle is in constant use, zero tends to remain fairly constant, unless the rifle is damaged in transport.

Any time the rifle is dropped or seriously bumped, zero should be checked. Seasonal checks are also wise, especially when the summer prairie dog rifle becomes a mid winter rabbit gun. Extremes in temperature and humidity can change point of impact by altering wood density, and therefore bedding characteristics.

Any time rifle performance slips (for example, too many missed shots, or shots continually off to one side), resighting under controlled conditions should be done. Sling pressure, too, can shift groups by pulling down on the delicate forend, creating pressure on the forward guard screw. So the answer is simple—sighting should be checked every time prior to using the rifle. This not only ensures top performance of rifle and load, but also gives the shooter a disciplined workout. All will benefit.

Likewise, a rifle's group with a particular cartridge will not markedly change. Shooters burning up large quantities of commercial ammunition must pay attention to lot numbers and brands. Separate batches of the same ammunition can behave differently. Manufacturers know this, so they assign codes to their batches. All commercial ammunition contains a stamped number on the box flap or somewhere inside the box. These are coded dates and batch or lot numbers. When purchasing ammunition check to see if all boxes are of the same lot, and where possible try to buy lots with the same number as your previous ammunition. Manufacturers make huge quantities of ammo, and it's simple to shoot from one lot over the course of a year or more. Much of this depends on the turnover in your local area. Product variation in lots will contribute to shifts in point of impact.

Ammunition of differing bullet weights, even of the same manufacture, will grossly alter group location on the 100 yard target. If you have spent any time in remote rural areas, one of first things you learn about is the scarcity of commercial ammunition.

Rural people conserve ammunition as if it were water. In doing this they mix bullet weights of all kinds of cartridges. At close range, and shooting with iron sights, it doesn't make much difference to a deer knocked over at 75 yards or rabbits shot at 60 feet. However, modern long range shooters won't have the same luck with small game at anything over 100 yards. Shifts in impact as little as one-quarter inch at 100 yards will cause misses on prairie dogs and woodchucks standing at 150 yards.

It's true that some rifles are not susceptible to shifts in impact with different bullet weights. The .250 Savage has this reputation, and the odd .270 is known to do it as well. The old .303 British, the never-mentioned cartridge that once killed more game than any .30-06, digests all bullet weights, placing them within a three-inch circle at 100 yards. However, this ability is a unique combination of the particular rifle and cartridge. It happens almost by accident, since rifles of the same model, shooting the same ammunition, will not necessarily perform this way. The cartridges mentioned here have a tendency to group in this manner, but there is no guarantee this occurs with similar rifle and cartridge combinations.

Shooters whose rifle groups varying bullets weights to the same point of impact are indeed lucky. Don't let such rifles out of your hands. My ancient .303 military P14 will do this every time—even when mixed bullet weights are fired into the same group. However, rifles consistently performing like this are exceptions.

My .243 Winchester Model 70 will place 75 and 87 grain Hornady bullets to the same point of impact, but not the 100 grain varieties. It does the same stunt with Speer bullets, but when it comes to shooting the 85 grain, solid base, boattail Nosler, compared to the same weight semi-spitzer partition Nosler, the results are vastly different, and it's necessary to resight and move cross hairs. However, shooters with rifles delivering this kind of performance have a more versatile firearm, one capable of covering more applications with no resighting.

Bullet groups also indicate the health of the load. Many rifles group better with one brand of ammunition than another. This is frequently a function of the powder or other components used. Groups obtained with reloaded ammo can be improved by changing both type and amount of powder used. Shape of a group can often be controlled by changing to powder of different burning rates. In varmint cartridges, fast burning powders are favored over slower kinds, but any shooter experiencing problems should move to slower, older powders like IMR 4064 or IMR 4320.

Sometimes rifles characteristically print groups with one flyer. Incorrect powder for the rifle or the bullet combination can create this. Sometimes incorrect primers are a possibility. This is especially the case where magnum primers are used but not necessary. Cartridge cases can also contribute to this, and it shows up most clearly when mixed lots of reloaded cartridges are used.

Finally, groups can be improved by fine tuning, using half grain increments to alter loads. Downloading may also improve grouping and is perhaps the single most effective way to tighten groups in the varmint shooting class of cartridges.

Tracking and Stalking for Success

Many hunters believe that only big game must be watched, stalked, and tracked to make hunting successful. They feel that small game can be found on any hillside, and that hunting techniques are much simpler than needed for big game. This is not true. All animals live by their wits, and this is particularly the case with small game. Most small game is prey for many different

Bullet groups indicate the health of the load. Shoot frequently and be consistent in your shooting habits.

predators. Unlike deer, it's rare to find rabbits, squirrels or rodents in the open, far from cover or protective burrows. These animals have evolved through eons of time with the predator as a major factor in their lives. Indeed, for most small game, predators exert the same kind of evolutionary pressure that was common before the days of the white man. This means that small game species actually live under a more natural (if it could be called that) environment than do many ungulate populations that no longer suffer much predation. The predator has maintained its evolutionary presence in relation to the small game animal. The result is predator-wise small game, alert for subtle changes in their environment, and constantly testing their environment for the predator's presence. For hunters, it means these animals are wise to man's activities and must be hunted using techniques similar to those used for big game animals.

Animals have no difficulty discerning disturbance in their habitat and responding by reflex action to these changes. These actions, honed by centuries of survival next to the predator, are easily used to defeat man. In order to take these animals on their own terms it's necessary to be a good observer, stalker, and tracker. In terms of skills demanded of the hunter, small game animals are equal to any big game species.

Small game is as tough to find, bring into rifle range, and bag as any white-tailed deer. The hunter needs techniques and skills to successfully locate and stalk these animals. It's not enough to simply drive into the country and casually look for rabbits, squirrels, and prairie dogs. These animals have to be systematically sought, and, when found, tracked and stalked with care and attention.

Everybody has heard of plinkers—casual hunters who do not aggressively pursue their game, usually small game animals. They take a relaxed approach to their hunting, placing no great emphasis on finding live targets or the quantity of game taken. For them, shooting their rifles is the high point of the hunt experience and equal pleasure can be taken from tin cans or live small

Animals know what poses a threat, and cattle grazing the grasslands offer little threat to the gopher.

game. This group will not particularly benefit from the information that follows. The goal here is to present detailed field information that can help serious hunters to consistently bag small game.

Fundamental in this kind of hunting is knowledge about the animal. The old English saying of "know your quarry" applies well here. The hunter must always carry with him a clear idea of exactly what he is looking for. It's critical to read books, study magazines, and gather information about the animal. Local lore and beliefs about the animal, its behavior, its favorite haunts, and its preferred foods all help to give hunters a better picture of where the chosen game can be found. It turns time afield into productive shooting time. Natural history knowledge is practical information that can be applied to help find sign, sort out animal activity, and guide the hunter in locating game.

It's important to know how to observe in the outdoors. Most observation is based on familiarity. Hunters have to know where to look. When everybody lived on a farm, it was simple to be intimately familiar with the countryside. Animals, their behavior, and the sign they left behind were always around to see. Yet certain sign was only found in characteristic places. As kids we knew where to look for gophers, for frogs, or white-tailed deer. We could find snakes with no problem. We were familiar with, and always knew where to find, whatever we might want. Today, when most hunters are city dwellers making weekend forays into the countryside, it's more difficult to observe well and understand what's actually being seen. Most hunters lack familiarity with countryside even close to home, and for some a trip into rural areas is like being in a foreign country. A hunter staring vaguely across the countryside will see only the most obvious signs. Hunters must learn how and where to look for sign.

Worse yet, city living breeds a defocused eye, or at least teaches us not to look or observe closely. It's a kind of passive consciousness. In our culture, staring is unacceptable behavior, and making eye contact is permissible only under certain circumstances. These cultural traits hamstring the hunter in the field, so for many serious hunters it's necessary to relearn how to make good observations.

Observation is a process requiring patience and practice. It's little more than concentrating the eye on a particular spot and mentally disciplining the mind to make an interpretation of the information available. Most people simply don't pay attention to details in their surroundings. There are many reasons for this, but the key to bettering our ability is simple training. It is important to begin focusing on our surroundings. Sorting out trees, shadows, boulders, and other vegetation requires practice. Through frequent observation a new understanding of the environment soon develops. Observation becomes easy through practice. How the environment fits together becomes clear, and it is easier to interpret what is seen and how the pieces fit together like a puzzle.

With some effort most animals are easily distinguished from their surroundings. Many keen eyed sportsmen will tell you that, although nature has successfully developed protective coloration to a high degree, there is always some part of the animal that fails to blend with the environment. Most keen observers readily notice the glint of light of an animal's eye. Photographers always try to capture this.

More commonly, some appendage will appear out of place. An ear that juts above the vegetation, an exposed backside that reflects light, a shiny claw or a tail that moves at the wrong moment. The trained eye looks for these oddities and the brain makes a decision. Doctors call this ability "perceptual skill". Once good perceptual skills are developed, game will be easily sorted from the background and seen.

Developing these skills can be done anywhere, even in the heart of the city. One trick is to become familiar with the silhouettes of the animals you hunt and try to recognize these from

Know your quarry. Study natural patterns of the animals you hunt. Know their foods, where they water, and how they live.

as far away as possible. In the field it will become easier to identify objects at great distances. Key in this is recognizing objects before they are clear, and being able to recognize parts of objects. The head, tail, or feet of the animal will always be spotted before the entire animal. These tricks improve visual acuity and can be learned in the living room.

Moving your eyes correctly is important. Eye and head movement improves depth perception. Eyes moved from side to side, up and down, are more likely to spot oddities and alert the brain. Shift your focus as you move, and always look well ahead rather than constantly down at the ground. Blink frequently, keeping eyes moist for optimum light transmission, and to prevent eyes from becoming adapted to the surroundings. Keep the eyes alert and sensitive through movements of both eyes and head.

These movements don't have to be exaggerated. Simple short distance head movements or fractional eyeball movements are all that's necessary to keep the eyes alert for long periods. Moving eyes will take in more of the world around them, and in the process turn up a lot of animal sign.

In seeking small game there are certain optical illusions that can fool the most careful hunter. Objects viewed over a hot plain will seem to waver and bend. Long range varmint hunters throughout the west will see this on hot summer days out on large prairie dog towns. Another illusion is the appearance of large lakes some distance away. Brightness, haze, fog, color contrasts, shadows, snow, heat, and mountains can create illusions of distance. Animals tend to seem closer when spotted against dark backgrounds, such as mountains or forests, while they give the illusion of being farther away when seen against light surroundings like snow or ice. By the way, optical instruments like scopes, binoculars, and spotting scopes won't have any effect on the illusion.

All sign is easier to find when the hunter is moving into the sun. In this way all light bearing down on the ground is used to illuminate any tell-tale marks. Take advantage of the sun by using the early morning and pre-evening periods for animal sightings. During summer the period from one hour before sunrise until about seven in the morning is simply the best time to be afield locating small game. Much sign is found at this time because animals are seeking food or checking territories. As the morning matures, the world changes. Animals become less active and the light quality decreases.

Wise hunters use the midday period to find dens, burrows, loafing sites, feeding areas, and

Walk carefully in the outdoors. Place the feet in accordance with the kind of cover in the area. Lift the feet so you don't bump logs and rocks.

animal trails. These are major signs of activity, but less obvious sign can also be found. Tracks can be located when the sun is overhead. Kill sites and the remains of meals can be clearly found. Locating these types of sign narrows the area where animals will be found.

The midday period is when most hunters are active, but it is also the time of day that hunters out stalking and tracking should be cautious in their movements. All game will be what trappers call "holed up", that is resting in loafing areas, not always near dens or burrows, but well within the established limits of the home range. While holed up, all game remains alert for predators and man. During this time noise, errant breezes carrying scent, and visual contact will alert animals quickly and easily, many times unknown to the hunter.

Good field techniques are as critical as observational skills. It's important to stalk and move slowly, lifting feet high to avoid kicking stones when crossing cultivated fields. Place your heel down first when walking dry pastures or woodland areas to prevent noisy grass or leaves from signalling nearby animals. Always take care when moving through shrub or bush, as branches scraping on clothing or snapping back into surrounding vegetation can alert game. When hunting on rocky ground, be sure to place the toe down first to avoid stumbling or dislodging rocks.

In mountainous or gravelly country, watch that movement over loose stones doesn't create noise. Hunters moving on snow must place their foot squarely on the snow and lift each foot sharply out of the snow crust. These minor considerations will let the hunter move quietly and reduce the odds of alerting game.

Always make good use of cover and ground. Big game hunters learn this, but it's equally important with small game. There's no mystery about the use of cover or ground. It is used to conceal your presence and achieve surprise, especially on colony-living animals. Gophers or prairie dogs post sentinels specifically to watch for predators and man. Gopher colonies and prairie dog towns will produce more targets when hunters remain unnoticed by the sentinels. Whenever possible shoot from cover. Even though the animals appear to hear the rifle's report, it seems that two modalities must be stimulated before these animals react to overt danger. Noise plus visual contact or smell would send the animals scurrying. Noise alone, especially from mild cartridges, has less effect. The correct use of cover provides this opportunity. The skilful use of cover lets the hunter get closer to targets and remain in position longer.

Wise hunters also use cover to conceal movements. Never be afraid to crawl or creep when placing yourself in position for using binoculars or shooting. In tall grass, move carefully, always planning where you will come out from cover. Walk upright in tall woods, crouch down in thickets, and use hands and knees in sparse shrub.

Wise hunters are conscious of their silhouette and the shadows created as they move. Never silhouette yourself against the skyline when moving from bush to bush or across valley walls or coulee tops. Always be alert to your own shadow. Silhouettes and shadows are important to small game animals. In our lives shadows mean nothing; most of us don't even notice the shadow we cast as we move about our daily activities. Not so in the animal world. Sorting out shadows is a survival skill all small game animals learn at very young ages.

If you think about it, most animals are well outfitted to interpret the shadows that characterize their world. Rabbits have large eyes, and prairie dogs are very adept at living in dark burrows, as are gophers. Squirrels, with contrast sorting eyelids, live their entire lives in the shadows of big trees and dense vegetation. For these animals shadows are an important piece of environmental information that is quickly recognized. They create a response, either positive or negative. Predators are identified by the shadow or silhouette they cast. For burrowing species,

Study the topography of your hunting area and learn the various cover types.

shadows mean airborn predators in the form of hawks and owls. For rabbits, well defined silhouettes mean fast moving predators.

Remember, too, that the early morning hours, when animals are most active, are characterized by well defined, long and obvious shadows. All animals grow up in this environment. As the day progresses and changes, it is more likely for small game to respond to a shadow or silhouette than to nearby disturbances. This is hard for the hunter to understand, but it is true.

Fundamental to carrying out good observations is the ability to see across broad areas. Wise hunting requires that a triangular shaped area at least 200 yards long be visible to the shooter at all times. For many small game species, the effective shooting range will be much less, but in general terms 200 yards clear visibility will give the hunter sufficient room to both study sign and maneuver for shooting position. At short ranges, snap shooting skills are necessary, and at greater distances long range skills are a must. However, being able to see clearly for some distance is required in either case.

Giving the eyes room to work is a function of terrain and ability. Military handbooks call the areas you can't see "dead ground". Animals react to reduce the visibility available to the hunter—to create dead ground. All species accomplish this by two simple methods. They either move quickly, or they remain still and hidden until the hunter passes.

General Custer's defeat at the Little Big Horn River was a classic case of not having sufficient visibility in which to maneuver. Caught in a series of slopes that severely reduced visibility, he was soon overwhelmed. Perhaps it was small game animals that taught the Indians how to behave on that fateful day. Today's small game, descendants from those same gene pools, still teach us the same lessons. Develop the ability to move in ways that put your eyes in the best possible position to let you see animals or their sign. Without this ability you will only have dead ground in front of you and few targets for the day's effort.

Always be wise to your movements in the field. It's not enough to saunter down some abandoned back country road toting an expensive scope-outfitted rifle and expect small game animals to pop out at you from the surrounding countryside. That won't happen. The finest rifle won't help a monkey in the woods, and while the best clothes may keep you warm, they will do nothing to put rabbit on the table and squirrel in the freezer. Always be conscious of your movements and take your cue from the Indians. Move like the animals you are stalking—take a few steps, stop, observe, test the environment both for the sight and sound of animals, listen, and then repeat the pattern. These techniques are simple but are highly rewarding.

There are often several types of cover that must be dealt with. Areas of broad open plain are frequently juxtaposed by small woodlands or steep coulees. Both hardwood and softwood forests can have openings several acres in size, and many rivers are accompanied by bush-covered shorelines and silted-in deltas.

Generally, close country provides the best hunting for rabbits and squirrels. Open plains are home to the burrowing rodents. Undulating ground is also common. Hedges and orchards are part of the picture. Intermittent stream beds, irrigation ditches, old logging roads and dry slough bottoms all provide a changing complex of surroundings for the hunter. Much land hunted today is checkerboarded with crop and cereal lands. Several skills have to be combined in order to making stalking successful. Game animals are capable of using a complex of vegetation types to call home, and the hunter has to be equally flexible.

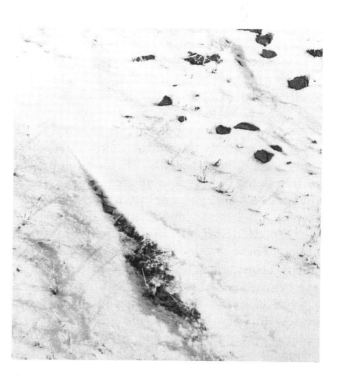

Learn from your mistakes. Here a missed short range shot has cut the soft snow. A miss like this can be more informative than a hit. How did hunter, rifle, and animal behave at the crucial moment?

The smell of success

Most hunting books today say little about the importance of wind in moving the hunter's scent toward loafing or holed-up animals. Military handbooks dismiss wind as nothing but a weather nuisance, failing to address the tactical values of wind as cover. Shooters know wind for the bullet drift it creates. Few outdoor orientated magazine articles ever discuss the role of wind in modern hunting, usually referring to wind as something that must be endured, a kind of inconvenience. The result is that today's hunters are wind ignorant.

In the simplest sense, wind blows the hunter's scent all over the countryside. In doing this, it provides an alert to scent-sensitive animals. All small game, even prairie dogs and gophers, have well developed senses of smell. Amazingly, even crows are scent sensitive. Scent plays a major role in the lives of all animals, being used for communication, reproduction, identification, territorial boundaries, and defensive survival.

The portion of the brain dedicated to olfaction (smell) is large in all small game species. Animals react quickly to foreign odors and those communicating danger are particularly noticed.

Why do animals respond strongly to scents? Odors are a common fact of life for all animals. For free living creatures there are no pleasant or unpleasant smells, just smells with certain characteristics. These characteristics come to together to elicit very specific responses from the animal. These are not thinking processes in human terms, but rather complex reactions that have been genetically programmed into the animal and geared to its survival and that of the species. In very simple terms, the animal responds because nature has set this out.

This all boils down to a need for the hunter to be wind wary. Always keep in mind that the wind is carrying additional information to the game that lies ahead. Animals don't break from cover at the mere presence of human scent. Many parts of the countryside are saturated with human odor, and animals become accustomed to this. An individual animal may easily smell an approaching hunter and take no further action. The computer like-brain simply files away a piece of information—"human nearby".

Animals react to a combination of incoming information. A rabbit, for example, sitting in its form, catches a strong whiff of human from a breeze passing near the ground. The animal remains unperplexed by this, while the brain, in its chemical way, flashes "human". The approaching hunter snaps a twig 100 yards up the trail and the noise perks the rabbit's ear.

This is now too much information for the brain to shrug off and store. Driven by this new information, in combination with the recognition of human presence, the rabbit quietly slips away along a well hidden path leading to a broad marsh and much cover. The hunter is ignorant of the event. The rabbit has given this hunter the slip, and nature has allowed this rabbit to survive another day.

When other factors are equal, watch that wind does not betray your presence. Whenever stalking, or tracking, or just looking for animals, take into account wind direction and intensity. Plan your movements to take advantage of wind. On prairie dog towns or gopher patches, try to set up so that you shoot directly into the wind. Plan your hunt movements to let the wind carry your scent over areas you have already worked. All of this is simple and seems to require no explanation, but each year hunters spread their scent at random throughout the countryside. The key is not to be one of those.

The other side of this coin is that wind, especially gusting winds, also acts as good cover for stalking and tracking work. Walking into strong winds masks a lot of noise. Crushing leaves and breaking dry twigs are neatly disguised by strong winds.

Out on the prairies tugging winds are a daily fact of life and can be made to work for even casual hunters. Animals know they are at disadvantage during these times and will restrict their movements. This will translate into rabbits that hold until the last possible second before bursting from cover. Wind gusts will also camouflage rifle report out on dog towns and woodchuck colonies. Squirrels are less likely to move from tree to tree, tending to remain in a smaller defined area when winds are high.

Finally, remember many small game species, especially rabbits and predators, will use wind to betray the hunter. Prey species do this all the time with predators and predators do this with humans. The animals will circle a moving hunter, attempting to get a downwind whiff and nail down the exact location of the intruder. Once this is established the animal either moves out or holes up.

Animals take advantage of the wind by being familiar with their home ranges. For example, any rabbit in his own environment will instinctively know the best locations for picking up errant scents carried in the daily winds. Many prey species loaf or sleep with their noses pointing into the wind specifically to pick up strange scents. Many waken several times during a rest period to re-orient themselves and position their sensitive noses into the wind. They use the wind currents as long distance communicators of danger. Outdoorsmen must learn to use the wind both as cover and provider of information.

In most areas of North America, differential heating of the soil and air creates two winds each day. One wind usually takes place in the early morning, while the second is after midday. Trips can be planned around these thermal events. Wind wise hunters move more during times of strong wind and less during quiet times.

Wind favors the hunter in much the same way it helps small game. Sounds carry better toward a hunter moving into the wind. Noise of an approaching hunter causes cautious game to hole tighter for longer. Hunters will see situations where rabbits have obviously heard the approaching hunter, yet remained tight in their forms. Wind is a factor in these instances.

There are hunters that claim to be able to smell wild game at a distance. They use the winds and air currents much the way any animal does. Anybody can smell a dead skunk at ten feet, but there are some outdoorsmen who have developed their smelling sense into a reliable information gatherer. It's hard to do, and very difficult to do well. A lot of time in the outdoors and training by association are required. Few hunters can smell a single rabbit 20 yards off a trail, but it's easier to nose the characteristic odor of a prairie dog town or bedded groups of large game. Practice is required, as is recognition that the human nose can never approach that of the animal, large or small. The sense of smell, at least in survival terms, is simply not important in our lives. Humans seem more concerned with the quality of odor, pleasant or unpleasant, than in any message the odor may be passing along.

Anyway, if you are one of those hunters who can, with some degree of reliability, use the winds to sort out game, then continue to develop your skill. If you are not in this group, then use the wind to cover your approach and disguise your hunting intentions. Forget about locating small game animals by wind-carried scent and learn to use other means.

One of the last things many hunters fail to consider is the extreme importance of seeing game animals before they see you. When this occurs the balance shifts, for the first time, in favor of the hunter. Prior to this all advantages belong to the animal. Seeing game before it sees you is the ultimate hunting experience. With the game unaware of your presence, you have ample time in which to shoot. This is fundamental to continued success in this type of hunting where the goal is not only to find animals, on their terms, in their environment, but also, by using well honed skills, to put meat on your table. All animals can be stumbled upon, located in general ways and found by just being present in their environment, but this is accident, not skill, and does not consistently result in success.

But the real mark of hunting skill is spotting game before it sees you and repeating this effort, time after time. This can only be achieved by vigorously applying the principles and good field techniques outlined here. Game caught off guard is game in the pocket.

Remember, too, that animals always remain alert and wary for changes in their environments. Watch animals closely for any subtle change in their behavior. Freeze any motions at the slightest sign of alarm. Wind may have alerted the individual animal, but more likely another animal—usually unseen by the hunter—will have become wise to some change and passively signalled the animal under observation. Control your breathing and movements during these times to remain as still as possible. Sometimes it's wise to back out of the scene, regroup, and await another opportunity. Finally, never deliberately scare an animal—you may want to hunt it another day, and unnecessary alerting only trains the animal to be wise to human tricks.

Chapter 10

Preparing Game

Perhaps the single greatest advantage to hunting is the freedom to prepare your own kills for the supper table. No butchers or middlemen are necessary in this step of the small game hunting process. There is a growing trend among big game types to simply turn over butchering to so-called professionals—usually would-be guides. These same hunters then wonder why game they worked hard to get possesses strange tastes and unrecognizable smells. Small game hunters will want to prepare their own game whenever possible to ensure quality and correct handling. They are in the best position to handle game first. There are numerous historical precedents for home preparation of game; even famous frontiersmen like Daniel Boone and Davy Crocket field dressed their own game.

Hunters of every type are wise to save game meat. Rabbits, woodchucks, and squirrels have a history of being superior pot meats. However, ground squirrels and prairie dogs can also be used in interesting ways to experiment with the palate and produce culinary masterpieces. Everybody has heard of eating crow, but crows, too, can be saved and turned into delicate treats. A skilled hunter is judged on how he treats game after it's down. Hunting and shooting are really only part of the package, and another set of skills is needed once game is in the hand.

To many hunters, small game meat tastes odd or seems to lack consistency in taste from one trip to the next. A common complaint is that rabbit never tastes the same twice. The same has been said of other game. In the past everything from field dressing techniques to recipes has been blamed, and the complaints have not gone away. Over most parts of North America, hunters will find rabbits taken in late summer taste entirely different from those shot during a cold, wintery February.

There are reasons for this. All game reflects the foods it has consumed. A sweet corn-fattened rabbit will taste markedly different from one living on river bank willows or another having spent several months dining on cured alfalfa. Time of year dictates an animal's physiological state. Those taken during breeding periods or while raising young will taste vastly different from those putting on winter fat or preparing to go underground. During the winter, metabolic patterns within the animal alter. Usually, nature has it planned that less energy is required to stay alive during this time, and body metabolism greatly slows. For these reasons a winter-taken rabbit or squirrel will not taste the same as one taken in the late summer. Food habits and physiology account for much of the so-called gaminess found in small game animals.

Old woodsmen will tell you that as an animal's food habits move from fresh herbs to more browse or twigs, there is an increase in wild taste. The shift in food habits is seasonal and reflects the changing physiological state of the animal.

For every rule, however, there are exceptions. During good mast production years squirrels will taste better than during years with poorer production. This is related to the quantity and quality of food found. There are times when there is sufficient good food, even under rough conditions, to leave taste unaffected.

Animals will select the most nutritionally complete food available. In rabbits, the classic example is a comparison between jackrabbits living only two or three miles apart under nearly identical winter conditions. One rabbit finds a good supply of spilled grain within its home range, while the other lives on tag alder and willow. The jacks, taken on the same day, will taste different, with the grain-fed specimen having more appeal than the willow fellow.

Good tasting small game is the result of learning the best places and times to hunt. There are few general guidelines, and trial and error will teach the hunter when to be afield for pot meat. Corn and grain fields produce better tasting game than cedar swamps and slough bottoms. Late summer tends to produce the best tasting game meat overall, but there is significant local variation. On our farm in central Saskatchewan, jackrabbits were good nearly any time except late January and February. On my uncle's farm in the Texas panhandle, rabbits taste best in January. The best advice is to experiment in your area.

Our tastes have become conditioned over the years to expect fat in our diet. In general, game meat does not produce the marbling and fat layering common to domestic stock. Over years of hunting you will encounter the odd animal, especially in squirrels, carrying much fat, but it's not common. Modern cattle management ensures that the meat we receive is at the correct stage of growt with the right combination of fat, muscle, and bone. When the hunter throws his rifle to his shoulder no such assurances are in place. Don't expect fat on game meat.

In animal physiology, fat plays an important role. It represents stored food that is brought into use during times of prolonged nutritional stress. In most rodent species brown fat is put down before white fat accumulates, and this brown fat is used as a food reserve for winter hibernation and spring reacclimation.

Fat build-up on all animals follows well defined patterns. First, fat accumulates around the internal organ suspension system (called mesenteric fat), followed by kidney fat (called omental fat), then fat around the the outside of the body (called subcutaneous fat) and finally marbling (called intramuscular fat). How far this accumulation sequence goes is a function of nutrition. When times are good, small game animals store fat supplies; when nutritional quality is down, less fat builds.

Proper game handling is a four step process requiring hunter attention from field to kitchen. *Field dressing* comes first, followed by *treatment in camp*, *handling in transit*, and finally *at home storage and preparation*. Most hunters think of only the first one or two steps, but reaching the goal of good tasting meat means close attention to all processing steps.

Aging small game meat has to be considered as part of correct handling. Depending on the field situation, meat can be aged at once or left for further treatment. Some hunters feel that most small game meat can be quick frozen and that removes the need for proper aging. Others say all meat must be cured or it's not tasty. Nearly all meat is improved by aging, although it is not as critical in small game as in big. Aging controls muscle fiber breakdown by enzymes and micro organisms. Controlling the process—the real skill in aging—will determine how the meat finally tastes. Even poorly cleaned meat can be improved with correct aging.

Most game meat is aged at 40 degrees Fahrenheit for varying periods of time. By the way, aging is often referred to as "hanging" and originates from the practice of suspending meat from hooks along rails in coolers. The average steer receives about 14 days of controlled aging, but the much smaller game meat requires less time. Large jackrabbits will taste better if allowed to hang for two days at 40 degrees. An average sized cottontail will age sufficiently for most tastes with a half day at 40 degrees Fahrenheit. Personal taste and time of year are important factors in deciding how long an animal should age.

Once game is taken, hunters must ensure their animal is dead. All game except for rabbits are capable of giving the hunter a nasty bite that can lead to other problems, so some caution is always wise when approaching downed game; even a wounded ground squirrel can deliver a vicious bite or scratch. Make sure the animal is dead. With small game, the bleeding process is usually not important. High power varmint cartridges with fragile bullets do an excellent job of opening an animal. Bleeding is done almost instantly and formal blood letting—the throat slitting ceremony—as practiced by big game hunters, is not normally required.

Critical in getting good tasting small game meat is cooling the carcass quickly. All small game going into the pot should be gutted and skinned immediately. This ensures the best possible tasting meat and reduces chances for contamination by digestive juices or enzymes. Often high power bullets damage some meat and spill gut contents onto edible portions of the carcass. Quick, on the spot cleaning eliminates the chance for further spoilage and stops chemical damage created by strong digestive juices.

Cleaning game immediately following shooting has other pluses. First, it lightens the load

carried back to the vehicle or lets the hunter continue on with a lighter pack. There's the added benefit of giving the hunter an opportunity to relax and take stock of the game and the surroundings as he goes about his chores of preparing game.

The hunter has to do his part well in the game cleaning process. More good quality game has been ruined by poor field dressing than any other single factor. As a game biologist I worked field checking stations and was able to observe up close the clumsy or hurried cleaning job hundreds of hunters performed on their game. I doubt whether much of this meat ever found its way to the table and into the mouths of wives and children. Most wouldn't have been pleased, and I couldn't blame them. The secret is to learn proper technique and practice until you are comfortable and competent. It may take a half dozen rabbits before the average hunter adequately learns the procedure, but any hunter will be handsomely rewarded with good tasting game.

Once the animal has been confirmed dead, check its health. Study the coat and hide condition of your animal. Dull, lackluster coats or a patchy appearance suggest health problems. These can range from light parasitic loads to dangerous diseases. Check closely for signs or extent of disease—look for lumps or thickenings along the underside, or open sores around face and ears. Don't be surprised to find scratches, bite marks, fleas, and ticks, especially on rodent species. This is the result of a colonial life where animals frequently come in contact with each other to re-sort territories and re-establish home burrows. However, an over abundance of abrasions and contusions can reveal an animal in a weakened state.

Once an animal is opened, a further assessment of condition and health can be made. Look at the internal fat supply. Is much mesenteric fat present? If not, it's a sure sign the animal was having a hard time and is usually a direct reflection of current food conditions. As mentioned

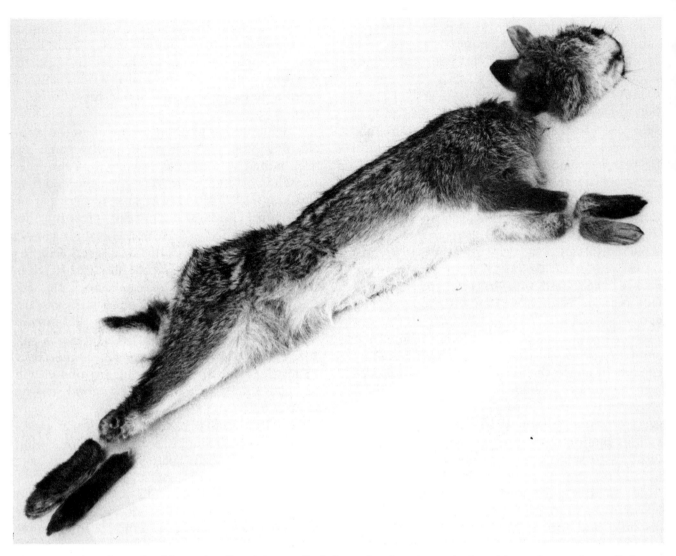

Sever the head, preferably at the first joint, called the axis. Cut through the skin and muscle until the knife blade touches bone, then twist the head to find the joint. Work the knife around the joint, twist once or twice more, and the head will be free. Cut the hind legs free at the first joint, then cut the forelegs at the first joint.

previously, fat is reabsorbed when an animal's nutritional plane drops below a certain point. Fat is quickly mobilized to keep body engines running.

Internal organs also reveal condition. In all animals the liver, the large light brown to red organ that sits under the diaphragm, tells all in health. It's easy for a hunter to check this vital organ and reach conclusions without being a veterinarian or field biologist. The liver protects the body and stores glycogen. As a result, anything happening in the body will be recorded in the liver. It should be firm, clear, smooth, free of spots, and not blotchy. If it appears off-color, bury the carcass at once, and wash your hands.

Animal condition and health are important

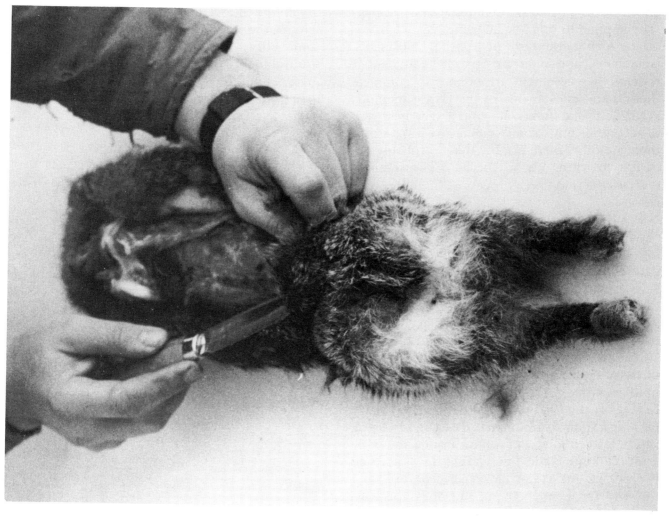

Make the cut follow the backbone and run the length of the body, ending at the base of the tail. Don't cut into the meat, but rather cut under the skin.

considerations when meat is prepared for the table. A competent hunter checks his game closely to ensure quality. Any animal with a coat in poor condition, inadequate fat supplies, or an infected liver should be discarded. Wash your hands and tools after handling infected game, and be careful not to let fluids contact cuts or abrasions on your hands and wrists as this is the entrance way for most animal to man transmitted diseases.

More Than One Way to Skin...

There are several skinning and dressing out methods developed for small game. The three most common methods are known as "torn", "cased", and "open". In some areas of the country one technique is preferred over another, and some methods are associated with particular regions. Any used for cleaning rabbits or other small game are pretty much a matter of personal choice. These same procedures can be universally applied to other small game.

The *torn* method can be used for cottontails, jackrabbits, and squirrels as well as any other rodents. It takes about 15 minutes to complete the job and rates as one of the fastest methods available to the hunter. It's also a very neat way of accomplishing a sometimes messy task. Again, there are other methods, but this is probably the easiest to learn. It's fast because it essentially reverses the traditional process of skinning small game.

Begin by laying the game out on a flat clean surface. It's possible to perform this entire cleaning procedure without the game leaving the hand, but beginners will want to use a surface. Start at the head. Sever the head, preferably at the first joint, called the axis. Cut through the skin and muscle until the knife blade touches bone and then twist the head to find the joint. Work the knife around the joint and twist once or twice more and the head will be free. Cut the hind legs free at the first joint. Then cut the forelegs at the first joint, as well. A small, sharp hunting knife will accomplish this. Use a twisting action at each joint and follow around the bone with the knife blade, freeing first the skin, then the sinews. An axe or cleaver can be used but this will fragment the bone and does not leave as neat a job as a knife.

Step two is done with a sharp knife. Pinch the skin on the back, and make the cut follow the backbone and run the length of the body, ending at the base of the tail. Don't cut into the meat, but rather cut under the skin. Hold the sharp edge of the knife upward and cut the skin. Pull the skin open and down the sides of the animal.

On jackrabbits the hide along the rear is tough to remove. The hide adheres strongly to the muscle layer. However, this method reduces the difficulty as the rearward cut entirely exposes the back. The hunter can then get a firm grip on the hide and pull the skin down toward the belly. Compared to case skinning, this method is faster and easier.

Pull the hide downward with the free hand to remove the skin from the carcass. This will take some effort on a jack, while a cottontail or squirrel hide will peel off with little more effort than peeling a banana. Completely remove the hide from the carcass, being careful not to spread

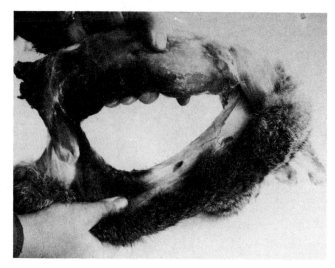

Pull the hide downward with the free hand to remove the skin from the carcass.

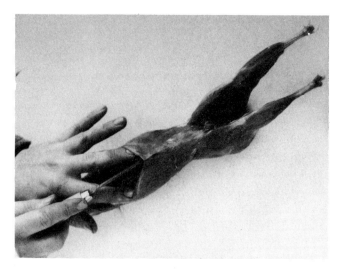

With hide removed, open the body cavity and remove the entrails. The cavity can be opened with a small knife.

hair. Hair is later difficult to remove and will ruin the taste of the game meat. Tear the hide clear of the neck and the hind legs.

With the hide removed, open the body cavity and remove the entrails. The cavity can be opened with a small knife, in the same fashion as preparing any other game. Run the knife from neck to pelvic area. Use the knife point only, being careful not to cut or nick the intestines. Cool the carcass.

It's critical that entrails—guts, if you will—be removed in their entirety. Reach into the cavity with the thumb and forefinger and pull the diaphragm and attached entrails forward. Usually this movement will clear most insides. Pick clean any areas missed.

Once the body cavity is cleared, wipe the carcass with a paper towel or grass to remove remaining tissue or fluids. Straw works particularly well for this operation. Some hunters wash the body cavity with snow. If the animal has been poorly hit and a lot of blood is present, this trick works well. The idea is to clear away fluids that might alter the meat's natural taste and clean

Rabbit fully prepared and ready to be broken down for cooking.

areas punctured by bone or bullet. Following this, cut away tissue damaged by the bullet or fragmented bone.

The *cased* method, traditional in the preparation of small game, involves treating the carcass much like a big game animal. The game is hung from some convenient perch and case skinned. Hide hunters will want to use this method for prime jackrabbit or squirrel. Case skinning removes the hide much the same way a sock is pulled off a foot. The main advantage in this method is that the hide is taken off in one piece and can be placed handily onto a stretcher. From a hide buyers point of view this is preferable, since strips are more easily cut from a uniform piece during the manufacturing process. This method favors the hide while the previous technique is aimed at quick access to the meat.

Cut around the rabbit's ankle joint and then follow through with a cut that runs inside of the left leg to the anus, then onto the right leg to the first joint. This cut opens the skin and gives the hunter a surface to pull down from during the skinning process. The tail area, or that zone around the anus is circled with a knife, then cut, leaving a tuft.

It's critical that the entrails be removed completely. Reach into the cavity with the thumb and forefinger and pull the diaphragm and attached entrails forward.

A second method is to treat the carcass much like a big game animal. The game is hung from some convenient perch and case skinned.

Case skinning a hide is like taking off a sock.

The skin is worked down the length of the body. Upon reaching the front shoulders, each leg is pushed up into the hide and pulled through the skin. Each front leg is cut at the first joint and removed.

Once skinned, entrails are removed by opening the body cavity. Make a cut beginning at the pelvis and running forward to the rib cage. Then cut the diaphragm completely free from where it fastens to the inside of the rib cage. As in the previous method, use the thumb and forefinger to free the entrails. Be sure to wipe away any material and blood.

Once the hide is removed and the entrails

plucked, allow the carcass to cool. Hang it in a shady spot or bring along ice and a cooler. Let your game cool.

The third method, referred to as *open*, is usually used when a carcass cannot be completely dressed in the field. A cut is made from the anus to the last rib and the entrails are removed. The skin is left in place. Once the hunter returns to home base the hide is removed by extending the cavity incision to the throat. A cut is made up the underside of each leg from the end points of the ventral cut. The hide is then pulled off. The head can either be removed in the field, or when the animal is skinned.

Once cool, break down the carcass into smaller pieces. The extent to which game is cut up or broken down depends upon the size of the animal, the recipe used, serving requirements, size of the pot and individual taste. There are also regional preferences. Field circumstances also vary. Large animals are usually partially broken down in the field to give the hunter less bulk to transport. At any rate, game must be broken down before cooking.

The patterns shown here can be used for any small game animal. Squirrels and rabbits can be cut up directly from the diagrams shown. Wood-chucks and prairie dogs also follow these rules, but leg portions are much smaller. The idea remains the same—each leg is separated from the carcass.

Certain similarities are common to all methods. The head is always removed and discarded. Excess fat is trimmed, and any shot areas are also cut away. Check the carcass one more time for bone, bullet, or shot fragments. Remove any adhering hair and rewash the carcass.

Work the skin down the length of the body. When you reach the front shoulders, push each leg up into the hide and pull it through the skin. Cut each front leg at the first joint and remove it.

Critical in getting good tasting small game meat is cooling the carcass quickly. All small game going into the pot should be gutted and skinned immediately. This ensures the best tasting meat possible, and reduces chances for contamination by digestive juices or enzymes.

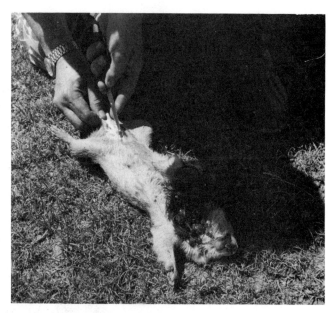

This prairie dog is being dressed out within moments of being taken. All meat benefits by getting the hide and entrails quickly removed.

Northern hunters learn early that a slightly frozen rabbit or hare will be easier to cut into pieces. A knife cuts through partially frozen flesh much more easily than a soft, warm carcass. Hunters taking winter game use this knowledge to their advantage when cutting and breaking down their game.

The methods outlined here are based on the size and weight of game. Anything under five pounds can be simply broken down in five simple steps, leaving behind five basic pieces of meat. This method renders game into frying and roasting size pieces. It's quick and handy.

Begin by cutting off the head. The most important cut is then made through the body, separating it into two halves. Shoulder and forelegs are removed as one piece. The rear legs and haunch are likewise removed as one piece. It's optional whether or not to cut the haunch in half to give six pieces. Small squirrels, young rabbits, and woodchucks can be broken down this way for quick frying in the field.

A large hare or rabbit, one over six pounds, can be cut into two basic parts—front and rear—leaving the front for cutting into stew sized pieces and the rear for roasting. A larger animal makes this easy. The heaviest muscling is toward the rear and this is best used for roasting. The forward portion can vary greatly in size and degree of muscling, and for this reason is recommended for stewing purposes.

Animals dressing larger than eight pounds are not common, but the lucky hunter that collects game this size is in for a real treat. A particularly

Sharp cutting tools are a must in cleaning game. Be sure your axe and knife are well sharpened before going afield. Sharp tools are safer to handle and easier to use. Touch up all tools after extended usage.

large woodchuck could yield eight pounds of meat, as could a large jackrabbit. Animals this size offer the hunter much opportunity.

Usually, game skinned, cleaned and cooled at once can be broken down and cooked directly without aging. Bring a supply of plastic bags to hold the pieces. One bag per piece works best.

When travelling, game meat is best stored in ice. Quick freezing works well when it can be done close to the field. Where your small game hunting is done in association with lodges or hunting camps, facilities for this are usually available. A close, air tight wrap is necessary to prevent freezer burn and retain freshness. Special freezer bags should be used for long term storage. Make sure the meat has been deeply chilled before it goes into the freezer. Quick surface freezing creates insulation on the surface of the meat and this slows down freezing in the center of the package.

This might be a good place to mention record keeping. Write on the package or an accompanying tag exactly what is in the bag, and the date. In this way a kind of quality control can be practiced over your game. Always use the oldest cuts first. Also, good record keeping lets you choose exactly what you want to eat. There are no surprises when the package is thawed.

Sharp cutting tools are a must in cleaning game. Be sure your axe and knife are well sharpened before going afield. Sharp tools are safer to handle and easier to use. Much small game can be broken down using a sharp pair of scissors or shears. Touch up all tools after extended usage.

Principles of Small Game Cooking

There is no single area of animal preparation that has become more individualized than game cooking. There are dozens of books covering nearly every aspect of game cooking. However, some forget that simplicity is paramount in obtaining good taste from your game. Many ignore basic principles that determine how game tastes and how it should be prepared to maximize flavor. The bottom line to getting good tasting game meat is knowing the basics of smart cooking.

The chronological age of game influences flavor and cooking methods. In general, young of the year and yearling animals can be cooked by roasting, broiling or frying. Older animals, large adults and animals subjected to some chase, require slow cooking either by stewing, pot roasts or fricassees. This simple rule of thumb is fundamental to good meat on the table.

A second principle often forgotten is that due to the leanness of most game meat, fat usually must be added during cooking to bring out the flavor. Squirrels and rabbits are very active animals and fat reserves accumulate only during certain seasons. The result is a lean muscled animal that can offer tough chewing at certain times of the year. More sedentary animals, like woodchucks, carry more fat for most of the year. Some animals possess a natural oiliness that helps

the cooking process. A naturally fat squirrel or rabbit is a treat.

Adding fat is necessary with most small game. This is called oiling and is done by rubbing the individual parts with pork fat. It can also be done by tying slices of fat directly to the meat surface. Yuppie cooks know this as barding, and rabbit roasts, even the domestic kinds prepared in the finest downtown bistros, are often barded. This is the secret to making a lean winter jackrabbit taste delicious. Side bacon, cut into half-inch slabs four to six inches long are excellent for providing the right amount of fat needed in cooking lean game animals. Small rabbits of any species, frequently cooked whole, are barded by filling the body cavity with fatty bacon.

Meat can be made tender by slow cooking. Low heat, especially in stews, tenderizes the meat. It mellows because juices within the cell walls are released during the heating. Fast cooking purges these juices too quickly. Heat under stew should be kept as low as possible. The best stews simmer for several hours, usually from two to four or five. Slow cooking is perhaps the biggest secret to successfully preparing small game for the table.

Game meat taste is greatly influenced by the food habits of the animal. Our small game feeds low to the ground on a variety of vegetation, usually varying with plant availability and season. These plants impart tastes to the meat—usually in the fat layers. Most are favorable and become characteristic of regions and times of year. This is most applicable in rabbits, but over the spring to fall period all small game meat tastes will undergo some change. As a cook, keep this in mind.Roasting may be favorable at one time of year while stewing may be the only way to go during other seasons. Don't let tastes influence your hunting, but do learn how to cook for the different seasons.

Meat texture is important as well. Most small game features finely textured meat. Although the meat becomes increasingly coarse with age, it all still rates as fine compared with deer or other big game. Finely textured meat is healthy and a source of good nutrition. However, it must be cooked gently. It responds well to special treatment like marinades. Cook this meat carefully to avoid disappointment and becoming "turned off" to game meat.

The instructions presented here are a jumping-off point for experimental cooking. The recipes are only one step in making small game suit your palate. The information here is pared to the bone so that anyone can begin with little effort. A major principle in any cooking is innovation and appeal to taste. Apply the ideas here to your own area and unique field situation.

Dutch Oven Cooking

The Dutch oven cooker is a traditional piece of outdoor equipment. For many it's not a new tool. Alleged to have been invented by the those from Holland—just like the Dutch clock, Dutch chair, Dutch cheese and the Dutch hoe—it was used extensively by early pioneers and trappers.

For some time now I have been using a Dutch oven and it has become my favorite method for cooking small game. There are a number of reasons for this. First, it provides the right kind of environment for cooking most small game. Low, moist heat delivered over a long period of time lets the meat mellow and develop its own unique taste. It allows the user to apply all the principles of game cookery in one easy package. Second is versatility. A Dutch oven can cook anything—from bread to roasts and stew. This makes it an excellent camp tool. Third, this tool is easy to use. I learned from an old cowboy, but anybody can become expert by applying a few simple techniques. Fourth, this oven removes much of the guesswork from cooking small game. Timing is critical only toward the end of the cooking session. Fifth, it does not require close attention during the cooking process. When set up correctly it takes care of itself, allowing the hunter to get on with hunting rather than spending time on the details of cooking. It

can be set up in the morning and left until evening when a meal is ready for tired hunters.

What does a Dutch oven look like? A typical pot is a big, heavy, squat looking thing made from cast, low grade iron. Most are about one-eighth to one-quarter inch thick and have an uneven, rough outer surface—the result of the casting process. The sides slope upwards giving the pot a look that is inconsistent with today's modern kitchen ware. The lid is important—it must be heavy and tightly fit the pot. It is dome shaped and has a rim around the edge. The lid has a small cast iron handle, while the oven has a heavy bail-type handle.

There are several oven models currently on the market. The recent fireplace craze has meant that several semi-decorative models are now available. Avoid these, as many are poorly cast and this contributes to uneven heating and the creation of hot spots, which in turn can cause meat to stick to the pot and burn. When this happens the oven is very unforgiving and a burned taste will permeate the entire mixture.

Many models come from the factory with three legs. These serve a very useful purpose. When the oven is set into fresh coals the legs keep the pot up off the hottest coals in the fire pit. This helps control the temperature and leaves the coals some breathing room. There are also many good quality pots on the market without iron legs. My pot lacks any such legs, yet works extremely well. If possible, choose a model with legs, but don't let their absence prevent you from buying a good quality oven.

Size and weight are important. Eleven quarts has proven correct for most use, but smaller models can be utilized. A good sized jackrabbit will take up half of my 11-quart oven. Good models have the capacity cast onto the lid.

A heavy pot will transfer heat more evenly than a lighter version. During cooking, the heat produced by the coal bed will vary greatly. Sometimes one side of the coal pit will be hotter than the other, or some coals will die out prematurely. Others will form as small bits of wood

A typical Dutch oven. A shovel is also necessary to help place coals on the lid and to bury and retrieve the oven. The Dutch oven is easy to use.

smoulder and develop into coals. The heavy weight transfers the varying heat evenly to all parts of the pot. My 11-quart model weighs just under 20 pounds, not exactly great for go-light hunting trips, but necessary for good heat distribution and flavorful cooking results.

New Dutch ovens and those not used for long periods of time must be seasoned. Begin by thoroughly cleaning the entire pot and lid with soap and water. New ovens often come from the factory covered with protective wax, and this must be removed. Rinse thoroughly and dry.

Seasoning is little more than covering the oven with cooking fat to fill all casting pores in the metal. The same trick is used with new cast iron

frying pans and can be easily accomplished by cooking some heavy, fatty foods.

Cooking a large batch of french fries will season any cast iron utensil, but those wishing to season as a separate step can cover the inside of the oven and lid with fat. Then place the greased Dutch oven in a conventional oven at low heat for a couple of hours, or the oven may be buried in hot camp fire coals. When the heating is finished, wipe all surfaces, but do not wash.

Once completed, the oven shouldn't need reseasoning unless foods are cooked in water. A small amount of water should not affect the seasoning. If the oven is stored for an extended

The greased oven can be heated over a campfire to season. In this way, the grease soaks into the pores of the metal.

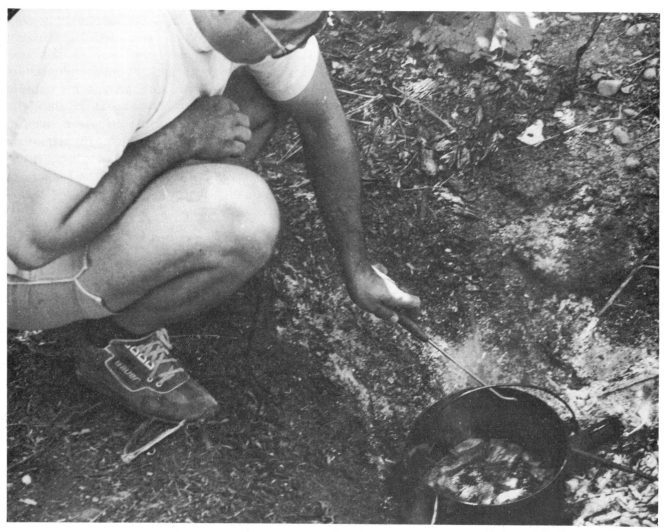

Brown each piece in the Dutch oven. Stir the pieces about, being sure that each side is browned, then remove the Dutch oven from the coals.

period of time it is wise to wash it well and reseason it, thereby avoiding any bad taste from rancid fat. However, an oven used regularly, wiped out after each use, and washed in mild soap and water occasionally will prove serviceable for years.

The Dutch oven is easy to use and produces both good food and more free time for hunting. Here's how to do it: Have a coffee break at about ten in the morning, and while it brews, clean and cool the morning's take of game. Then stoke up the fire, giving a large bed of coals, and sit down to coffee. Following coffee, the cooled carcasses can be broken into pieces and the fire pit prepared. These tasks are easily divided among hunting partners.

Prepare the fire pit by digging into the bed of coals with a spade, making a hole large enough to accept the Dutch oven. Move some coals into the bottom of the hole. Set the empty Dutch oven, with lid removed, into the coals. While the cast oven heats, collect the broken down carcasses. Add a small amount of fat to the Dutch oven and brown the meat on all sides to lock in the flavor.

Once all the meat is browned, remove the Dutch oven from the coal bed and begin preparing your stew or roast. Using stew as an example, add the various desired vegetables and seasonings to the pot, then add a small amount of water, not quite covering the ingredients in the oven.

Now put the lid in place and lower the oven into the hole. Cover the oven lid with hot coals. This is important to the success of the meal. The thick exaggerated lip on the lid serves to hold the coals in place.

Finally, there must be coals surrounding the entire oven—below, above, and beside. Be sure

The key to Dutch oven cookery is in adding the correct amount of water. Add enough to almost cover the contents.

that coals envelop the oven, then bury it with a mixture of ash, coals, and dirt. Place enough solid earth on top to retain heat. Test the coverage by holding your hand over the mound. Most heat should be held underground for cooking, and very little should be felt above ground.

How long do I wait? Usually, two medium sized rabbits in the 11-quart oven require six hours of cooking, depending, of course, on the size of the meat chunks. Roasts take longer than stew. Cooking times can also vary in accordance with the heating quality of the wood used.

Coals for my camp fires have usually been from poplar, pine and sometimes oak trees. Once in Wyoming I used dead and very dry Russian olive trees from a shelter belt and found they worked very well. In Ontario I used cedar successfully. Some trial and error is required in discovering the correct cooking times with various kinds of woods.

Once the Dutch oven is covered, the shooter is free to continue hunting since the entire system needs no further checking or handling. At about six in the evening a warm meal of freshly taken rabbit is ready. Dig out the oven, being careful not to bump the lid. If this happens dirt will get into your stew. Clean any remaining coals, ashes or dirt from the lid, and slowly lift the oven from the fire pit by the large handle. A shovel will work to do this.

After the meal the Dutch oven is emptied, cooled and wiped out. Placed in the back of my four wheel drive, it's ready for future trips. These ovens are reliable and take the guesswork out of preparing any kind of small game. The only negative is the heavy weight, but, as with other gear, trade offs are made.

By the way, the Dutch oven can be used during the winter. Instead of burying it in a hole, simply cover it with ash and embers. Cut shrubs, green wood or large pieces of bark to cover over the ash and oven in a kind of tent or hut arrangement. Heap lots of snow over the cover and firmly pack it down. Some snow melts, but this does not hurt the oven or interfere with cooking.

Now put the lid in place and lower the oven into the hole.

The oven works well under all hunting conditions, and there is just nothing finer than a jackrabbit cooked to perfection in it.

Recipes

The following recipes cover the basics of small game cooking. but also includes one advanced recipe for rabbit. Hunters are encouraged to modify any to suit their personal tastes or those of their family. Use herbs and spices that are on hand or add to the variety with new choices. Game meat provides a wonderful opportunity to experiment with new and different tastes and ideas in seasoning.

Woodchuck Chili

Four pounds of ground woodchuck cut from the rear of the animal are best for this recipe. Woodchucks feeding on alfalfa haylands in late summer will have an excellent taste.)
    5 cloves minced garlic
    5 tablespoons chili powder
    1/4 tablespoon paprika
    1 tablespoon salt
    1 tablespoon white pepper
    2 quarts water
    3 14-ounce tins beans
Brown the meat in the bottom of a Dutch oven or cast frying pan, adding the chili powder,

paprika, salt and pepper. Stir in the water. Cook slowly for three to four hours. Add the beans. This recipe can be halved or quartered. In the field the recipe can be adapted to a small camp stove by reducing the portions. Keep the camp stove at low heat.

Variations:

- A small amount of cooked rice can be added to the mix.
- The haunches of two ground squirrels cut into small pieces with sharp hunting knife can be substituted. Reduce other proportions accordingly.

Oven Fried Squirrel

This is a traditional recipe used, in one version or another, for most game. However, it works best with squirrel.

    half dozen squirrels
    flour to coat squirrels
    fatty bacon
    one bay leaf
    powdered onion

Cover the top of the oven with hot coals. This is critical to success. Note how the thick lip on the lid holds the coals in place.

one can mushroom soup

1/2 can evaporated milk

Preheat oven to 325 degrees. While waiting for the oven to heat, flour the broken down squirrel carcasses and brown them with the bacon in a hot Dutch oven or frying pan. Once browned, place the meat in a casserole. In a small bowl mix the seasonings with the canned milk and mushroom soup. Pour this over the squirrels. Cover and cook for one and one-half hours or until the squirrel meat is tender to the fork.

Sweet and Sour Small Game for a Slow Cooking Pot

This is another basic recipe that can be used with any kind of small game. For those who want to experiment with different kinds of game, this is a good beginning. For example, if you have not tried prairie dog or woodchuck or rockchuck, this recipe will get you off to a correct start. The long, slow cooking period will soften the red muscled meat of small to medium sized squirrel or cottontail rabbit. Prairie dogs can be used in this recipe, too.

One small to medium sized small game animal (woodchuck, rockchuck, prairie dog, old jackrabbit or cottontail)

salt to taste

1/4 cup brown sugar

1/4 cup vinegar

1/4 cup soy sauce

1/4 cup chili

1 cup water

Liberally salt the game meat and place in a Dutch oven or large frying pan with a tight fitting lid. Mix the remaining ingredients and pour over the meat. Cook on top of the stove on low heat for one and one-half to two hours, or until tender. Check closely and add more water if needed. Cook for eight hours. For an interesting variation on this recipe, leave out the soy sauce and add a can of stewed tomatoes to the mix. Be prepared for excellent eating.

Curried Woodchuck

This is a top recipe and many sophisticated palates can be fooled into believing they are eating chicken. This recipe also works with tree and ground squirrels.

Break down the woodchuck or squirrel into bite sized pieces. One woodchuck or rockchuck or three ground squirrels work well for this recipe.

1/4 cup cooking oil

1 woodchuck or 3 ground squirrels

seasoned flour

1 large onion, chopped

1/3 cup dry red table wine

2 teaspoons curry powder

2 tablespoons white sugar

1/2 teaspoon pepper

water

Heat cooking oil in a heavy pot. Coat the meat with the flour and add it to the hot oil along with the onion. Brown the meat. Reduce heat and add the curry powder, sugar, pepper, wine, and water to almost cover the meat. Simmer until tender, about two hours.

Hasenpfeffer

If there is one traditional rabbit dish it must be Hasenpfeffer. There are probably more variations on this basic recipe than quills on the proverbial porcupine. It continues to be popular with all ages and a surprising number of people—hunters and non-hunters alike—will own up to having filled their bellies with Hasenpfeffer on more than one occasion. First-time game cooks are advised to use this recipe. It is usually a success and even those not fond of game meat will at least try Hasenpfeffer. If the beginning game cook wants to impress someone, this is the recipe to follow.

In the traditional Hasenpfeffer recipe a marinade is required. Some feel these remove all the natural taste from the animal, but their purpose is to tenderize the meat. As a group, marinades

Large rabbits can be turned into the traditional dish called *Hasenpfeffer*. There are probably more variations on this basic recipe than quills on the proverbial porcupine.

enhance natural flavors.

The marinade consists of equal parts of white vinegar and water to cover the rabbit. Sugar is dissolved in the liquid in a ratio of four teaspoons for each cup of liquid. Peppercorns are added and salt is mixed in at the rate of one half teaspoon per cup of liquid. Sliced onions and some onion salt are added to taste. Two celery stalks, two carrots, and two or three juniper berries are chopped and mixed in along with three whole cloves and two bay leaves. The marinade is stirred and allowed to sit for a few minutes to allow flavors to mingle.

The rabbit is broken down into serving size portions and placed in the marinade. Small animals, freshly taken, can be marinaded in a cool place for 24 hours. Older, larger animals should be given two days time, also in a cool place. The pieces are turned two to three times per day. The marinade should also be stirred from time to time.

Next the meat should be browned. Drain and

Begin with simple recipes and work up to more complex offerings. Experiment with your own tastes and ideas. Few meats are as open to experimentation as small game.

dry the meat chunks, then roll each in seasoned flour (salt and pepper mixed into flour). Brown in a Dutch oven or frying pan with bacon drippings or strips of whole bacon. When all the pieces are browned, add the marinade, along with the vegetables, to the Dutch oven or large pot. Bring to a quick boil and then lower the heat, simmering until the meat is tender. Remove the rabbit to a platter. Put the sauce and vegetables through a sieve and return the sauce to the heat. Blend in one tablespoon of flour and one-quarter cup of sour cream. Heat, but do not boil. Then pour the sauce over the rabbit and voila, bon appetit!

Basic Roast Rabbit

This is the basic recipe for outdoorsmen interested in one quick method of cooking rabbit or any small game quickly and without much preliminary effort. For this method to be successful a well cleaned rabbit is necessary. All bullet-damaged meat must be cut away and the surrounding areas washed with cold water. Entrails have to be removed quickly and cleanly. The carcass must be cool.

Wash and dry the rabbit and sprinkle with salt and pepper to taste. Fill the body cavity with the stuffing of your choice. Place strips of fat bacon across the top of the carcass. Roast, uncovered, in a 325 degree oven until tender. It usually takes about 30 minutes per pound of meat.

Roast Gopher

1 medium sized gopher
12 whole cloves
1 medium sized onion
1/2 cup water
salt and pepper to taste
1/2 can tomato juice
Combine ingredients in a casserole and bake in a 300 degree oven for 3 hours.

Jugged Jackrabbit

This recipe represents the ultimate in rabbit preparation. Some might consider this too much trouble, but the rewards are there for those taking the extra time and following the instructions closely. This is an advanced recipe—recommended for those with considerable experience in preparing small game. Use this recipe to impress important people and display your finely honed culinary skills.

one jackrabbit, four to six pounds.
one pound fat bacon
one pound button onions
one cup chopped carrots
one cup chopped onions
two cups cooked mushrooms
one glove garlic
one bundle of herbs (to taste)
one-half liter red wine
one tablespoon olive oil
one-half cup flour
salt and pepper
one can undiluted consomme soup
one cup red currant jelly
one-half pound croutons
one-quarter cup bacon drippings
one-quarter cup chopped parsley
one large wine glass of port

This recipe calls for the rabbit blood to be saved. This must be done in the field. Chill the fresh blood as quickly as possible. Also save the liver. Remove the gall bladder and any adhering tissue. Cool the liver at once. Remember to inspect the liver closely for signs of disease. Those appearing clean can be retained and used in this recipe. Break down the rabbit as outlined in chart two. Each piece should be about three ounces.

In a suitable bowl place the meat, and salt and pepper to taste. Add the sliced carrot, onions, garlic, faggot, olive oil and red wine. Cover the bowl and allow to soak in a cool place for several hours.

Fry the bacon and mushrooms. Drain the

liquid off the rabbit and save. Now fry the onions and carrots in the bacon drippings. Add flour and continue frying until a golden color.

Dry the meat on a cloth and add to the fried onions, carrots and flour. Add the reserved liquid and consomme. Bring the meat to a boil, then simmer for two hours or until tender.

Strain the meat, saving the sauce. Force the vegetables through a sieve and add to the sauce. Place the meat chunks in a saucepan. Add the bacon strips, button onions, and mushrooms and keep hot.

Skim fat from the sauce, and reduce, if necessary, until it will coat the back of a spoon. Remove from heat and add the blood, if desired. Heat the sauce, but do not boil or it will curdle.

Check the seasoning, add the red currant jelly and port wine, strain and pour over the rabbit.

Heat gently.

Remove to serving platter. Surround with heart shaped croutons which have been fried in butter with their points dipped in chopped parsley. Serve immediately.

Jugged jackrabbit is sometimes accompanied by liver forcemeat. A recipe follows:

One-quarter pound rabbit liver
One-quarter pound sausage meat
One cup breadcrumbs
One-half teaspoon mixed herbs
One-half teaspoon dried, chopped parsley
Salt and pepper to taste

Clean the liver. Chop it finely. Mix with other ingredients except breadcrumbs. Form into small balls. Roll them in breadcrumbs. Fry in deep fat to a golden brown and serve with jugged jackrabbit.

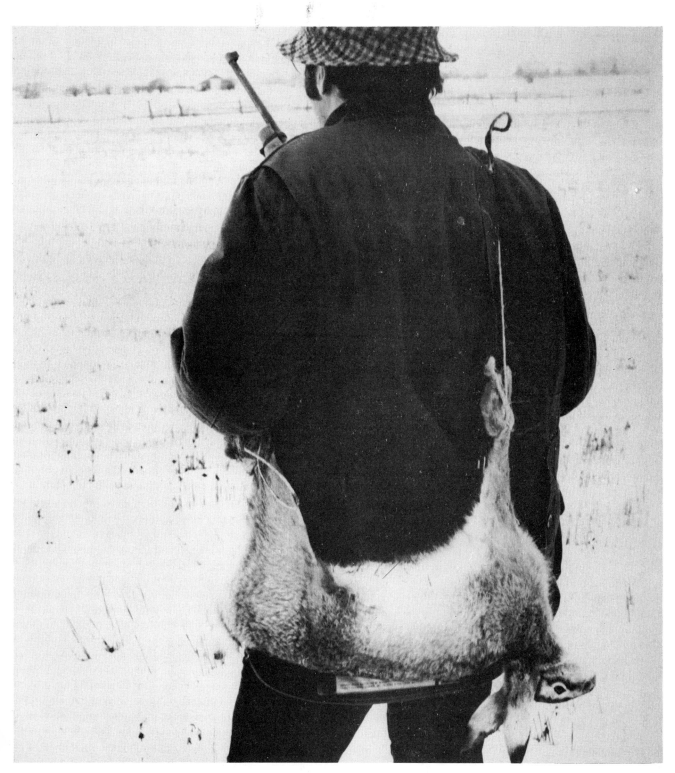

Another successful "shopping" trip.